THE BIG 50
TORONTO BLUE JAYS

THE BIG 50
TORONTO BLUE JAYS

The Men and Moments That Made the Toronto Blue Jays

Shi Davidi

TRIUMPH
B O O K S

The Library of Congress has cataloged the previous edition as follows:

Names: Davidi, Shi, 1975– author.
Title: The big 50, Toronto Blue Jays : the men and moments that made the Toronto Blue Jays / Shi Davidi.
Description: Chicago, Illinois : Triumph Books, [2016]
Identifiers: LCCN 2016000330 | ISBN 9781629372082
Subjects: LCSH: Toronto Blue Jays (Baseball team)—History.
Classification: LCC GV875.T67 D37 2016 | DDC 796.357/6409713541—dc23
LC record available at http://lccn.loc.gov/2016000330

This book is available in quantity at special discounts for your group or organization. For further information, contact:

Triumph Books LLC
814 North Franklin Street
Chicago, Illinois 60610
(312) 337-0747
www.triumphbooks.com

Printed in U.S.A.
ISBN: 978-1-62937-891-6

Design by Andy Hansen
All photos courtesy of AP Images unless otherwise indicated.

To my parents, Frieda and Israel, for encouraging me to love a sport totally foreign to them, and then learning to love it with me; my sons, Adyn and Zev, who are just discovering how much fun baseball can be; and to my wife, Stacey, for being the teammate I always wanted.

[Contents]

[Foreword]

I was there. Honestly. I know hundreds of thousands of people say they attended the inaugural Blue Jays game, but I really did—although I'm told I asked to leave after five innings because of the cold. (At least I can say I made it to official game status.) The day before that game, I'm not sure I could have told you anything meaningful about baseball. But April 7, 1977, was a day that, although I certainly didn't realize it then, would come to play a major role in my life.

I loved baseball from the moment I was introduced to it as a 10-year-old. I loved the stats, the strategy, the endless conversations you could have during and after a game about what had gone on and what was likely to happen the next day. And I could scarcely believe my good fortune: a major league team had come to my hometown. Sure, we already had the Maple Leafs—a team I worshipped as a child—and sure, I was aware there was already a Major League Baseball team in Montreal, but I never once thought Toronto would get a team to call its own.

As soon as the Blue Jays arrived, I took full advantage. I would go to a game with my parents or family friends whenever they would take me, and as soon as I was old enough to go with my own friends—well, then the horse was really out of the barn. The route from my home in Willowdale was the 53 bus to Finch Station, the subway down to King, the streetcar across to the CNE, and then a walk to get to Exhibition Stadium. Back then, shocking as this may seem, there were scheduled doubleheaders. Not day-night. And not because of rain. Try to find a better way for a bunch of kids to spend their Saturday or Sunday. It can't be done.

THE BIG 50

I can recall various periods of my life by the connection I had to baseball at that time. In 1986, we had a surprise 50th birthday party for my dad at a Blue Jays game, and Tony Fernandez hit a foul ball that hit me right in the hands. Error Shulman. When I was working as a lifeguard in the late '80s, I'd take control of the radio on my shifts. Bye-bye music, and hello ballgame. Just out of university, I went on a baseball road trip with some buddies, and by sheer luck we wound up at Dave Stieb's no-hitter in Cleveland. And then, just two years later, somehow I found myself sitting in the broadcast booth with Tom Cheek and Jerry Howarth as I waited to do *Jays Talk* after the game.

Little did I know then that in 1995 I would start calling Jays games on TSN. I vividly remember the first at-bat of my first spring training game, between the Jays and the Orioles. I was so nervous, I willed Brady Anderson to do something easy, like hit a ground ball to second, so I could get the first batter out of the way. But it wasn't meant to be. Anderson hit a moon shot to right centre, I lost it in the sun, and I blew the first home run call of my career. Fortunately, my bosses stuck with me and let me work through some rookie jitters. Now 20 years later, I guess I've come full circle, as I have the opportunity to come back home and call some Jays games for Sportsnet while still doing baseball and college basketball for ESPN.

Kid or adult, fan or broadcaster, baseball is as enjoyable to me now as it has ever been. I've gone to dozens of games with my parents, and dozens more with my sons. There have been good Toronto teams and bad, overachievers and underachievers, open roofs, closed roofs, and (way back when) no roof at all. But as much as anything in my life, for almost 40 years now, baseball—and the Blue Jays in particular—have been there. And I'm sure, like I have, that many of you have sat around and reminisced about the memorable moments in Blue Jays history that are detailed so well by Shi Davidi in this book.

Enjoy *The Big 50: Toronto Blue Jays*, and relive the good times all over again.

—Dan Shulman

[Introduction]

Major League Baseball very nearly came to Toronto in the form of the Giants, the history-rich National League franchise struggling to make a go of it in California in the mid-1970s. Horace Stoneham, the franchise owner out west, had a deal to sell the Giants to Labatt Breweries along with R. Howard Webster and CIBC, the group seeking to bring a second club north of the border. An announcement of the $8 million sale, plus $5.5 million more to buy out the 19 years remaining on the lease at Candlestick Park in San Francisco, was made January 9, 1976, and a rivalry with the Montreal Expos loomed on the horizon. Imagine for a moment how different the Canadian baseball landscape over the past 45 years might have been had that deal reached fruition.

The sale of the Giants fell through when San Francisco Mayor George Moscone obtained a temporary court order preventing the National League owners from voting on the deal. Hours before the order's March 1 expiry date Bob Lurie, who'd been seeking a partner to keep the team in the Bay Area, joined with Bud Herseth and bought the club for $8 million. For Labatt, which had previously made runs at buying the Baltimore Orioles and the team in Cleveland, and Webster, who had tried to buy the San Diego Padres, their collaboration with CIBC on the Giants deal marked yet another near miss.

"It was probably the most depressing time for me in all my public life," said Paul Godfrey, the former Blue Jays president and CEO, who at the time was chairman of the Metropolitan Toronto council and had aggressively pursued a team for years. "I had the Giants in the palm of my hands. There was great excitement in the city, and then victory was snatched from us."

But Godfrey wasn't deterred, nor were Labatt president Don McDougall and Herb Solway, a partner at the law firm Goodman and Goodman, which represented the brewery. Soon after the Giants deal fell through, Godfrey got a call from Kansas City Royals owner Ewing Kauffman saying he wanted Toronto in the American League. Years earlier, Kauffman's Toronto-born wife, Muriel, had overheard the trio chatting at a bar after a baseball meeting and offered to use her influence with her husband to help their cause.

Meanwhile, the junior circuit in February 1976 awarded a new franchise to a group from Seattle, seeking to ward off a $14 million lawsuit from the city. A week before the 1970 season started, the Seattle Pilots had been abruptly sold to a group led by Bud Selig (who would later become baseball commissioner), and moved to Milwaukee, where they became the Brewers, prompting Seattle's legal action. The birth of the Mariners in 1976 resolved that, but left the American League with 13 teams. As such, another club was needed to balance out the schedule. So, during a joint meeting of baseball's 24 owners on March 20, 1976, the American League voted 11–1 in favour of expanding north to Toronto. The National League didn't take kindly to that, and at the same meeting announced that it would actively consider a franchise in Toronto for the 1977 season in spite of what had just happened.

Bowie Kuhn, baseball's commissioner at the time, continued to press the matter. As he tried to find a way to get Toronto into the senior circuit, the American League went about choosing between the Labatt ownership group and another headed by Toronto businessmen Phil and Irv Granovsky. A secret session was scheduled for March 26 in Tampa to settle the matter, where both applicants made presentations before the 12 established American League owners. Eventually they settled on the Labatt group due to what Detroit Tigers owner John Fetzer, chairman of the loop's planning committee, described as "solid, sound economics. You can't run baseball on a shoestring. The Labatt people gave this part of the equation, and that makes it viable."

The purchase price was $7 million. The official announcement came later that day, seemingly marking an end to a trying two-year process for Labatt, and setting off celebrations in Tampa and Toronto.

Having done his part to land the team during the presentations, Gord Kirke, the prominent Toronto sports lawyer who at the time worked with Solway at Goodman and Goodman, left the festivities early to get back home and tend to other duties, but not without some shenanigans at the Toronto airport first.

"I went to go through customs and was in a very celebratory, overserved state of mind," he recalled, "and the customs officer said the usual, 'Did you buy or receive anything of value while you were in the United States?' To which I responded, 'Yes, very much so,' and he said, 'What is the approximate value of what you got while you were in the States?' I said, 'Seven million dollars.' And he said, 'Please, sir, it's been a long day and I don't want to make this day any longer than it needs to be for either of us. What did you buy while you were in the States for seven million dollars?' And you know, [he was] being very doubtful that I had really spent seven million dollars. I said, 'The baseball team,' to which he again scoffed at the answer and said, 'Sir, I don't want to have you to go the separate room and have them deal with you. You seem like a nice guy. Why can't you tell me the truth?'

"I said I was, and dug in my briefcase and came up with some pins that Labatt had made up about Toronto baseball as part of a campaign to get a franchise, and I gave those pins to the customs officer. I've heard that those pins on the collectible market are worth quite something today, so the customs officer turned a bad day into a pretty good day."

As good as it was, more headaches remained. Commissioner Kuhn remained unhappy with the American League's expansion to Toronto because he was under pressure from the U.S. Congress to put a team back in Washington, and wanted to put both new franchises in the National League. Godfrey said Kuhn's plan was for New Orleans to join Seattle in the American League. On March 29, the National League voted 10–2 in favour of expanding into Toronto and Washington, but the nays cast by Philadelphia and Cincinnati killed the motion because it required a unanimous decision. Despite that, some of the owners urged Kuhn to use his powers to protect the best interests of baseball, urging him to rule the vote a legal majority. Instead, another vote was scheduled for April 26, and this time the tally was 7–5 in favour, effectively settling the matter. "What happened is once some of the owners saw there were votes against it in the first vote, they decided to let Cincinnati and Philadelphia be the bad guys," said Godfrey. "They didn't want to alienate the commissioner. But when the commissioner kept pressing, three more decided, 'Screw the commissioner.' And that's how the team ended up in the American League."

An accountant named Paul Beeston became the Toronto franchise's first employee on May 10. After Peter Bavasi was named executive vice president and general manager June 18, he lured over Pat Gillick from the New York Yankees to run player personnel. And on August 12, "Blue Jays" was selected by the board of directors from more than 4,000 suggestions and 30,000 entries into a name-the-team contest.

Another popular suggestion was Blues, although potential names were all over the map, from Exhibitionists to Island Ferries. During a board meeting on potential names, some members began to favour "Beavers," given that the animal is known for its hard work, is on the Canadian nickel, and is symbolic of the country's wildlife. The younger participants in the room, however, cringed, since "shooting beaver" was a vulgar euphemism commonly used by athletes at the time to describe the pursuit of women. They could only imagine the headlines. Only after some delicate explanations of the slang from a team-management member (some board members initially took the euphemism at face value and thought it was silly to think players would actually hunt beavers), the group decided against the name and John Robarts put forth Blue Jays. Just that morning the former premier of Ontario had seen a blue jay in the trees through his bathroom window, and he became enamoured with the chatty, aggressive, and very Canadian bird. Dr. William Mills of Toronto had officially submitted the name and ended up winning the contest.

From those convoluted, backroom beginnings to consecutive World Series championships to a 21-year postseason drought to the captivating playoff runs of 2015 and '16 to the weird, wild pandemic season of 2020, which played out of Buffalo's Sahlen Field, the Blue Jays have certainly been, as Godfrey described the expansion process, "the most extreme roller-coaster ride."

THE BIG 50

TORONTO BLUE JAYS

1

THE 1992 WORLD SERIES

At the pinnacle, after Otis Nixon bunted, and Mike Timlin pounced on it, and the Toronto Blue Jays and their fans held their collective breath as the relay went to Joe Carter at first base, and Jerry Crawford signalled out, and the World Series he'd spent 16 years trying to win was at long last agonizingly won, the thing Pat Gillick felt most was relief. Certainly there was joy, elation... all the stuff you'd expect. But after all the work put in to building an expansion franchise from the ground up, after all the losses during those years of development and all the heartbreak during the winning seasons, the Blue Jays had reached the summit. "I've never climbed Mount Everest or anything," said Gillick, "but it's sort of like climbing a mountain, and when you get to the top, you take a deep breath and say you finally made it."

That's precisely how it felt on the night of Saturday, October 24, 1992, as Carter took Timlin's toss to end Game 6 of the World Series and CBS broadcaster Sean McDonough declared that, "For the first time in history, the world championship banner will fly north of the border. The Toronto Blue Jays are baseball's best in 1992." Winning the season's last game—4–3 in 11 innings over Atlanta—triggered the kind of never-been-done-before high that players, coaches, the front office, and fans can experience only once. Improving from expansion doormat in 1977 to American League East champion in 1985 was fun; waiting another seven years to make the jump from division winner to World Series champion was excruciating. Along the way cruel labels like "Blow Jays" were attached, and the battle scars accumulated. For many, the euphoric dog pile on the Atlanta–Fulton County Stadium infield was cathartic.

"Even though I wasn't here in '85, '87, and '89, we all knew that baggage was there," said Carter. "The year before, when we got beat by Minnesota in the ALCS, we took it upon ourselves, [me] and Pat Tabler. We said, 'You know what? We're coming to spring training and next season we have one goal, and that's to win the World Series. Not get there. Heck, I don't want to get to the World Series, I want to *win* the World Series.' So all the history, we put it behind us, and we said we're going to focus on now. And when you win that first one, it's a big relief."

The five-game loss to the Twins in the previous October stung deeply, and in many ways it shaped some of the key moves that pushed the Blue Jays over the top in 1992. Gillick felt the '91 team had been superior to Minnesota, which needed seven games to beat Atlanta in the World Series, yet his group wilted at the moment of truth. The free-agent signings of workhorse starter Jack Morris away from the Twins, as well as designated hitter Dave Winfield, were designed in part to address that lack of killer instinct. Veteran infielder Alfredo Griffin, another free-agent addition, added a cool and savvy presence in the clubhouse to complement Morris' toughness and Winfield's determination. Morris' pre-signing conversation with Gillick was succinct: "The only words out of [Gillick's] mouth were, 'I got tired of having you beat us,'" Morris said.

Morris joined a rotation that also included Juan Guzman, Jimmy Key, Todd Stottlemyre, and, at different points, Dave Stieb, David Wells, and Pat Hentgen. Eventually the staff would be bolstered by the acquisition of David Cone. Wells and Hentgen pitched mostly out of a bullpen that also featured the dynamic duo of Tom Henke and Duane Ward. Together the pitchers posted a 3.91 ERA, just below league average but ninth in the American League. The loop's second best offence with 780 runs (11 fewer than the Detroit Tigers) helped cover the gap. The lineup featured seven players with at least 11 home runs, led by Carter with 34. Carter drove in 119 and Winfield 108, while the dynamic Roberto Alomar did a little bit of everything with a team-best .405 on-base percentage, 177 hits, 105 runs scored, 76 RBIs, and 49 stolen bases to go with his Gold Glove defence. "You better be able to win with all that," said Tabler.

Win they did, from Opening Day onward, spending only six days all season out of first place in the American League East, and none after May 24. At no point did the Blue Jays trail by more than a half game. Even though they finished only four games ahead of the Milwaukee Brewers, they were in control from start to finish, a sense of purpose carrying them through the grind.

"I had been on two world championship teams and I looked around and said, 'This is another one,'" said Morris, who became the franchise's first 20-game winner. "I just sensed it, and everybody in the locker room was committed early to winning. They had tasted the postseason, the guys that were here. Of course Winfield and I were new, and Dave wanted it as bad as I wanted it. In general, there was an atmosphere of, 'We're going to win this thing,' and that was predetermined from way early in the season, not just late in the year."

Still, the regular season was not without its challenges. Stieb, coming off a neck injury that cost him nearly the entire 1991 season, struggled with elbow and shoulder issues and finished the year on the disabled list. Kelly Gruber's offence disappeared and was never to be found again. And the Brewers and Baltimore Orioles simply wouldn't go away.

Despite being in command, the Blue Jays never led the division by more than five games. They were just 2½ games up on the Orioles when they acquired David Cone from the New York Mets in a stunning waiver deal on August 27. The price was steep: infielder Jeff Kent, who ended up having a Hall of Fame–calibre career, and outfield prospect Ryan Thompson, who flamed out despite being the piece Gillick was most reluctant to part with. "We thought about it and we said, 'You know, David Cone is a guy that we think can put us over the hump,'" said Gillick. "And at the same time, it kind of deflates your competition if you can do something like that. Psychologically, I think it has that effect on the people that are pursuing you."

Cone went 4–3 with a 2.55 ERA in eight games, including one relief appearance, down the stretch while stabilizing the rotation. The Blue Jays clinched the American League East on the penultimate day of the season with a 3–1 victory over the Detroit Tigers, and the focus shifted to exorcising postseason demons. Their opponent was the Oakland Athletics, a team that bested them in five games in the 1989 American League Championship Series.

"Among ourselves, when we put us up man-to-man, we were better than most teams," said centre fielder Devon White. "As a team and the chemistry we had with each other, it was without a doubt the best during that period."

The definitive turning point against Oakland, and in some ways one for the franchise as a whole, came in Game 4. Up 2–1 in the series but down 6–1 through seven innings, the Blue Jays rallied for a three-spot in the eighth and had men on second and third with two outs. Ed Sprague hit for Manny Lee, and Hall of Fame closer Dennis Eckersley struck him out, but on his way off the mound he pumped his fist and then pointed and stared aggressively at the players in the Blue Jays' dugout. While Eckersley's theatrics were commonplace for him, this crossed the line. The Toronto players were furious. The next inning, White led off with a single before Alomar turned on a 2–2 fastball and ripped it over the wall in right to knot things up. Immediately after finishing his swing, he dropped his bat and thrust both arms in the air, fingers pointed to the sky. "It was a big hit for us," said Alomar. "It turned around the series, and from that point on we were a different ballclub."

The Blue Jays completed the comeback in the 11th, when Derek Bell led off with a walk against Kelly Downs, went to third on Candy Maldonado's single, and scored on a Pat Borders sacrifice fly. Henke closed out the bottom half for a 3–1 series lead, and they booked the first World Series trip in franchise history at home three days later with a 9–2 win before 51,355 in Toronto. Alomar, in no small measure because of his Game 4 home run, was named the ALCS MVP.

"Just a great, clutch at-bat against the game's best at the time," said Morris. "Eck had done a lot of showboating on the mound, and talking to him years later [he said] that was never his intent, it's just the way he was... but it rubbed all of us the wrong way. So, when Robbie hit it, it was like the ultimate revenge. It's like the baseball gods wanted to remind everybody that nobody is too good." Added manager Cito Gaston, "Without Robbie hitting that home run we don't make it."

The World Series, which opened in Atlanta, was uncharted territory for the franchise and its jubilant fan base, and more heroics were needed early on to keep things from going sideways. Damon Berryhill's three-run homer off Morris in the sixth inning of Game 1 put the Blue Jays down 1–0 in the Series, and they trailed 4–3 with one out in the ninth of Game 2 when Bell came to the plate for Lee against closer Jeff Reardon. Bell, an energetic, 23-year-old fourth outfielder, worked an eight-pitch walk

Joe Carter is mobbed by his teammates after catching the final out of the 1992 World Series. (Rusty Kennedy)

and Sprague, the catching/corner infield prospect called up midsummer, batted for Ward. Gaston had told Sprague in the previous inning to be ready to pinch-hit, so he'd had plenty of time to prepare. During the gap he asked Rance Mulliniks what he looked for against Reardon, and the utility infielder told him to be ready for a high fastball. On the first pitch, that's what he got—and he belted it over the wall in left-centre field to put the Blue Jays up 5–4. After Henke survived a nervous ninth, the trajectory of the entire Series changed. "It was like, oh my God, we could be down 0–2 to Atlanta, and this might be our last chance," said Tabler. "And then for him to homer, we were so excited."

There was more excitement to come. Game 3 on October 20 was the first World Series contest ever played outside the United States. It started with a Marines unit from New York carrying out the Canadian flag before the game. (Before Game 2, the Maple Leaf was brought in upside down in Atlanta. U.S. president George Bush issued an apology for the flap.) By the eighth inning of Game 3 in Toronto, the Blue Jays faced a 2–1 deficit with Steve Avery dealing on the mound. Gruber, who had just two hits in the postseason to that point, led off, battled the lefty for seven pitches, and then turned on the eighth offering for his only homer of the playoffs. As he rounded third he pointed to some friends in the stands, plus his mom and popular Canadian musician Anne Murray, who sang the national anthem before the game. "She's a friend," he said afterward.

That set the stage for more drama in the ninth. Alomar led off with a single against Avery and then, with Mark Wohlers pitching, stole second, leading to an intentional walk for Carter. Winfield sacrificed the runners over for John Olerud, bringing in lefty Mike Stanton. Gaston countered with Sprague, leading to another intentional walk, Reardon came in and Maldonado belted an 0–2 pitch over Nixon's head in centre to win the game, triggering pandemonium. The next night, a 2–1 win in Game 4 behind 7⅓ dominant innings from Key gave the Blue Jays a stranglehold on the series, but John Smoltz beat Morris 7–2 in Game 5 to send things back to Atlanta.

Cone got the ball for Game 6 and held Atlanta to one run over six strong frames, leaving with a 2–1 advantage thanks to Maldonado's solo shot off Avery to open the fourth. That lead held until the ninth, when Nixon's two-out ground ball single got through the left side off Henke to knot things up.

In the 11th Charlie Leibrandt, who'd beaten the Blue Jays with the Kansas City Royals in Game 7 of the 1985 ALCS, took over for Atlanta. He hit White with one out. Alomar followed with a single. After Carter flied out, up came Winfield, who in his 19th big-league season was still chasing his first championship—and who had just seven RBIs and a .200 average in 25 career playoff games to that point. "You get the full range of emotions, but the positive outweighed anything in the past," Winfield said of stepping into the batter's box. "It took me 19 years [in] the professional ranks to be able to put my imprint on a World Series. So I thought about when I was 12 years old, when you just finish practice, men on base, last game of the season, and you want to do well. I thought about that, I thought a little about the last time I was in the World Series with the Yankees, [when] we came up short, which was 11 years before that. But I just thought it was a great opportunity, and you just think positively and want to come through. You don't know how, but it's, 'Just get a hit, make a difference.'"

With the count 3–2 after a good take on a breaking ball low and away, Winfield made a difference, hooking a ball down the third-base line for a two-run double, his first extra-base hit in 44 World Series at-bats. White and Alomar scored easily. Pivotally, Atlanta third baseman Terry Pendleton was playing well off the line, which gave him no shot at knocking down the ball. A crowd of 51,763 went silent while the Blue Jays celebrated in the dugout. "We were fortunate they weren't guarding the line," said Winfield. "I remember that once it got past the infield and it kicked around in the corner, I said, 'That's two guys in.' And I'll just tell you, some people think that hitting a home run to win the game is the ultimate. But when you're on the road and you get a hit, and you put a dagger in the opposition like that, and you're standing in the middle of the field, that is a great feeling, because you silence 50,000 people, and the only people out cheering are your teammates, and a small section of people who happened to get tickets for your team."

Still, three outs remained, and the Blue Jays had already used both Ward and Henke. Key, who came out of the bullpen on short rest to get two outs in the 10th, was back out for the 11th and allowed a leadoff single to Jeff Blauser before Berryhill reached on a Griffin error. After a Rafael Belliard sacrifice and a run-scoring Brian Hunter groundout, Gaston came out to visit Key. Nixon, 8-for-23 in his career against the lefty, was up next. When Gaston asked him what he was thinking, Key admitted that he hadn't had much luck against the speedster. So Gaston brought in Timlin, the right-hander with all of four big-league saves under his belt. Nixon fouled off the first pitch, then dropped a bunt up the first-base line on his second. Timlin pounced on it, and the World Series came to an end in the glove of Carter, who was playing first base during the games under National League rules so that Winfield could play right field. "That last out, biggest game of my career, biggest game in Toronto Blue Jays history and I'm like, 'What am I doing at first base?'" said Carter. "The thing I'm most impressed with was after catching the final out and jumping on the pile, the celebration went on for about two minutes on the field, and I'm in the pile, the bottom, the top, jumping and everything, and not once did I drop that ball. The ball was in my glove the whole time."

Said Winfield, "It was the fulfillment of a dream... and it took me a long time to get there. I prepared my best, every day, every day of every year, but you need a team, and we had a team. And then once we were celebrating and all the energy was gone, I remember after hugging all the guys, I looked for Cito Gaston, because he helped me when I was a kid. We were roommates briefly in San Diego, and from a roommate, all of a sudden you're playing for your friend as the manager. I was as happy for him as I was for myself."

At the end of the celebrations, Timlin approached Carter and asked about that ball. "I'm like, 'It's right here,'" relayed Carter. "He said, 'You've got to give it to me, that's my save.' I'm like, 'Okay.' So I gave it to him. He had it all encased and wrapped up and everything. That was a big moment for us."

For many, it was the biggest. A moment that, just like the ball used for the final out, is well worth preserving.

2

THE
1993
WORLD SERIES

"A swing and a belt, left field, way back, Blue Jays win it! The Blue Jays are World Series champions as Joe Carter hits a three-run home run in the ninth inning and the Blue Jays have repeated as World Series champions. Touch 'em all, Joe! You'll never hit a bigger home run in your life."

—Blue Jays broadcaster Tom Cheek, October 23, 1993

The day after a swing and a belt to left field way back, and touch 'em all—and the delirious bedlam and the joyous party— there was a parade and a rally in Toronto. An estimated 1 million people flooded the city streets the night before to celebrate the Blue Jays' second straight World Series title on the Carter walk-off home run. The only other World Series to end on a homer came in 1960, when Bill Mazeroski's Game 7 drive off Ralph Terry handed the Pittsburgh Pirates a 10–9 win over the New York Yankees. This moment of childhood dreams come true arrived at 11:39 PM Eastern Time, and sent a generation of fans spoiled by success to a new level of ecstasy. "The ball disappeared," said Paul Molitor, who was on base at the time, "and I thought, 'We win, we win, we win, we win.'"

Revellers from the previous night barely had time to sober up by the time a motorcade started at Queen's Park the following afternoon, wending its way toward SkyDome along downtown roads lined with 750,000 people. A crowd of 50,239 awaited the team's arrival at the stadium, while the CBC dropped coverage of a Canadian Football League game to carry the festivities live. Among the speech-makers was starter Todd Stottlemyre, who told Philadelphia mayor Ed Rendell, "You can kiss my ass" after the mayor claimed he could hit the right-hander.

Another championship banner was unveiled. "The first thing I'm thinking is how can they make it that quick? It's pretty big," remembered Carter. "Then, when you see the banner hanging, it's an accomplishment that you did as a team. It gives you a great feeling of respect, a great feeling of admiration, that as long as there's the Toronto Blue Jays, that banner will be up there. And it represents 25 guys who played their hearts out."

Right then and there, with consecutive World Series championships capping a run of 11 straight winning seasons and five American League East titles, the Blue Jays were at their zenith. No one could have fathomed then that 21 futile years would follow, the franchise steadily dragged through a painful nadir. On that stage, there was talk of a threepeat. Pat Borders mused about a ring for each bling-lacking finger. He may have been serious; nothing seemed out of reach.

Indeed, there was no reason to think otherwise, not after the Blue Jays retooled so cleverly following their first World Series triumph. Gone from the '92 team were Dave Winfield, Jimmy Key, David Cone, Tom Henke, David Wells, Candy Maldonado, Kelly Gruber, and Manny Lee. Replacing them in 1993 were Paul Molitor, Dave Stewart, Darrin Jackson, Darnell Coles, Dick Schofield, Danny Cox, and Tony Castillo. With Pat Hentgen and Ed Sprague emerging as major contributors and John Olerud developing into a batting champion, hitting .400 into August before settling in at .363, the Blue Jays simply kept rolling. "Even though everyone knew we were the team to beat, we never paid any attention to that," said centre fielder Devon White. "We just went out and won the ballgames that we needed to win."

Still, the Blue Jays dawdled in the first month and a half of the 1993 season, falling all the way to fourth place and 4½ games off pace following a 13–8 loss to the visiting Detroit Tigers on May 12. It would be their largest deficit of the season. Their turnaround started right after that, a 16–5 stretch giving them a share of the top spot after a 4–3, 10-inning walk-off win on June 4 against Oakland. Three weeks later, on June 26, the Blue Jays took sole possession of first place from Detroit with a 3–2 win at Milwaukee, with Juan Guzman outduelling Cal Eldred. From then on, they went to bed out of first just once: on July 20, after a 2–1 loss to the White Sox.

The production from the top five hitters in the lineup—White, Roberto Alomar, Molitor, Carter, and Olerud, collectively dubbed WAMCO—was the driving force behind that. With only one shutout loss, 44 comeback wins, and eight walk-off victories, the offence was a force to be reckoned with. The June 11 reacquisition of Tony Fernandez from the New York Mets in exchange for Jackson added depth to the bottom of the lineup. "After a little acclimation period things went well," said Molitor. "We had a good team. We were professional. We knew we had a chance to defend a championship."

Still, there were inevitable bumps. Jack Morris, a 20-game winner the previous season, fought through shoulder and elbow pain for most of 1993; his ERA bloated to 10.22 on June 6 before a lengthy run took it down to 6.19. He missed a considerable amount of the season after that. From June 30 to July 17 the Blue Jays lost 12 out of 14 games, but somehow dropped only two games in the standings, ultimately ending up in a tie atop the East with the New York Yankees.

Exactly two weeks later, general manager Pat Gillick pulled off another trade-deadline masterpiece, acquiring Rickey Henderson from the Oakland Athletics for Steve Karsay, one of the club's top pitching prospects, and outfielder Jose Herrera. While the Blue Jays didn't need more offence, there was no arguing against adding the greatest leadoff hitter of all time, even if it meant upsetting the WAMCO combination, which up to that point had largely carried the load.

To ensure there were no hard feelings, manager Cito Gaston called all five players in for a meeting, and asked them to write out their vision for the ideal batting order including Henderson. "They knew what kind of player he was. He certainly wasn't going to hurt us. He was going to help us. But you like to keep guys where they're comfortable," said Gaston. "They pretty much came back with the lineup I was thinking."

For the most part, it simply meant slotting in WAMCO in order behind Henderson (although against lefties Molitor moved up into Alomar's spot and the second baseman dropped behind Olerud). No matter what combination they used on a given day, everything the Blue Jays did seemed to work. They closed out the season 35–22 in August and September, and a nine-game win streak from September 10 to September 21 pushed their lead from one to five games over the Yankees. The Bronx Bombers never got closer than three games after that.

TORONTO BLUE JAYS

A 2–0 win on September 27 at Milwaukee clinched the Blue Jays their fifth American League East title, and they cruised to a 95–67 finish in the final week. The locale was fitting for Molitor, who had been part of the 1982 Brewers team that lost the World Series in seven games to the St. Louis Cardinals and hadn't been back to the playoffs since. "Strange," he said afterward. "All these years here and now I'm doing this in the visiting clubhouse."

The early clinch afforded Gaston the chance to set up his playoff rotation exactly the way he wanted for the ALCS against the West-champion Chicago White Sox. He lined up Guzman, Stewart, Hentgen, and, somewhat controversially, the up-and-down Stottlemyre.

The series lacked the drama of the previous year's matchup against the Athletics. The Blue Jays won the first two games in Chicago, then dropped the next two at home before rallying for wins in Games 5 and 6. Both Guzman and Stewart, who won MVP honours after allowing just three runs in 13 innings, went 2–0. There was a strong MVP case to be made for Molitor, who went 9-for-23 in the six games with a home run, five RBIs, and seven runs scored. But the real prize was being on a hot streak for his return to the World Series, where the Philadelphia Phillies, who had dispatched Atlanta in six games, awaited. "When we got through the White Sox series and got into the World Series, I really kind of intentionally told myself to make sure I absorb all the moments," said Molitor. "My first World Series, 11 years removed, had been too much of a blur for a young kid, and I wanted to really savour the opportunity that I had. In doing that, the peripheral benefit was that it helped me slow the game down. I was 37, and everything kind of went at a really nice pace considering how fast Major League Baseball can be, and it helped me capture the moment, it helped me be relaxed in a situation where some people might not be able to call upon that emotion. And thankfully for me, it translated into good play."

The Fall Classic against the Phillies was an all-out slugfest. The games averaged a combined 13½ runs and only one contest featured fewer than 10 runs: a 2–0 Phillies win in Game 5 behind a Curt Schilling five-hitter against Guzman. Schilling's gem came after the Blue Jays took a 3–1 Series lead with a 15–14 Game 4 victory in one of the craziest World Series games ever, when they rallied from a 14–9 deficit with a six-run eighth. Stottlemyre started that game after getting dissed by Philadelphia's mayor, gave away a 3–0 lead in the first by walking four—three of them consecutively—then got thrown out trying to go first-to-third on an Alomar single to end the second inning. His chin slammed into the ground during his awkward slide, opening a gash. He pitched an inning with the injury before his night ended. One can only imagine the hashtags and memes had Twitter existed at the time.

Al Leiter matched the six runs Stottlemyre surrendered in 2⅔ shaky innings of his own and Tony Castillo also surrendered a pair in 2⅓ frames before the Blue Jays went to work against Larry Andersen and Williams in the eighth. Molitor's RBI double started the rally, Fernandez's run-scoring single gave him five RBIs in the game, Henderson's two-run single pulled the Blue Jays within one, and White's two-run triple cemented the final margin of victory. Mike Timlin and Duane Ward nailed down the final six outs to put the Blue Jays on the verge of a repeat. "I didn't play in Game 4," said Hentgen, "but after we won, I remember the atmosphere in the locker room. It was the most incredible atmosphere that I've ever been a part of."

Asked afterward if he'd ever experienced something similar, the ever-quotable Stottlemyre quipped, "I went to the University of Arkansas. Every game there was like this."

Schilling's gem postponed the champagne toasts, and two nights later in Toronto the Phillies looked set to force a decisive seventh game when they turned the tables on the Blue Jays, scoring five in the seventh off Stewart and Cox to take a 6–5 lead in Game 6. Borders left the bases loaded in the eighth, but that rally set the stage for the ninth since the lineup had turned over. Mitch Williams, who saved 43 games in the regular season but was nicknamed "Wild Thing" because of a career walks-per-nine rate of 7.1, got the ball in the ninth looking to make amends for Game 4. Instead, he opened the frame by walking Henderson on four pitches, and never recovered. "It started auspiciously when Rickey stepped out and Mitch kind of flailed off the mound and he didn't throw a pitch," recalled Molitor. "And it was just, 'Here we go.'"

White followed with a nine-pitch at-bat that ended with a fly ball to centre before Molitor delivered a single, making him 12-for-24 with two homers and eight RBIs in the six games. "I remember being in the on-deck circle when Devon was up, and I had this thought of all the days when you're a kid, and you're in the backyard and you think about coming up in the bottom of the ninth with a chance to hit a home run to win the World Series, and I was about to live that moment," said Molitor. "I said to myself, 'Put that thought out of your mind. That's not what you do.' I hadn't done much against Mitch in my career, I hadn't faced him a ton, but I knew he had been tough on me. So to go up there thinking about hitting a home run to win the World Series, that's the last thing to be thinking about. I said to myself, 'Just go up there and have another good at-bat like you've been doing,' I got a pitch that I was able to hit into centre field and it got down. I had a little conversation about it with John Kruk at first, and I remember saying, 'This is unbelievable how much fun this is.' He goes, 'I'm not having any fun right now.'"

Carter, 0-for-4 in his career versus Williams to that point, followed, taking a fastball outside for ball one, a fastball high for ball two, and a third heater on the outside corner for strike one before swinging hesitantly at a breaking ball that nearly dipped into the dirt.

Then, history.

"I had a bit of a flat-footed swing on the 2–1 pitch, I lost track of the ball because Mickey Morandini was right behind second base," said Carter. "I had just moved the umpire over, because umpires like to stand on the first-base side of second base with a guy on first. But against a left-handed pitcher, it comes right out of the umpire, but you can't move the defender out of the way. The breaking ball looked pretty good when he first threw it, and once I picked it back up after it went through his jersey, I saw it was a ball. But I had already committed, so it kind of looked like a feeble swing. In my mind, I'm thinking, 'Okay, he's going to come back with a breaking ball. He has to the way I swung at that one.' Then he shook off the first sign, and I'm like, 'Wait a minute. He just shook off the breaking ball, because I knew Darren [Daulton] put down breaking ball, he had to, and [Williams] shook him off.' One thing Bobby Bonds always taught me was to trust your hands. If you're ever looking breaking ball and get a fastball, trust your hands. So I said, 'Okay, I'm still looking breaking ball.' He threw a fastball that he was trying to get up and away, but because he did the slide step, he kind of jerked it and threw it down and in. Ninety-nine out of 100 times I would either swing over that ball, foul it off my foot, or hit a line drive into the third-base dugout. But because I was looking breaking ball, everything slowed down. They say you have $1/16^{th}$ of a second to make a commitment or adjust to the ball, I think I went probably about $1/20^{th}$ of a second. All I did with the fastball in was just react and drop the head [of the bat] straight down. When I looked up all I saw was a bank of lights."

As the ball sailed toward the wall in left, iconic Blue Jays broadcaster Tom Cheek shouted into his microphone: "A swing and a belt, left field, way back...."

Molitor was taking his lead at first base: "I wanted to be ready in case Rickey took off from second. Joe makes contact, and I take off running because I'm just not sure. I'm watching Pete Incaviglia in left field and I'm thinking if the ball hits the wall, I score and we win. I was probably just about rounding second when I saw Incaviglia drop his head just a little bit, and then it was just a matter of making my way around and getting ready for the celebration."

White was in the dugout: "When the ball went up we all came out and we didn't even look for the umpire to say it was fair. We knew it was fair. We were all just yelling, 'Get up, get up,' because it was a low line drive. We all were standing on the top step."

Morris was in the middle of the dugout: "I jumped out. When Mitch cocked and loaded nobody knew if it was going to end up in the upper deck, behind home plate, or in centre field. He was the true Wild Thing. Joe squared it up, hooked it down the line, and the party started. I was probably the first guy to high-five him as he was coming around third base."

Hentgen was in the corner of the dugout, charting pitches: "When Joe first hit the ball I thought for sure it was going to be foul, because he hooked everything, and he was a dead pull hitter. It was amazing that he kept it fair. And I remember thinking, 'Just stay fair, just stay fair.'"

Alfredo Griffin, who came in as a pinch-runner for Olerud in the eighth, was on deck: "Cito called me and he had a matchup list. He goes, 'Listen, I'm not going to pinch-hit for you. If Carter gets on or whatever happens, you're going to hit. You own this guy [3-for-10 career].' I said, 'Hey, that's fine with me,' but I said to myself, 'Please, God, help me. Let Carter do it.' I wasn't afraid to go up and do it. Just I was at the end of my career, I wasn't the same player I was in my prime. So Carter hit a home run and I said, 'Oh, God, thank you.'"

As the ball cleared the wall and Carter hopped around the bases, Cheek continued his unforgettable call. The crowd of 52,195 was rocking as the Blue Jays dog-piled at home plate. Molitor peeled off, tears in his eyes.

"I make my way home and we pound Joe, we have the pile, and then little by little the group starts to break up and people are hugging, and then the emotion of everything that had gone on the past seven-and-a-half months, and even longer, because the decision to come here was emotional, getting acclimated to a new team after 15 years was emotional, trying to fit in, being embraced by the fans here, it became very emotional for me, and I wasn't expecting it," said Molitor. "It went from elation to still having that celebratory feeling but at the same time kind of a drain that hit me on the field. I could feel that players were coming up to me almost intentionally, one after the other, saying, 'I'm so happy for you, I'm so happy for you.' And I'm thinking, 'I'm happy for us.' But people thought enough to let me know that [they were really] happy I had a chance to win a world championship—that meant the world to me. And the embrace I got from Cito on the field. It was kind of [before the] hugging era we're in right now, but it was as comfortable [as] I ever felt really giving a man a hug, one who had done everything for me to help make what happened happen."

For the second October in a row, Carter was the man of the final moment, his jubilant teammates pulling him in a million directions. "We enjoyed the second one more, even the celebrations," said Carter. "Once we won the first World Series, we said, 'Now we can enjoy this.' And then the World Series here, it was even bigger. We had a great time."

3

2015
AMERICAN LEAGUE
EAST CHAMPIONS

Periodically, between the excruciating fits of angst, Alex Anthopoulos turned away from the game that consumed him to take in his surroundings. The Rogers Centre crowd of 49,742 was raucous but uneasy during the Toronto Blue Jays' do-or-die Game 5 of the American League Division Series against the Texas Rangers in 2015. A 2–1 deficit for baseball's best offence, even against ace lefty Cole Hamels, was by no means insurmountable. But being on the razor's edge in the postseason can be both exhilarating and exhausting. The tension can be hard to manage. "There would be times in the third, fourth, fifth innings, I'd stare at the crowd, stare at the [American League East championship] banner and try to remind myself, 'Hey, we wanted this. Win or lose, it's a good moment for Canada, for the fans, for the organization,'" said Anthopoulos. "I kept trying to remind myself to enjoy it."

The Blue Jays and their fans certainly wanted it—desperately. After 21 years without a trip to the postseason, they certainly enjoyed it, too. On this night, the Blue Jays were triumphant, notching an unforgettable 6–3 win over the Rangers. But just nine days later, with a Game 6 loss to the Kansas City Royals in the American League Championship Series, it was all over. The loss stung all the more because the Jays went 0-for-12 with men in scoring position that night at Kauffman Stadium. Even so, that hurt is far better than sitting out on the sideline when baseball matters, an experience that generations of fans knew all too well. "We had a tremendous year," said catcher Russell Martin. "We didn't have the finish we wanted, but we're going to hold our heads high. I'm proud of this group. I'm proud of how we fought."

Fought is the right word, too, because it hadn't been a wire-to-wire run from Opening Day to the American League East crown; no, it had been a grind. The $82-million, five-year deal Martin signed as a free agent the previous winter marked the start of the club's makeover from also-ran to division champion, and the changes just kept coming. Josh Donaldson, Marco Estrada, Justin Smoak, and Chris Colabello were also in place by the time spring training started, and each of them helped transform the club's personality. Then there was the energy of the six rookies who'd end up breaking camp with the team: Aaron Sanchez, Roberto Osuna, Daniel Norris, Miguel Castro, Devon Travis, and Dalton Pompey. Finally, there was the pre-trade deadline push that landed David Price, Troy Tulowitzki, LaTroy Hawkins, Mark Lowe, and Ben Revere, an array of moves that patched over an underachieving 50–51 team's flaws and ultimately spurred it to a 43–18 finish. Even after the trade deadline passed, Anthopoulos kept adding, picking up Cliff Pennington when it became apparent Travis' injured shoulder wouldn't heal in time, and Darwin Barney when Tulowitzki fractured his shoulder blade. "Credit to Alex on those moves, but we also played better," said slugger Jose Bautista, who delivered another stellar season. "The guys that were here before [the deadline] played much better than we had in the first 100 games. Playing better and the additions led us to this point."

Through the first 100 the Blue Jays had been a baseball enigma, a middling team in the standings with the positive run differential of a champion. On July 28, when they sat 50–51 and eight games back of the New York Yankees for the division lead, Toronto had scored 530 runs and surrendered 436. Only the 64–36 St. Louis Cardinals, at +106, had a better run differential than their +94. Projection models suggested the Blue Jays should have been 58–43. Indeed, they were a much better team than their record suggested.

But cracks in the foundation continually undermined the overall structure. The bullpen frittered away several games in April and May as roles were juggled back and forth; the closer's job went from Brett Cecil to Castro back to Cecil and eventually to Osuna. Meanwhile, the assignments bridging the gap to each of them shifted accordingly each time, too. Then there were the defensive problems. Jose Reyes' range fell off drastically at shortstop and cost the team at least a couple of games. Bautista's shoulder injury—aggravated by an aggressive throw to first in an emotional game against Baltimore in late April—combined with Pompey's demotion forced the Blue Jays to use a combination of

Colabello, Danny Valencia, and Ezequiel Carrera in the outfield corners. Fly balls hit to them often should have been accompanied by circus music. A handful of games disappeared there, too.

The collective issues prompted Donaldson, in the midst of a season-high five-game losing streak that stretched from May 13 to 17, to issue a rallying cry that resonated all season: "This isn't the 'try' league, this is the 'get it done' league. Eventually they're going to find people who are going to get it done."

The low point came June 2, when the Blue Jays lost the first game of a doubleheader to Jordan Zimmermann and the Washington Nationals 2–0, dropping them to what would be a season-high seven games under .500, at 23–30. Max Scherzer loomed in the nightcap, but Kevin Pillar took him deep twice in a steadying 7–3 win, and an 11-game win streak began.

Still, the Blue Jays continued to spin their wheels until reinforcements came in. With Tulowitzki at shortstop, Revere in left, and a healthy Bautista in right, the defence suddenly became airtight. The extra pitches and outs the gloves saved the pitchers made the staff more consistently effective. And the offence just kept on bludgeoning opponents. "Obviously [the trade deadline moves] were the turning point on paper," said R.A. Dickey. "But I felt like we were just waiting, like all of us were just waiting, the pitching staff was just waiting, and when they kind of put the chips all in, it did something to us, and we took off."

A four-game series against the Royals from July 30 to August 2 also proved pivotal. In the testy Sunday finale, the Blue Jays felt Donaldson was thrown at by Edinson Volquez, and the benches cleared. The incident provided a galvanizing moment. "At the time we were in the mix but hadn't established ourselves yet," said Tulowitzki, "and that sent a message across baseball and definitely to them that we had a good team."

The Blue Jays then swept the Minnesota Twins—who had entered the four-game series holding the second wild-card spot—in part of another 11-game win streak. "We made the trades, we played the Royals, I was so confident going into that Royals series," said Anthopoulos. "Knowing we won three out of four, we could have swept them, then I was really confident we were going to play well against the Twins. I was just confident that, 'Man, we've got a really good team.'"

The tipping point came when the Blue Jays took 9 of the 13 games they played against the Yankees in August and September. During a three-game sweep in the Bronx from August 7 to 9, Toronto allowed only one run in 28 innings of baseball. A gruelling doubleheader sweep September 12 in New York helped give the Blue Jays three of four during another visit to their former house of horrors. From 2012 to 2014 they had lost 17 straight games at Yankee Stadium. Things got so bad that Anthopoulos instructed travel secretary Mike Shaw to change the team's hotel in New York in an attempt to alter the team's fortunes. Eventually he started staying away from the clubhouse himself, wondering if he was the jinx. Then in 2015, the Blue Jays propelled themselves to the postseason there.

The final blow was a three-game set from September 21 to 23 in Toronto. The teams had split the first two games of the series before Marcus Stroman outduelled Ivan Nova in the finale, with Martin breaking open a 1–0 game in the seventh with a three-run homer in a 4–0 win. Trailing by 3½ games, the Yankees ostensibly surrendered the division at that point. "To see the chase was the best part," said Anthopoulos. "The last two months were more fun than the playoff games."

A week later, the Blue Jays clinched the American League East with Stroman on the mound in a 15–2 victory over the Orioles in the first game of a doubleheader. But they waited until after the second game to celebrate. A charge out of the clubhouse onto the Camden Yards infield for a group shot infuriated a groundskeeper, who yelled at the Blue Jays to get off her lawn. Instead, they chanted, "We are heat" and "Bush party," the latter a term Munenori Kawasaki made famous during a tamer party the previous weekend, when the team had clinched a playoff berth.

At long last, the playoff drought was over. Then the comeback from a 2–0 series deficit against the Rangers and the loss in six games to the Royals followed. A week later, Anthopoulos turned down an extension offer citing concerns about "fit" with incoming president and CEO Mark Shapiro. Everything happened so fast.

"When you reflect on some of the teams of the past, even [in 2014], we were in first place for quite a bit, then a lot of guys got hurt. I felt we had talented teams. And what was the piece we didn't have?" said Anthopoulos. "The more we self-analyzed and we reviewed it, we felt [character] was the one element we might need to place a little more emphasis on.... It was challenging because we really wanted to stay diligent with the philosophy, and at times we thought about bending a little bit, but we didn't, and I'm proud of our group that we stayed with it the entire way."

The end result gave the Blue Jays and their fans something to be legitimately proud of.

4

1985
AMERICAN LEAGUE
EAST CHAMPIONS

Doyle Alexander delivered, Ron Hassey swung, a lazy fly ball gently fell into George Bell's glove, the left fielder dropped to his knees in rapture, and pandemonium ensued. On October 5, 1985, in their ninth season, the Toronto Blue Jays came of age with a 5-1 victory over the New York Yankees to clinch their first American League East title, completing the transformation from expansion chumps to deserving champs. An Exhibition Stadium crowd of 44,608 erupted as teammates mobbed Alexander on the mound, while Bell yelped, "Tony, you're hurting me, man," because Tony Fernandez hugged him so hard in shallow left. "He almost broke my neck," Bell said, laughing at the memory. Slowly, hundreds of fans ran from the stands to join the festivities despite the PA announcer's admonishment, "Ladies and gentlemen, please stay off the playing field." After years of losing, this party belonged to everyone.

"That was just a great year, it really was. It was the year that we just took off," said Lloyd Moseby, the spark-plug centre fielder who was also one of the club's spiritual pillars. "We knew we were good, we understood that we were good, and we weren't afraid to say we were good, so I think that took us over the hump. Before we were like a Canadian team who thought, 'Well, somebody's going to think we're bragging,' but sooner or later we just said, 'Hey, what the heck, let's just go beat somebody up.' And, it was a great year, it was a lot of fun, too."

Winning 99 games during the regular season had to have been fun, especially after the Blue Jays began their existence with six consecutive losing seasons. They suffered at least 102 losses in each of the first three years before finally breaking through after consecutive 89-win campaigns left them knocking on the door. "I think we're going to be around for a while. I think we're going to reckoned with," said catcher Ernie Whitt, one of a handful of original Blue Jays remaining on the '85 club, amid the champagne showers.

He was right. From 1985 to 1993, the Blue Jays would play only 12 regular-season games in which they had been eliminated from contention for the division crown. During that span, they won the East four more times. Meaningful baseball went from pipe dream to given for Blue Jays fans, and that first title marked the beginning of a golden era that would only be fully appreciated during the 21-year playoff drought that followed 1993. "As I talk to former Blue Jays employees as I go around, I don't think anybody understood how good it was in the mid-80s to early '90s," said Gord Ash, a player personnel official in 1985 who eventually succeeded Pat Gillick as general manager. "I don't think we appreciated it as much as we should have or could have, because it was pretty special to be that successful for that length of time. It doesn't happen very much anymore now."

Bell, Whitt, and Moseby are among those who wonder if the Blue Jays might have won their first division crown sooner. They believe a leaky bullpen held them back in both 1983, the club's first winning season, and '84, when the Detroit Tigers opened the season 35–5 and cruised the rest of the way. Gillick made a point of addressing that pitching void in the off-season, acquiring right-hander Bill Caudill from the Oakland Athletics in exchange for beloved shortstop Alfredo Griffin (a move made possible by Fernandez's emergence) plus speedy outfielder Dave Collins and cash. He also added left-hander Gary Lavelle from the San Francisco Giants in exchange for righties Jim Gott, Jack McKnight, and Augie Schmidt. Both Caudill and Lavelle helped immensely. But the real finishing touch was the late-July promotion of Tom Henke, the fireballing righty plucked from the Texas Rangers with their pick for Cliff Johnson in the free-agent compensation draft. Henke was so dominant in 28 appearances—only nine earned runs allowed over 40 innings, with 42 strikeouts—that people nicknamed him the "Terminator." "We didn't know who the guy was until we saw him pitch and we went, 'Damn, we've never seen that before,'" said Moseby. "That's what we needed."

Also crucial was Jimmy Key's seamless move into the rotation after spending 1984 in the bullpen. Workhorse righty Jim Clancy underwent an appendectomy early in the season and later suffered shoulder tendinitis that would limit him to one inning in the postseason, while

Luis Leal pitched so poorly he was demoted in early July and never returned to the big leagues. That left a heavier load for Alexander and ace Dave Stieb to carry, and the Blue Jays might have broken had Key not delivered a 14–6 record with a 3.00 ERA over 212⅔ innings in 35 games, three of them in relief. "We called him Pee-Wee Herman because he looked like a nerd, but he was actually like an assassin," said Moseby. "He was the most unflappable young guy we had ever seen. He was the best thing that ever happened to us as far as starting pitching goes, because we were kind of lacking in that department."

Smaller but surprising contributions came from the likes of Tom Filer, who was 7–0 with a 3.88 ERA in 11 games, and Dennis Lamp, who went 11–0 with a 3.32 ERA in 53 games, while logging 105⅔ innings. Despite the early uncertainty, the Blue Jays ended up leading the league with a 3.31 ERA.

A deep, balanced, and dynamic lineup (think of the 2015 Kansas City Royals) ensured that all that pitching didn't go to waste. Six players had double-digit home run numbers, led by Bell's 28. He also paced the team with 95 RBIs and joined Moseby and Jesse Barfield in what was dubbed the "Best Outfield In Baseball." Fernandez, playing stellar defence while contributing a .730 OPS, and Damaso Garcia, second on the team with 28 stolen bases, formed a dynamic pairing up the middle. Ernie Whitt was steady in a platoon with Buck Martinez behind the plate, while Willie Upshaw at first base and Rance Mulliniks and Garth Iorg at third handled the corners. The midseason acquisitions of Al Oliver and Johnson in separate deals helped bolster the DH spot and bench. "The '85 team was as good as any team we had," said Fernandez.

The Blue Jays grabbed a share of first place in the American League East after a 9–5 win over the Seattle Mariners on May 12 and they didn't relinquish it the rest of the way. On August 4 they stretched their advantage to a season-best 9½ games. But the Yankees cut that to just 2½ games at the beginning of a four-game set in New York on September 12. The race got even tighter after Toronto dropped the opener 7–5, a Yankees six-spot in the seventh erasing a 4–1 lead. But the Blue Jays bounced back to win the next three games and push the advantage back up to 4½ games. The division seemed to be in hand again when a 6–2 win over the Boston Red Sox on September 24 extended the gap to seven games, but the Blue Jays struggled to close out the title—an issue that would become familiar in the years to come. They lost six of their next nine games, including the opener of a season-ending three-game series at home against the Yankees.

The 4–3 loss October 4 was especially tough to take, as Butch Wynegar's two-out fly ball to right off Henke in the ninth was pushed out by the gusts to tie the game at 3–3. A single, a walk, and a Don Mattingly fly ball to centre dropped by Moseby brought home the go-ahead run and delayed the celebrations. But there was no pushing back the party the next afternoon. Alexander grabbed the game by the throat, solo shots by Whitt in the second and Moseby and Upshaw in the third put the game out of reach, and the division was clinched. "I've been here from the beginning," Iorg said afterward. "From worst to first. It's just great."

The Blue Jays' first appearance in the American League Championship Series followed, and on paper the matchup against the Kansas City Royals appeared great, too. The Blue Jays owned home-field advantage by finishing nine games ahead of the West winners in the standings. They capitalized on that early, Stieb throwing eight innings of three-hit shutout in a 6–1 Game 1 win, and Oliver capping a seesaw Game 2 with a game-winning, two-out, two-run single in the 10th inning for a 6–5 victory.

George Brett, who ruined October for a generation of Blue Jays fans, put on a tour de force in Game 3, going 4-for-4 with two homers and three RBIs in a 6–5 win. But Oliver delivered more heroics in Game 4, ripping a go-ahead two-run double in the ninth inning for a comeback 3–1 win. In previous seasons, that victory would have sent the Blue Jays to the World Series, but in 1985 the championship series were changed from best-of-five to best-of-seven affairs, a switch that saved the Royals, who went into rally mode. Danny Jackson's eight-hit shutout in Game 5 sent the series back to Toronto, where Brett's go-ahead homer in the fifth inning of Game 6 paced a 5–3 victory. And in the decisive seventh game, Jim Sundberg's wind-aided, three-run triple capped a four-run sixth that sent the Royals to the World Series after a 6–2 win. Over a span of four days, the exhilaration of an imminent berth in the Fall Classic turned into the kind of sporting agony that is only borne out of unimaginable defeat. "I spent a week in my basement," said Cito Gaston, the hitting coach for that club. "I wouldn't come out, I was so depressed." Adds Fernandez, "We should have won it all. We know that."

To this day, the pain and frustration linger. "I need some therapy because of that," said Barfield. "That still bothers me. I never want to second-guess a manager but I question why we even pitched to Brett [during the series]. I saw him with our ring on, and I asked him, 'Are you taking care of our ring?' He laughed. But that's baseball." Moseby feels the same way. "You still kind of turn over at night sometimes and think, 'Why did we pitch to George Brett?'" he said. "It's a lifetime of wondering and hurting because that was our time, nobody could beat us at that time. We knew that, and we didn't have the best pitching, we didn't have the best 'this,' but nobody could beat us, we just had what it took to win. But they went into the next series against the St. Louis Cardinals and did the same damn thing [rallying from a 3–1 series deficit], so it was meant for them to win."

Maybe it was, maybe it wasn't, and maybe it depends on which sports narrative you buy into. Regardless, the Blue Jays won in a meaningful way for the first time in 1985, discovering in the process that enjoying the spoils of success also exponentially intensifies the torment of failure.

5

FRANCHISE ICON: PAT GILLICK

om Henke was the fallback to the fallback plan for the Toronto Blue Jays in the 1985 free agent compensation draft. Pat Gillick's initial target for the pick—received after Cliff Johnson signed with the Texas Rangers—was Donnie Moore, but the California Angels scooped up the right-handed reliever first. The Blue Jays then locked in on Bill Cutshall, a right-hander in the Montreal Expos' system who had pitched in 13 A-ball games during the 1984 season, striking out 88 batters in 69 innings. No one was going to be on him. "He was a prospect at the time," recalled Gillick. "We saw him in the instructional league, and we liked him a lot." Toronto was set to pick him until the St. Louis Cardinals selected shortstop Angel Salazar from the Expos. Since teams could lose only one player during the draft, Cutshall was suddenly off the board and out of reach. "Son of a bitch, we lost the guy," Gillick shouted in the Exhibition Stadium office where he and a group of scouts were gathered. Under the gun, he quickly turned to Wilbur "Moose" Johnson, the scout who years later would push for the pursuit of Roberto Alomar and argue strongly in favour of sending Fred McGriff and Tony Fernandez to San Diego for Alomar and Joe Carter. "Moose, who should we take?" Gillick asked. "He said, 'There's a guy down in Texas, I saw him late in the season. A hard-throwing guy. His name is Tom Henke.' That's how we got Henke."

While the December 5, 1990, acquisition of Alomar and Carter is widely regarded as Gillick's masterstroke, and understandably so, it's the smaller, more clever pieces of business, such as the Henke acquisition, that are at the heart of his Hall of Fame run as general manager of the Blue Jays. The low-key Californian with the photographic memory and uncanny eye for talent was all Moneyball decades before Moneyball became famous, aggressively scouting Latin America, stealing future stars in the Rule 5 draft, and leveraging every method of player acquisition long before the rest of the league caught up. The farm system he meticulously developed from the

Blue Jays' inception in 1977 fuelled and sustained a run of 11 straight winning seasons. He made impact trades to augment and eventually revamp the team's core, despite earning the nickname Stand Pat while going from August 31, 1987, to April 30, 1989, without making a single trade. And when the time called for finishing touches, Gillick used free agency brilliantly to help deliver World Series championships in 1992 and '93. The vast majority of the Blue Jays' high-water marks came under his watch because he built a deep and talented baseball operations department that left no stone unturned.

"That was our thinking, to cast a wide net and try to get as many players as we possibly could," said Gillick. "We thought it would take us 10 years to get to where we wanted to be and we had very good support from our ownership on a long-range plan. They were very patient. It ended up that we got there a little bit sooner than 10 years [winning the American League East for the first time in 1985], but we wouldn't have been able to do what we did if it wasn't for the patience. It took time, but it worked out in the end."

Among the players drafted during the Gillick era were Dave Stieb, Lloyd Moseby, Jimmy Key, David Wells, Pat Borders, Pat Hentgen, Mike Timlin, John Olerud, Jeff Kent, Ed Sprague, Shawn Green, Shannon Stewart, and Chris Carpenter. Tony Fernandez, Carlos Delgado, Luis Leal, Nelson Liriano, Junior Felix, Luis Sojo, Sil Campusano, and Kelvim Escobar were signed out of Latin America. Willie Upshaw, George Bell, Jim Gott, Jim Acker, Kelly Gruber, and Manny Lee were Rule 5 pickups. Alfredo Griffin, Damaso Garcia, Fred McGriff, Cecil Fielder, Duane Ward, and Juan Guzman were acquired via trade while still prospects. Gillick also made "win-now" trades for the likes of Bill Caudill, Gary Lavelle, Al Oliver, Cliff Johnson, Phil Niekro, Mike Flanagan, Al Leiter, Mookie Wilson, Devon White, Alomar, Carter, Tom Candiotti, David Cone, Darrin Jackson, Fernandez, and Rickey Henderson.

That alone is a Hall of Fame résumé. Forget that after leaving the Blue Jays following the 1994 season he also built playoff teams with the Baltimore Orioles, Seattle Mariners, and Philadelphia Phillies, winning another World Series in the City of Brotherly Love in 2008.

Gillick's evolution into a Hall of Fame executive began in 1964, after arm problems ended a five-year pitching career in the Baltimore

General manager Pat Gillick at a 1989 press conference in Toronto. (Hans Deryk/The Canadian Press)

Orioles system. During those days he earned the nickname "Yellow Pages" because, as legendary manager Earl Weaver once said, "if you wanted to know anything all you had to do was ask Gillick." Weaver managed the lefty in the minors and called him Wolley Segap—Yellow Pages backwards—but Gillick's ability to instantly recite stats for various league leaders served him well. He started out as an assistant farm director with the Houston Colt .45s (who later changed their name to Astros), branching out to scouting in 1968. In 1974 he took over as scouting director, then joined the New York Yankees in the same role in 1975.

Shortly after Peter Bavasi was named vice president and general manager of the Blue Jays in June 1976, he approached Gillick, whose contract with the Yankees expired at the end of October, about coming over. The aim was to get someone in place before the season ended in order to do some scouting ahead of the expansion draft that November. Yankees owner George Steinbrenner didn't let him go easily. What happened next demonstrated the type of shrewd, at times cutthroat, negotiator Gillick could be. "[The Yankees] finally agreed in late July to let me leave, and there were some terms and conditions that had to be met," said Gillick. "At that time they were using telegrams, so I said, 'Send me a fax so I know what to say on the telegram.' So they sent me a fax and I returned the telegram verbatim. Then I got a call back from [president and GM] Gabe Paul saying that's not sufficient, Mr. Steinbrenner doesn't like it. I told him send me something else, what Mr. Steinbrenner prefers, and basically it said I couldn't take scouts, couldn't take personnel, couldn't take front office people with me. I could go but can't sabotage the organization. So they sent me another fax, I sent another telegram, and they called me back and said this isn't good either. I said, 'Well I complied twice. I don't know what to do. You tell George that if he doesn't want to let me out of this thing I'm going to go to the *New York Times* and tell them exactly what's going on.' Consequently, maybe about an hour later, I got a call back and they said, 'Okay, we'll let you go.'"

Gillick came over as vice president of player personnel, but essentially operated as the general manager. He immediately began focusing on the expansion draft—picks Jim Clancy, Ernie Whitt, and Garth Iorg hung around long enough to play key roles on the '85 squad—while diving into Latin America. Bavasi overruled Gillick once that first year, preventing him from dealing away Bill Singer to the Yankees for a young left-hander named Ron Guidry. "Bill Singer was our Opening Day starter, he'd won 20 games (for the Dodgers in 1969 and Angels in 1973), he was our only $100,000 player our first year, but he was basically broken down by then," said longtime Blue Jays PR man Howard Starkman. "Pat had sort of made the deal. He knew Guidry because he'd been in the Yankees system and Bavasi turned him down because he was afraid the media would say why are we getting rid of our one big name. It was a bad move, and after that Bavasi basically told him, 'I won't interfere.'" Guidry went on to win 16 games in 1977 and 170 in all during a 14-year big-league career. Singer was 2–8 with a 6.79 ERA in 13 games in his last season in the majors.

Though he missed on Guidry, Gillick steadily lifted some of his other favourites from the Yankees' system in the years to come, Garcia, Upshaw, and McGriff notably among them. The first two were part of the slow build to the first American League East crown in 1985, the ecstasy of finally breaking through quickly juxtaposed with the agony of blowing a 3–1 lead to the Kansas City Royals in the American League Championship Series.

Still, that period marked a definitive turning point for the franchise, and not just because the doormat years were left behind. The Detroit Tigers ran away with the division in 1984 and it would have taken a spectacular comeback to chase them down after a 35–5 start, but in some ways the Blue Jays never really gave themselves a chance as their bullpen continually squandered wins. They had 24 blown saves and 13 walk-off losses that year, which is why Gillick acquired Caudill from Oakland and Lavelle from San Francisco for 1985. As it turned out, it was Henke that ended up making the difference after he was called up at the end of July and dominated from his first appearance onward. Then, on July 6, 1986, Gillick acquired a hard-throwing prospect named Duane Ward from Atlanta for Doyle Alexander. Ward stuck for good in 1988, emerging as a dominant setup man for Henke in what was a precursor to the current power-arm bullpen model.

"We were not able to close out games, and there can't be anything more frustrating to an offence," said Gillick. "They would start thinking, 'Well, how many runs do we have to score to win a game?' That has an effect on the whole team. As we all know, bullpens are built differently today. At that time, [Dan] Quisenberry was closing out games, Henke was closing out games, [Goose] Gossage was closing out games, but it was one guy. The fact that Ward and Henke were a tandem, one guy in the eighth and the other in the ninth, I don't think we could have gone and won a World Series without those two guys closing things out."

Before the Blue Jays got to that point, there was a lot of heartache to endure, from the collapse of '87 to the American League Championship Series drubbings from the Athletics in 1989 and Twins in 1991. At the 1990 winter meetings in Rosemont, Illinois, Gillick had decided it was time to start turning over the core, looking to change the mix of players that couldn't get over the hump together. Moose Johnson banged on the table for Alomar, leading to the December 5, 1990, blockbuster with the Padres. In hindsight it was Gillick's signature move, but it was met with plenty of disapproval at first—especially from his wife, Doris, who implored him to "come home before you screw up the team more" when he broke the news to her.

"That kind of calibre of trade takes big balls, as we would say in Texas, and certainly Pat had them," said Gruber. "You're either going to look great or you're not, and if you give away two proven players, especially players people liked, you're climbing uphill. But Pat knew what he was doing."

Indeed, the trade was no flight of fancy. John Olerud was coming at that point and Gillick wanted to open up first base for him. George Bell had become a free agent, leaving the Blue Jays in need of a right-handed slugger. "We probably would have done a McGriff for Carter one-for-one," said Gillick. "But it was on the third suggestion by San Diego that I asked them if they would talk about Alomar. And they said, 'Well, if you would talk about Fernandez,' and so that's the one that got [it] going."

After the flameout in 1991 against the Twins, Gillick made his boldest forays into free agency by signing Jack Morris and Dave Winfield for the 1992 season, and then Paul Molitor and longtime nemesis Dave Stewart for '93. In-season deals for David Cone in '92 and Rickey Henderson in '93 bolstered the two championship runs. Gillick left the Blue Jays after the strike-shortened 1994 season, having finished what he started.

"First you win your division in 1985 to get to the top of the mountain, but then all these others hills are around, bumps in the road that we went through between '87, '89, '91. In '91, I thought we actually had a better team than we had in '92 and '93, but lost to Minnesota. Then finally to get to the top in '92, it was like taking another deep breath and saying, 'Well, it took from '85 to '92, but we finally made it to the top.'"

Not only did Gillick make it to the top, but with a brilliant Blue Jays legacy and a plaque in Cooperstown, he's staying there, too.

6

2016 AMERICAN LEAGUE WILD-CARD WINNERS

A bunch of renegades, John Gibbons called them, just before the corks started popping and streams of bubbly ripped through the cramped quarters of the visitors' clubhouse at Fenway Park. Moments earlier, the Toronto Blue Jays did just enough to survive a September swoon and clinch the first wild-card berth in club history in their regular-season finale. Two days later, Edwin Encarnacion would end an epic game against the Baltimore Orioles with a walk-off home run. The subsequent sweep of the Texas Rangers in a narrative-charged division series rematch gave further credence to what Gibbons told his players after the dramatic 2–1 win over the Boston Red Sox. "Keep it going," he shouted. "Watch out for this team."

As it turned out, Cleveland and its lockdown pitching staff blindsided the Blue Jays in the American League Championship Series. The second straight loss in the final four wasn't as close as the first one, but cut a little deeper after a 2016 season played out on unsteady ground. The new front office of Mark Shapiro and Ross Atkins operated in a dramatically different fashion from that of Paul Beeston and Alex Anthopoulos. Their win-now roster carried the American League's third-oldest position player group and second-oldest pitching staff, with several players approaching a best-before date. The looming free agency of organizational pillars Jose Bautista and Encarnacion represented a crossroads that loomed like a threatening storm on the horizon.

That's why, upon his arrival, Shapiro spoke of maximizing the short-term while needing "to manage against the long-term challenges" he felt were created by Anthopoulos' flurry of deals ahead of the 2015 trade deadline. Essentially, the organization ran on two tracks. On one, there was an attempt to keep the big-league club operating as similarly as possible to the previous year. On the other, the start of a total remaking of the farm system and entire organizational structure. With impact prospects too far down the road to replenish the existing big-league core, the clock was ticking on the big-league club. The effect of all that was a last-hurrah feel, especially as some of the fault lines (which, in 2018, triggered a full-scale rebuild) were revealed.

Hence, the entire setup, and the tumultuous path back to the postseason, made "renegades" hit just the right tone. "That's what we were," said Gibbons. "You had some cast-offs. Josh Donaldson was sort of a cast-off until he found a home. Bautista was, too. And those two guys weren't liked around the league. A lot of it was because they were so good. But they were animated. They were emotional. So they pissed some other teams off, big-time. They were our two main big boys, so that was kind of who we were, you know?"

Fittingly, the campaign was marked by a chaotic May brawl in Texas in which the Rangers, driven by shameful pettiness, exacted vengeance on Bautista for his postseason bat flip a year earlier. Later in the season there was another wild melee with the New York Yankees. Along the way, preseason extension talks with Encarnacion went nowhere, Chris Colabello was suspended 80 games after testing positive for a banned substance he denied knowingly ingesting, and Aaron Sanchez had to fight against a move to the bullpen because of workload concerns.

Through every twist and turn, "we were all focused on just continuing to win," said Bautista. "We had a great team in place with all the players Alex put together."

Tim Leiper, the first base coach at the time, concurred. "What was super impressive to me is that the focus was totally on winning," he said. "There was no other B.S. involved at all."

That focus was important, because the potential for disruption continued long after the split with Anthopoulos. Just as spring training started, a three-way trade that would have shipped out Michael Saunders (who went on to an All-Star season) and returned Jay Bruce fell apart, while Bautista declared that he had given the Blue Jays a number it would take for him to re-sign and he wouldn't negotiate off it. Encarnacion then told the Blue Jays he wouldn't engage in extension talks once the season started. Amid the external noise, Donaldson's arrival at camp with the proclamation that he was "pretty excited to be back with the boys and cause a little trouble" restored a sense of normalcy within the group.

"That's probably the year where I was the most confident and most excited to begin," Bautista said of the team's vibe. "We got it done the year before, with a successful run in the playoffs, two wins short of the World Series, having put the drought of 21 years to bed. Getting my first postseason at-bats, and for a lot of those guys in our group as well, and then coming back with that experience and the same group, if not even an enhanced group, felt pretty good. I showed up in spring training ready to rock."

The same didn't apply to the offence once the regular season started. While the rotation came out hot in April, the offence did not, hitting just .232/.314/.395. Compounding matters was that the early-season bullpen issues that nearly submarined the 2015 campaign resurfaced. Lefty Brett Cecil took five of the losses in an 11–14 opening month. Drew Storen, the former Washington Nationals closer acquired for Ben Revere in January, allowed nine earned runs in eight innings over 10 games. Gavin Floyd and Arnold Leon had hiccups in leverage. Nineteen of 37 inherited runners in the month were allowed to score.

Things didn't settle on that front until the end of May, when Cecil righted himself, Rule 5 pick Joe Biagini emerged as a trustworthy arm, and Jason Grilli was acquired from Atlanta and immediately delivered reliable set-up work in front of closer Roberto Osuna. That followed the Blue Jays' nadir—a season-high five-game losing streak May 14–18. Within that stretch came the infamous brawl game with the Rangers at Globe Life Park in Arlington, late in the final regular-season meeting between the clubs.

A week and a half earlier, the teams played four games in Toronto without incident, and though Bautista was booed heartily in Texas, the possibility of schoolyard nonsense had seemed to pass. If it was going to happen, the Blue Jays figured, it would have happened May 2 in their first meeting of the season. Gibbons remembered a conversation with Bautista beforehand, "and him saying, 'If they hit me, I'm just going to go to first base.'"

Instead, the teams played clean until the eighth inning of their seventh meeting, when reliever Matt Bush drilled Bautista on the left elbow with his first pitch, to the delight of the braying masses in Arlington. Home-plate umpire Dan Iassogna immediately issued warnings to both clubs, which only inflamed the situation. If he suspected the pitch was intentional, he should have ejected Bush right then and there. He didn't, and Bautista fumed at first base as the inning continued. Encarnacion flew out and after lefty Jake Diekman replaced Bush, Justin Smoak hit a grounder to third base that lit the tinderbox. Adrian Beltre threw to second to start a double play and Bautista, demonstrating his displeasure, slid aggressively through Rougned Odor. The second baseman tried to whip the ball at Bautista's face as he jumped to avoid contact, just missing. The two then squared up and after Odor shoved Bautista, he caught him in the jaw with a clean right, and then slapped Bautista's head with his glove. Beltre wrapped up Bautista and pulled him away, while Kevin Pillar and then Donaldson charged at Odor. A wild scrum ensued by second base, with Blue Jays bullpen catcher Jason Phillips exchanging blows with Sam Dyson, who surrendered the bat flip homer to Bautista the previous fall.

Gibbons and Leiper had both been ejected in the third inning and were in the manager's office, drinking a bottle of wine when Bush hit Bautista. Immediately, Gibbons put his shoes back on, sat on the edge of his chair, and as soon as the melee began, "gave the word, 'Let's go,'" Leiper recalled. "Just classic Gibby. I didn't go on the field because, listen, I'm a first-base coach, I'm going to get tanked if I go back on the field and I don't have any money. So I watched it from the bench. Gibby walked right out to the middle. He didn't run. He didn't walk fast. He walked like Gibby out to the field. It was one of the funniest, surreal moments that I was a part of."

Once at midfield, Gibbons checked on Bautista, who had been passed from Beltre to Ryan Goins. Then he began yelling at Rangers manager Jeff Banister, who made a sideshow of himself by clapping his hands together and yelling, "Let's go!" like he was in a WWE ring. The crowd broke out into an asinine "U-S-A, U-S-A," chant, finding a bizarre patriotism in a Venezuelan socking a Dominican. Gibbons shook his head in disgust as he walked off the field once the scene had calmed. "If I've got a problem, and we're going to do it the old-school way, we're going to hit somebody, you do it right away, man," he said. "That way everybody knows what's going on. But the way it all played out, nothing happened early, final game down there, [Bush] wasn't even a guy that was with the team [in 2015]. To me that was bush league. When you wait like that, it hamstrings us. I thought it was chickenshit, running scared, whatever you want to call it."

That sentiment was shared throughout the Blue Jays clubhouse. "What drives me crazy is the way to handle that is you hit Bautista in the first game, get it out of the way, and that's it. It's all said and done," said starter Marco Estrada. "But you wait until the eighth inning of the last game, you bring in your hardest-throwing reliever and he drills him? It blew my mind." Added Leiper: "Absolute garbage."

The Rangers tried to brush it off, Bush claiming the ball slipped, Banister denying any intention. But there was no doubt that they were settling a score. In the wake of Bautista's bat-flip homer, the benches emptied twice. Dyson ripped Bautista's antics after the game. Reliever Anthony Bass, who pitched for the Rangers in 2015 and the Blue Jays in 2020, pointed to the "two big-personality types on each team—Bautista and Odor," as being central to the feud. "When [Bautista] hit his home runs, it rubbed Odor the wrong way and he let the guys in the clubhouse know that he didn't want to put up with that."

Bigger picture, both Bautista's homer and the Rangers' reaction to it underscored the wider cultural divide in baseball around on-field celebrations and decorum. While bat flips are not only accepted but celebrated in Latin America and South Korea, they were frowned upon in the big-leagues. Bautista's toss, an emotional reaction after delivering in a pivotal moment, changed the discourse. As the MLB player base trended younger in the years since, acceptance has grown. "If Bautista does what he did today, it's not even talked about," said Estrada. "I mean, guys are throwing their bats two storeys up in the air now. I didn't think what he did was out of line and I'm all about not disrespecting anybody and I don't want to be disrespected. But in that moment, that big of a situation, if you get me then you earned it."

Major League Baseball certainly didn't reflect that in its discipline, giving Odor eight games and Bautista one. Bush received only a fine, even though the league deemed he "intentionally threw at Bautista, causing the warnings." Gibbons got three games and a $5,000 fine, while Banister went unpunished. Bautista deserved better. All he did was hit an iconic home run. The Rangers started a fight with him because their feelings were hurt.

"They dealt with it the way they dealt with it, and I'll let them answer to that," Bautista said of the Rangers. "We all know that our team would have handled it different had it happened in reverse. Do I wish I would not have gotten into the fight and the skirmish and got suspended and all that other crap? Yeah. I wish it would have never happened. Maybe there were things that I could have done to avoid it. Do I think they were looking for something? Obviously. They hit me and I don't know what else they expected or wanted to happen. But I feel pretty good about having beat them twice [in the playoffs]. That's what it's all about."

In the aftermath, the Blue Jays returned home and were swept by the Tampa Bay Rays, falling a season-worst four games under .500 at 19–23. But then they found their equilibrium with an 11–3 stretch against the Twins, Yankees, and Red Sox, the offence picking up to support a rotation that had emerged as the club's primary strength.

J.A. Happ, signed as a free agent after a strong half-season with Pittsburgh, continued a late-career bloom and became the franchise's sixth 20-game winner. Estrada was again masterful with his high-spin-rate fastball/Bugs Bunny changeup combination. Marcus Stroman rode out some bumps and found himself starting the wild-card game, while R.A. Dickey continued to reliably eat innings. Combined with Sanchez's progression to an ace-calibre starter, the Blue Jays had suddenly become a pitching-first squad. "As a staff, we were coming off a year in '15 where we were pretty darn good and nobody really gave us any credit," said Dickey. "We took it as a slight internally, that people didn't think that we could carry our club and it always had to be the offence in the American League East. [Pitching coach] Pete Walker did a good job of stoking the fire for that. I remember having conversations with Marco and Stro about how we knew we were going to eventually hit, that was going to happen. We just needed to be able to hold the fort down until we started producing offensively. That's kind of what happened."

Sanchez almost pitched too well. In 2015 he had thrown 109.1 innings, beginning the year as a starter before transitioning to the bullpen. When he broke camp in the rotation, there were questions about how big an innings jump he could handle. One thought was to ride him again as a starter for half a year and then transition him to a relief role, but as Sanchez dominated start after start, that idea became increasingly fraught.

Still, ahead of the trade deadline, the Blue Jays acquired Francisco Liriano from the Pirates so they could shift Sanchez to a relief role. Several players came out against the plan—"I've never been a big fan of having Sanchie go back to the bullpen," said catcher Russell Martin—and the right-hander pushed back enough that Atkins flew from Toronto to Houston to meet the team. Their solution was to run a six-man rotation into September and then shift back to five ahead of the playoffs. "We were pioneers, man," quipped Gibbons.

Initially, the move wasn't popular with the rotation. "None of us liked that," said Estrada, "but if he was good to pitch, which he was, we didn't want anything to change. And he felt bad that because of him we'd get that extra off-day in between." Still, it was a necessary evil to contain Sanchez's innings, even though he was showing no signs of fatigue. Top of mind was Washington's controversial decision to shut down Stephen Strasburg in September 2012 because he'd hit an innings cap coming back from Tommy John surgery. In hindsight, that was seen as unnecessary, and his absence was felt in the playoffs, when the Nationals were eliminated in the first round. The Blue Jays didn't want to risk similar regrets. "You're basically guessing, but you're guessing and you're taking probably arguably your best pitcher out of the rotation," said Leiper. "It's like, oh, holy crap, we're going to lose a guy from the rotation because he's over-performing? That's kind of a tough pill to swallow. What they ended up coming up with was really, really good and really effective."

There was no guarantee it would turn out that way. Liriano arrived as a question mark, carrying a 5.46 earned-run average. The Blue Jays believed they could get him right and viewed him as a lower-risk add than Rich Hill, the curveball-throwing lefty who was fighting blister problems. The Oakland Athletics planned to flip Hill and outfielder

Josh Reddick at the deadline and wanted a prospect package centred around Rowdy Tellez and Jon Harris, the 2015 first-round pick. Instead, the Dodgers ended up with the duo for a package that featured Jharel Cotton and Frankie Montas.

With Sanchez's status settled, the Blue Jays continued to roll in August. A 16–8 July had allowed them to touch first place in the division for the first time, and a 4–2 win August 13 against the Astros kicked off a 3½-week stretch in which they held the top spot. But as the calendar turned to September, their play flipped once more. They lost five of six games on a road trip to Tampa Bay and the Bronx, the finale dropping them a game back of Boston. Then they returned home to get thumped 13–3 on September 9 by the Red Sox in perhaps their worst game of the season. Having lost four games in the standings in nine days, their play was so concerning that they called a team meeting the following day. "Any time the players call a team meeting, it's a big deal," said Estrada, who started the loss to Boston. "It definitely was something we all needed. We just knew we were too good of a team to be crashing down the way we kind of were." Dickey remembered it as "a stay calm and keep trucking kind of meeting. Like, hey, this is all right. We've been here before. Nobody panic. Arrest the momentum."

"One of the things I loved about that team, we really were in a state of understanding about who we were," Dickey continued. "There was no need for Gibby to have nightly meetings to try to motivate us, or for JD or Bautista or whoever to yell at people or to give people space. Those guys all took turns saying their piece. But there was nothing that was aggravating about it. It wasn't, 'Hey pitchers, y'all need to get your butts in gear,' or 'Hitters, do this, we don't have any passion.' I don't think anybody thought to themselves, 'This isn't going to happen, we're going to lose a postseason berth.' We knew we we're going to play well. We just knew."

The Blue Jays rallied to beat the Red Sox 3–2 right afterwards, but fell 11–8 the next day. They didn't win another series until taking two of three from Seattle September 19–21, but by then the Red Sox had seized control of the AL East and would soon clinch the division. That left them fighting with a few teams, including the Orioles, for a wild-card spot.

Before Baltimore arrived for a three-game series in the final week of the season, the Blue Jays ended up brawling with the Yankees at Rogers Centre. This time the trouble started when Luis Severino grazed Donaldson on the left elbow. Whether or not there was intent, Happ decided to retaliate, throwing one pitch behind Chase Headley before catching him on the left buttocks with his second. The benches cleared but nothing developed, though Severino opened the next inning by throwing two pitches at Smoak, just missing with the first, before getting him in the thigh on the second. Everyone jumped in after that. "J.A. stuck up for a teammate at the right time at the right spot. And that was effective," said Leiper. "Not that I condone throwing at guys, but it was a good moment for us because we knew we had each other's backs."

It came at a cost, though, and one that extended beyond discipline, as reliever Joaquin Benoit, who had pitched well after being acquired from Seattle for Storen on July 26, tore his calf running in from the bullpen. His loss thinned out the relief corps just as the stakes were rising. The Blue Jays then dropped two of three versus the Orioles, setting up a do-or-die weekend in Boston. Before they left, Encarnacion sat in the dugout quietly, taking in his surroundings. "I don't want to leave here like that," he said. "I want to come back here to the playoffs and give everything I've got to the fans."

The Blue Jays did just enough against the Red Sox to make it happen. After dropping the first game, they won the second 4–3 on a ninth-inning sacrifice fly by Ezequiel Carrera. The next day they clinched behind seven dominant innings from Sanchez (two hits, one run) and a go-ahead RBI single from Troy Tulowitzki in the eighth that secured a 2–1 victory. "I know we lost the first night, but I thought we played some of our best baseball of the year," said Leiper. "The Sanchez game is easily the best regular-season game I've seen pitched. We obviously had a lot of good ones, but I can't say enough about how good I thought that game was."

Granted his wish of a return to Toronto, Encarnacion made the most of it in a tension-filled wild-card game against the Orioles.

Bautista homered in the second to open the scoring, Mark Trumbo countered with a two-run drive in the fourth and Carrera's RBI single in the fifth tied it up. The score stayed there until the 11th, when Ubaldo Jimenez allowed one-out singles to Devon Travis and Donaldson to put men on the corners.

Jimenez had handled Encarnacion well throughout his career—9-for-41 with only one homer, back in 2012—but Orioles manager Buck Showalter had Zack Britton sitting in his bullpen. The lefty had one of the most dominant seasons ever by a reliever, allowing only four earned runs in 67 innings, while converting all 47 of his save chances. But he was left idle as the Orioles failed to take a lead, even as the Blue Jays kept looking for him to start warming. "I can remember running out to first base every inning and going, 'Where is he? Like, why is he not pitching yet?'" said Leiper. "Putting my manager's hat on, I totally get why you do that. But there's also a time where it's like, 'Okay, man, I'm throwing my best guy out there.' At that point he's probably going to throw two innings, and then after that you just live with whatever you've got."

Showalter instead bet on Jimenez, presumably in the hopes of a double-play grounder. A crowd of 49,934 stood in anticipation, chanting "Eddie, Eddie, Eddie." Sitting in the bullpen, where he was stationed in case the Blue Jays needed an inning or two from him, Estrada told himself, "Man, this is it. Eddie's going to hit a home run right here." On the first pitch, that's exactly what happened. Catcher Matt Wieters set up low and away, looking for a rollover grounder. Jimenez missed middle-middle at 91 mph. Encarnacion got every last bit of it and the crowd exploded. "I was so emotional," he said. "It was crazy."

In the dugout, Gibbons was looking up some numbers, mapping out a potential 12th inning. "I heard the crack and looked up. Boom. Gone. See ya."

The change in fortunes for the Blue Jays was similarly fast. Four days earlier, they were on the brink of going home, a dismal September about to negate a season of promise. Now they were headed for a rematch with the Rangers, as video of the Bautista-Odor brawl looped on every sports network. Ahead of the opener, Odor tried to play down the history—"I think it's a normal series," he said—but no one was buying it. Elvis Andrus was more real about things. "It's really sweet facing a redemption this year, and [a chance to] beat those guys," he said.

On the other hand, the Blue Jays viewed the matchup as a pre-show bout rather than the main event. Dickey sensed that the Rangers were like a spent force after the brawl. "It played in a backwards way for them and in a great way for us." Leiper was even more blunt. "Listen, those guys hated us and they created so many narratives in their head about how garbage we were, which actually really affected them when they played us. It ended up costing them two playoff series."

The Blue Jays dropped the hammer on Cole Hamels in the opener, taking control with a five-spot in the third in a 10–1 win. Estrada, chasing the first complete game of his career, was masterful, allowing only four hits, but was pulled with one out in the ninth after Shin-Soo Choo's run-scoring groundout. "When Gibby came out in the ninth, he wouldn't even look up at me," said Estrada. "I was, telling him, 'Dude, this is my game. I got it. I'm not tired. Please let me finish.' And he just said, 'Dude, that's it.' I told him, 'Gibby, this is my game, you've got to go.' And he said, 'Listen, we need to save your bullets, you've thrown 98 pitches, we're going to need you.' After that, what else can you say?"

Ryan Tepera closed it out, and the next day, the Blue Jays jumped Yu Darvish, with solo homers by Pillar, Carrera, and Encarnacion in the fifth securing a 5–3 win. The series shifted to Toronto, where a 6–6 game stretched into the 10th inning and Bush took the mound for the bottom half. Donaldson opened the frame with a double and after Encarnacion was walked intentionally, Bautista struck out swinging. Martin, the next batter, hit a bouncer to short, where Andrus fielded it and flipped to second for the second out. Odor had to bend down to pick a low throw and with Encarnacion coming in hard but clean, he unwisely tried to make an off-balance relay to first. Mitch Moreland scrambled off the bag to block the ball from skipping by him, while Donaldson turned at third without breaking stride and charged for home. Moreland's relay to the plate short-hopped Jonathan Lucroy, who couldn't pick it as Donaldson dove in. Ball game. Series.

"When I saw Odor's arm action, I'm like, 'Oh, something really good's going to happen here,' because of the way his feet were," said Leiper, who credited Donaldson for his alertness. "He was ready for that play before it happened because of his instincts on the bases. That's the one part of his game that people never realized, how great a baserunner he is, how many great things he did. J.D. was a complete player."

For the second time in five days, pandemonium ensued as the Blue Jays advanced in the postseason with a walk-off win. That it was against the Rangers made it sweeter. One sign in the stands summed up the sentiment: "I'd rather get punched in May than knocked out in October." Said Estrada: "We just went about it the right way. We did it on the field. We completely destroyed that team. I mean, it was awesome." Perhaps for no one more so than Bautista, who had a homer and four RBIs in the three games. "I tried to focus on the task at hand," he said, "but that doesn't mean [the history] was non-existent for me. Yeah, 100 percent, when somebody makes it personal, it's hard to completely not think about it. It was a good feeling knowing that we ended up taking them out of the playoffs again."

The good vibes, however, didn't last long. Cleveland, coming off a sweep of the Red Sox, was up next, and their pitching was formidable, especially with dominant reliever Andrew Miller shortening games with multi-inning stints out of the bullpen. An offensive reawakening had fuelled the Blue Jays past the Orioles and Rangers. But in the ALCS opener, they repeatedly let ace Corey Kluber off the hook, going 0-for-4 with runners in scoring position through the first three innings. Kluber settled in after that. Estrada, pitching what he felt was one of his best games of his career, allowed just six hits in an eight-inning complete game. One of them was a two-run homer to Francisco Lindor in the sixth inning. In a portent of what was to come, the final was 2–0. "We had Kluber on the ropes and I was just thinking, all we need is a few runs," said Estrada. "I was feeling really good that day, but we just never scored those runs. Once Kluber figured it out, that's it."

The story was similar in a 2–1 loss the next night and a 4–2 setback in Game 3. The Blue Jays staved off elimination with a 5–1 win in Game 4, and a pathway to their comeback aspirations appeared when Cleveland named slop-tossing lefty Ryan Merritt to start Game 5. Infamously, when asked about facing a pitcher he'd never seen before, Bautista replied: "We'll try to look at video, look at some scouting reports, see how his ball moves. Not having seen him is something that can go either way, but with our experience and our lineup, I'm pretty sure he's going to be shaking in his boots more than we are. I like where we're at."

The quote went viral, clipped of its context and shortened only to the "I'm pretty sure he's going to be shaking in his boots more than we are" part. It was billboard material in the Cleveland clubhouse. When Gibbons saw it the next day, he thought to himself, "Oh, no, that's the kiss of death, man. You don't say those things. I was hoping he was right. Turned out he wasn't. [Merritt] was a lefty who could finesse it a little bit and he was really good that night."

Merritt worked 4.1 innings and allowed only two hits, handing the reins to the Cleveland bullpen. The Blue Jays mustered four hits the rest of the way, one of them a Bautista double in the ninth, in what had the potential to be his final at-bat with the Blue Jays. It wasn't, but Encarnacion's strikeout one batter later turned out to be his Toronto farewell. The 3–0 final ended their season with a whimper. "We were all really quiet in the dugout, and I'm thinking to myself, 'Wow, we have a rookie pitcher out there, why aren't we all excited? We're going to be okay,'" said Estrada, who gave up runs in the first, third, and fourth innings. "It's not good when you feel that way and I hate to talk about it even now. It was a tough series. We faced some really good pitching and it showed."

The defeat marked the beginning of the end for those Blue Jays. Encarnacion ended up with Cleveland after miscalculations on both sides bungled his return to Toronto. Cecil and Dickey also left as free agents. Age hit other parts of the roster in 2017. Bautista wasn't the same. Blister issues and subsequent complications derailed Sanchez. Tulowitzki tore up his ankle and never returned. Travis broke down. The seeds of Donaldson's departure were planted. Stop-gaps Kendrys

Morales and Steve Pearce didn't pan out. In many ways, 2016 very much was the last run of the renegades.

"I was used to chaos with some of them guys, man," said Gibbons. "There was always some kind of shit going on, but I loved every one of them. I played with those New York Mets teams in the 1980s, briefly. Though I was an outsider, I was kind of used to that. I thought if a team is good, your best players can be a little chaotic, a little bit volatile. You're not going to win with a bunch of choir boys. Sorry, you're just not. I look back now, and I love those years. It was just so much fun with this group, with this coaching staff. Even the chaos. It was a group that was a little bit dysfunctional—there's no doubt—but they worked together pretty good."

7

THE PANDEMIC SEASON

The Toronto Blue Jays secured their eighth postseason berth at a Triple-A stadium in Buffalo, New York. The crowd consisted of 2,857 cardboard fan cut-outs. Rather than dog-piling on the mound after a 4–1 clinching win over the New York Yankees, gleeful players exchanged high fives and bro hugs in a relatively orderly line. Artificial crowd noise and the Rogers Centre's familiar horn were piped in to complement their hooting and hollering. In place of a good-old champagne shake-and-spray in the clubhouse, a joyous and tentative celebration played out on the infield.

Leading the raucous ritual was an improbable master of ceremonies—depth catcher and quasi-coach Caleb Joseph, who appeared in all of three games all season. A more significant contribution came in the post-victory selection of three stars he conceived of and conducted. On this night, he shouted out the staff, the coaches, and, finally, the players. Then he bellowed, "Enjoy this moment. You never know when it's your last. And this will be the only time that all of us are here in this spot. The only time. Enjoy the crap out of it. These are the moments we play for. These are the moments we dream about. It's happening. It's a reality. Let's go out there and give it our all, leave everything on the field. And see where the chips lay because boys, it's going to be a good one, I can feel it." Two big claps and a Ric Flair "Woo" later, the collective group portion of the party fizzled out. COVID–19 protocols ruled all.

The surreal scene offered a rather representative slice of 2020 life, when everyone sought to graft pieces of normalcy onto pandemic reality. Baseball's return from its mid-March shutdown was among the more prominent displays of that phenomenon, with public squabbling over money between owners and players really making it feel just like old times. The Blue Jays ended up in Buffalo after the Canadian government rejected their plan to host games in Toronto, and state governments in Pennsylvania and Maryland shot down attempts to play in Pittsburgh and Baltimore. Outbreaks among the Miami Marlins in the first week of the season and the St. Louis Cardinals shortly after that nearly killed the entire program. Still, the TV-only campaign rolled onward amid ever-tightening protocols, ensuring the network dollars kept coming. All summer long, everything was great and terrible, and odd and typical, and joyous and grim at the same time. The many incongruities struck Joseph, a veteran brought in on a minor-league deal to serve as system depth, during the clinching festivities.

"It wasn't depressing, but there was almost regret, like, I just wish everyone could experience what this really feels like in a normal season," said Joseph, part of postseason teams with the Baltimore Orioles in 2014 and 2016. "When you're celebrating a clinch, you just never know when it's your last, so we really wanted to celebrate the mess out of it. Looking around, it was trying to explain to these kids that the feeling is amazing and the joy in everybody on the field is passionate and real and genuine. But there's more, though, and I kept thinking that I just feel so sorry that the kids that haven't experienced this before, that they're not getting the full, all-encompassing feeling."

There was no alternative but to make do. And if all goes according to the club's plan, the 2020 wild-card berth will be the first of several trips to the postseason for this Blue Jays core. While the vagaries of small-sample-size randomness made drawing precise conclusions from the shortened 60-game schedule impossible, the summer represented a massive leap for the club. They were coming off a 67–95 campaign that marked the low point of a rebuild that began two years earlier. The 2019 season was a soul-sapping, hard-knocks grind, in which the transition and growth of players like Vladimir Guerrero Jr., Bo Bichette, Cavan Biggio, Lourdes Gurriel Jr., Teoscar Hernandez, and Danny Jansen were the priority. Attempts to catch lightning in a bottle meant the likes of Socrates Brito and Alen Hanson received long, rank auditions. Ryan Feierabend, Buddy Boshers, Nick Kingham, and Zac Rosscup were among those enlisted to help the team meet its daily nine-inning obligation in quantity, if not quality. The final record was built on merit.

Some gain for all that pain was expected in 2020, especially after the Blue Jays augmented a tattered-rags pitching staff with ace lefty

Hyun-Jin Ryu, signed to an $80-million, four-year deal as a free agent. They also added starters Tanner Roark and Chase Anderson, plus relievers Anthony Bass, Rafael Dolis, and Shun Yamaguchi. A sturdier pitching foundation meant the team would be better equipped to leverage the promise of its young position players. That group entered 2020 with lofty expectations of a postseason berth. Never mind that the roughly 20-game improvement needed was like trying to long jump across the Grand Canyon. "I expect us to do really well," Bichette said at the beginning of camp. "We have a lot more talent than people realize. I don't think people are taking into account that some of our guys are going to take steps forward and become really impact players."

By the season's end, the Blue Jays had proven Bichette right, even if COVID-19 muddled the scope of their progress. Hernandez won a Silver Slugger. Gurriel raked and was a Gold Glove finalist. Biggio continued to grow into a reliable, stabilizing force. Bichette's 29 games, sandwiched around a knee injury, were elite. Randal Grichuk was the best version of himself. Guerrero, once he lost some of the weight he put on during the lockdown, flashed his ability to carry a team. In combination with a creative manipulation of the expanded 28-man rosters that allowed the Blue Jays to optimize their pitcher usage, they finished 32–28 to claim the eighth and final postseason seed.

Whether the Blue Jays would have sustained that pace over 162 games is an intriguing question. But given all they endured over the three months, it shouldn't detract from the achievement. "In my mind, this is just the start of it," said Biggio. "I mean, it's been a crazy year, not only for us, but for everybody. We could have easily looked at it in a negative way. We didn't. We took it with a little bit of a chip on our shoulders and we played with a little bit of an edge. What's going to make it special is doing this consistently and doing this for years to come."

In that way, the Blue Jays hope to benefit long-term from the upheaval and adversity they faced throughout 2020. Momentum began building during the first spring training. Ryu added gravitas and experience to the group. Guerrero arrived in great shape after a winter of hard work and looked ready to make strides at third base. Jansen's adjustments at the plate generated more hard contact. Top pitching prospect Nate Pearson and his triple-digit heat were tantalizing. As good things kept happening for the Blue Jays, COVID–19's insidious spread slowly began to upend the continent. Manager Charlie Montoyo was chilling at his spring apartment the evening of March 11 when word broke that Rudy Gobert of the Utah Jazz had tested positive. Shortly afterwards, the NBA announced it was shutting down. Montoyo had an uneasy feeling. "I remember thinking, 'Uh-oh. If they're doing it, it might happen to baseball, too,'" he said. But the next day, "We went about our business because nobody really knew, like okay, this may happen, this may not."

To that end, Montoyo stayed back in Dunedin, Florida, with one split squad for the annual exhibition against the Canadian junior national team, while the rest of the Blue Jays headed down to Bradenton to face the Pittsburgh Pirates. Midway through the game, Montoyo was summoned to his office. Waiting for him were president and CEO Mark Shapiro and general manager Ross Atkins. "They told me that spring training was going to be cancelled, and maybe the season, too," said Montoyo. "I remember an empty feeling and selfishly thinking, 'Oh, my gosh, this isn't good for our young guys, we need to keep playing, we're doing so well right now.' Now looking back, that was the right call, of course, with how bad things got."

The next few days were chaotic. Players at both big-league camp and on the minor-league side were told to go home. Major League Baseball ordered facilities closed, but the exact rules kept changing. No one was sure if they should hunker down in their spring locale or head home, wherever that may be. While some welcomed the safety measures, others complained that the closures were a gross overreaction to a virus that, if not a hoax, posed minimal threat. At a team meeting to discuss disbanding, Montoyo recalled "a disappointed look on their faces like, 'Oh, man, really? We're not going to play?' And then, just like life, there were some people that really didn't believe in what was happening. Baseball is like real life. Different opinions. Different backgrounds."

Jordan Romano remained in Dunedin, fearful of getting caught in Canada due to border restrictions if he went home to Markham,

Ontario. Ryu and his pregnant wife also remained in Dunedin. Yamaguchi went to Japan, Guerrero to the Dominican Republic. Prospects Santiago Espinal and Forrest Wall sheltered with Bichette at his family's St. Petersburg, Florida, home, creating a workout pod. Montoyo went home to his family in Arizona, taking extra precautions to protect his younger son Alex, who was high risk. They had never spent April, May, and June together before because of the baseball schedule. Unused to the desert spring, Montoyo's allergies flared up and the heat forced him to start his daily eight-kilometre runs earlier and earlier. When other joggers jammed his running routes, he started working out in his garage. "I just didn't go outside anymore," he said.

By June, Major League Baseball had developed the outline for a return to play, although negotiating the terms became predictably messy. On June 23, after weeks of acrimony, commissioner Rob Manfred imposed the season's structure on the players, with a July 1 report date for a second spring training, branded Summer Camp and sold off to a sponsor. Teams were to gather in their home cities. But for the Blue Jays, neither where they would hold camp nor host regular-season games was clear. A few days before the terms were set, the Blue Jays had a COVID-19 outbreak at their facility in Dunedin, which had been their backup plan for home games if border restrictions left Rogers Centre off limits. As infections surged in Florida, even training there came off the table due to risk of community spread.

The Blue Jays were already pitching what was dubbed a modified cohort quarantine plan for the regular season to the municipal, provincial, and federal governments. Now they also sought expedited approval to stage camp at the dome. Players who had booked flights to Toronto were rerouted to Dunedin to wait things out. On July 3, two days after camps opened around the majors, they got approval to come home, and three days later, they took the field in Toronto under an open roof. "There are going to be two types of teams," Montoyo told his players upon arrival. "There are going to be the teams that work together. They're going to follow the guidelines. They're going to work as a group. They're going to stay healthy. And that's going to help them win more games. And then there are going to be the teams that are going to complain about everything, lose focus, get sick, not be healthy, and they're not going to do very well. It's going to be a long 60 games."

The message proved prescient. A condition of being allowed to train in Toronto was that the Blue Jays limit themselves to the Rogers Centre's footprint, using a private pathway from the attached hotel to the field. To help keep everyone from going stir-crazy, the stadium's 400-level party room was converted into a lounge. A 200-level balcony was furnished with couches and turned into a patio. "It does get a little boring sometimes just sitting in bed," said right-hander Trent Thornton. "But if that's what we need to do to play, that's perfectly fine with me."

Meanwhile, the Blue Jays worked tirelessly to gain government approval for their regular season games. They proposed an additional 54 pages of protocols to the 113-page operations manual prepared by Major League Baseball. The city and province signed off July 16,

Blue Jays players, coaches, and staff celebrate the 4–1 win over the Yankees at Sahlen Field in Buffalo to clinch a playoff berth. (AP Images/Adrian Kraus)

leaving the feds as the only obstacle. But two days later, the Canadian government said no, citing the criss-crossing of the border, alarming infection rates down south and travel to-and-from hotspots. The Blue Jays were blindsided. Six days from the season's start they had no home. "We were pretty encouraged by both the mayor and the premier, like, 'You're going to be fine. You're going to be able to play here.' And we were training here, you know?" said Shapiro. "We were like, 'Okay, it's not that much of an extension to play here without fans and to continue the same sort of quarantined-off existence for visiting teams, too. Everything from the federal level was just not very clear and it didn't start to feel concerning until the end."

The rejection kicked off a wild scramble. The Blue Jays had invested $600,000 to improve the lights and make other upgrades at Dunedin Stadium, but that was off the table. In a meeting after the rejection, players asked the club to try and find a big-league facility they could share with another club. Only a few schedules matched up reasonably well, the Pittsburgh Pirates' being one of them. The previous off-season, the Bucs twice raided the Blue Jays front office, hiring Ben Cherington as their new GM and Steve Sanders as their AGM. Manfred did the initial outreach and Pirates president Travis Williams was all in. Officials from both teams began laying groundwork. Once they had a plan of how to split up PNC Park, Pennsylvania officials said no. The Blue Jays were playing an exhibition game in Boston that night, having left Toronto two days earlier with packed suitcases in the clubhouse, destination to be determined. "This is something we've never had to deal with in the past, but honestly, this season is all about [the challenges] that we experience and overcoming them," said Ryu. "It's going to be difficult, but I trust my teammates and I think we'll be able to rally around just because it's an unprecedented season."

The next day, the Maryland state government reacted coolly to plans to share Camden Yards with the Orioles. In the interim, New York senator Charles E. Schumer leaned into Major League Baseball to have the Blue Jays settle on Buffalo. Playing all 60 games at their opponents' stadium was considered again. But on Friday morning, hours before the Blue Jays opened the season at the Tampa Bay Rays,

Shapiro made the call. Sahlen Field it was. Happy Opening Day. "We were tired of it all and ready to play," Biggio said after a 6–4 win that night. "Even if it's in a Triple-A ballpark, we're still going to play with a chip on our shoulder and have some fun with it."

While the unease of the situation had taken a mental toll on everyone, there were some unintended benefits. The concentration of time together forged a cohesion that sometimes even a full season as a group doesn't create. As a by-product of regular meetings to discuss the latest developments and make decisions on player preferences, an intimate familiarity developed among the players. "We were being forced to come together, to do hard team work and culture building," said Joseph. "In the midst of something that seems like it was a divider, we were actually getting really close and really tight."

As that drama played out, the Blue Jays quietly began mapping out how to best deploy their roster across 60 games. An easy decision was moving Guerrero from third to first when he reported for camp at 282 pounds, after what Atkins delicately described as a "less than ideal" time between camps. While the extra weight had an obvious impact on his defence, it also hurt his offence. "It's really clear how much more dynamic his swing is when he is in the [235–240 pound] range that he's shooting to be in," said Atkins. Guerrero apologized to his teammates for letting them down and then diligently worked to rid himself of the extra weight, improving at the plate as he shed pounds.

The bigger question related to the pitchers. A truncated second camp meant starters had to ramp up much faster than usual. With several veteran arms, the Blue Jays had to tread lightly, but cancellation of the minor-league season meant they could also think creatively. Under normal circumstances, Thomas Hatch, Anthony Kay, Julian Merryweather, Ryan Borucki, and Jacob Waguespack would have been in the rotation at Triple-A Buffalo. But with the alternate training site in Rochester, New York, the only place to get them some work, the Blue Jays turned them into multi-inning relievers. And since expanded rosters allowed teams to add more bullpen arms, starters could be limited to twice through the lineup before handing off to fresh power relievers. Such an approach meant the Blue Jays could usually use pitchers in spots where they were most likely to succeed, and limit looks that favoured the hitter.

"[Assistant GM] Joe Sheehan said at one point, 'Hey, it's July 5th, we're tied for first place and there are 60 games left. What's the reality of being tied for first place and having 60 games left and how do we play that?'" recalled Shapiro. "It was thinking about every opportunity, whether it be the trade deadline, or whether it be the utilization of minor-league players in a way that we wouldn't normally. Once the opportunities were there, we were going to double down on them because the experience for our young players of playing in meaningful games, of playing in postseason, could elevate our timeframe long-term."

At times, the data-driven approaches the team often employed created friction, especially among veteran starters accustomed to a longer leash in games. Unusual batting orders elicited knowing glances and assumptions the lineup had been driven by the analytics department. But at the season's start, reality struck in another way. After the Opening Day win, the Blue Jays lost the next two to the Rays, both on late bullpen implosions, the second featuring an elbow injury to closer Ken Giles that would eventually lead to Tommy John surgery.

The Blue Jays rebounded with a pair of wins against the defending World Series champion Washington Nationals. But with Buffalo not yet ready, they played the back half of home-and-home two-game sets as the home team at Nationals Park, dropping both. Their next series was supposed to be another home-team-on-the-road affair in Philadelphia against the Phillies, but that was postponed due to the fallout of the Marlins outbreak. The Blue Jays practised at Nationals Park through the weekend before heading to Atlanta and Boston, dropping two of three at each city.

Meanwhile, a mad scramble unfolded in Buffalo. A workforce led by Marnie Starkman, the club's senior vice president of marketing and business operations, rushed to upgrade Sahlen Field with new lights, COVID-compliant dugouts and clubhouses, and Blue Jays branding galore. On August 11 it was ready. Barely settled into the hotel rooms that became their home, they delivered a 5–4 walk-off win in 10 innings over Miami. But they fell 14–11 in 10 innings to the Marlins the next night—despite rallying back from an 8–0 deficit—and then dropped two of three to the Rays. In the process, they lost Bichette to a knee injury.

At 7–11, three contests into a gruelling stretch of 28 games in 27 days, down two key players, continually making defensive mistakes and poor baserunning decisions, their season was in many ways on the brink. When the Blue Jays landed in Baltimore ahead of their next series, the coaching staff gathered in Montoyo's room to discuss their predicament. "The next day, the whole idea was to talk to players, like let's keep it going, we're doing fine," he said.

During the pregame hitters' meeting the next day, coaches took turns addressing the group. Third-base coach Luis Rivera preached the need for preparation ahead of the play, like knowing which base to throw to in advance, rather than being totally reactionary and making every decision on the fly. First-base coach Mark Budzinski urged the players to run the bases aggressively rather than recklessly, keeping in mind the game situation. Hitting coach Guillermo Martinez presented the group with reams of data that showed they were making quality contact. He urged them to trust that they'd be rewarded if they continued doing what they'd been doing. "That was, in my opinion, one of the most instrumental parts of the season," said Joseph. "These were really good insights that, with a younger team, you can't talk about enough. We just really hit on things that are going to make us successful. We had the talent. The only reason we weren't letting it rip and getting into a groove was because we were beating ourselves with our own mistakes."

The Blue Jays played a clean, crisp game that night, beating the Orioles 7–2. In their postgame celebration, a new wrinkle was added. Before the season, Joseph suggested a hockey-style three stars selection at the end of each victory to Montoyo and some clubhouse leaders as a way to build camaraderie. As a taxi-squad player travelling with the team in the event of a sudden injury, he didn't want to overstep his boundaries. But his teammates supported the idea. "A lot of the guys fell in love with it early," said Grichuk. Rather than highlighting the obvious, like the person who hit the winning home run or the pitcher who got the key outs, Joseph, with the input of others, pointed out small plays that helped win the game. For example, an outfielder throwing to the right base to prevent a runner from advancing to keep the double play in order. Or a batter grinding out an eight-pitch at-bat to set the stage for those behind him. Or the infielder who knocked down a grounder to prevent a run from scoring.

As the miscues mounted, Joseph and Montoyo thought they could use the celebrations to point out mistakes, as well. Joseph tried it that night in Baltimore. Discussing blunders in a light-hearted way after a victory allowed issues to be addressed without the tensions that tend to accompany a loss. "He did a really good job of pointing out if we're struggling at something," said Grichuk. "When we were in the bad baserunning spell, bad defence, he talked about that. He just has that feel. You see teammates that you say are going to be a manager one day or are going to be in coaching one day, just gets it, the personality, the communication, they see the game differently—he's one of those guys."

An avid Nashville Predators fan, Joseph came up with the three stars as an ode to the longstanding hockey tradition in the Blue Jays' home and native land, delivered with a dash of Ric Flair showmanship. "Because we created such a positive atmosphere, it was a great way to hold things accountable. It was about every single person on the team knowing what was unacceptable," he said. "When it's not really spoken about, sometimes it can grow legs and before you know it, you've gone two weeks, and you've made five other mistakes."

As the season progressed, younger players came to Joseph with suggestions for good plays to highlight. Meanwhile, Joseph kept adding creative ways to hammer on mistakes. He started picking boneheaded plays of the game, handing out the "awards" with a smile and a positive-reinforcement lecture.

A prime example came September 2 in Miami, when deadline-acquisition Jonathan Villar made two outs on the bases. Gurriel added a third, although he made amends with a two-run homer that Ryu made stand up in a 2–1 win. "That night we held a moment of silence for our baserunning and just put that to rest," said Joseph. "Like, we had the most atrocious baserunning today and we got lucky that we won this baseball game because our baserunning was so bad. We need to let that die right here, right now. Let's all just bow our heads in a moment of silence for our pitiful baserunning. We will never do that again."

Slowly, bad habits began to change. The Blue Jays swept the Orioles in that series, returned to Buffalo to sweep a makeup doubleheader, erasing a 7–0 deficit in the second game, and then split four against the Rays in Tampa. As August turned to September, they were not only holding a wild-card spot, but but would soon climb past the Yankees into second place. They ended up going 18–10 during the stretch of 28 games in 27 days, overcoming additional injuries of varying length to Pearson, Matt Shoemaker, Thornton, Romano, and Hernandez, who was performing at an MVP level. "Everybody contributed on different days," said Montoyo. "I can remember when Teoscar went down and then J.D. Davis, just called up, hits a home run to beat the Yankees. Stuff like that, when you've been around, you're like, yeah, that's how you make the playoffs, pick the other guy up. And we kept doing that. Santiago Espinal playing a good shortstop when Bo went down. There were so many examples of things you need to do to have a chance to make it to the playoffs."

The front office recognized that, too, which is why prior to the August 31 trade deadline, Atkins swung four deals, acquiring two rental starters in Taijuan Walker and Robbie Ray, pending free-agent infielder Villar, and swingman Ross Stripling, who came with two additional years of club control. They were clever, reasonably priced pickups, with only down-the-depth-chart prospects going the other way. The additions were nowhere near as splashy as the wild spree of the San Diego Padres, who made six trades involving 26 players, with starter Mike Clevinger as the centrepiece. But they marked a shift from the sell-offs of the past three deadlines and illustrated the club's approach in a win-now mode. "It's important to be measured, and there isn't one juncture where, in our view, that you put all the cards on the table," said Atkins. "For us it will be, hopefully, continuing to be able to build and have a system that continues to provide talent for us, and not just trade pieces. That's our goal."

Walker ended up pitching one of the most important games of the season, throwing six innings of one-run ball in a 6–3 win over the

Phillies on September 20. That stopped a six-game losing streak, one that began with the Yankees blitzing the Blue Jays by a combined score of 43–15 during a three-game sweep in the Bronx. The Yankees hit a record 19 homers over the three contests, among the 44 hits and 19 walks they collected in 24 innings of work. "I've never seen anything like that," said coach John Schneider. Third baseman Travis Shaw described the series as "a shell-shock in a way," one that lingered the next couple of days in Philadelphia. The Phillies took both ends of a doubleheader on the first day and when Montoyo noticed the clubhouse vibe sagged, he called a team meeting for the next day. "I felt the pressure on everybody, because we were supposed to make it now," he explained. "I knew a losing streak was going to happen sometime. The Rays went through a losing streak. The Yankees went through a losing streak. Ours just happened there at the end when you're supposed win. I think that puts more pressure on everybody."

The focus of his message, though, was a little different. He pointed out how back in July, before the season started, they would have gladly signed up for a four-game lead in the wild-card standings with nine games to play. Even after a rough week, that was their actual situation, not a hypothetical. They were fine. No need for panic, not a big deal. They lost again behind Ryu right after that, but Walker set them right in the finale, ahead of a rematch with the Yankees. "We hit a little skid, those are going to happen," Walker said afterwards. "I thought today was a huge win to give us momentum going into the next series."

That's precisely what took place. The Blue Jays pounced on the Yankees in the opener 11–5, and after a 12–1 loss the next night, they took the final two games 14–1 and 4–1, clinching behind a Ryu gem September 24. The ex-Dodger said the celebration that followed "was quite different." Speaking through interpreter Bryan Lee, he added, "Obviously there's no afterparty, the champagne and everything that comes with clinching a spot in the postseason due to the regulations. But we did get the [playoff] cap and the shirt, so that part still remained the same."

The Blue Jays drew the Rays in the postseason, bidding adieu to Buffalo after going 17–9 at Sahlen Field, a place that turned out to offer a strong home-field advantage. "Our people did a great job, along with our players, of making the most of Buffalo," said Shapiro. "I'm not sure it could have lasted for 162 games. But for 60 games it was a good alternative and our players had the right mindset and mentality to not make it an excuse." Their wild-card stay in St. Petersburg, Florida, was brief, with losses of 3–1 and 8–2 ending their season. There was lots of talk about lessons and progress and growth and pride. But it had also been a long slog. "It's weird," said Jansen. "Honestly, at times it felt like it was 200 games and at the same time, it's just 60 games in 69 days, so it happened fast. My body felt like it was game 200. Wild season."

How much they were forced to adapt really hit home once it was over. After elimination, players were free to leave, no more constant testing for COVID-19, no worries about the so-called bubble the Blue Jays had operated in. Suddenly, after three months of precautions and discipline, of being unable to see families without meticulous planning, of spending lots of time in isolation, they were free. It was a trip. "It was not romantic in any sense," Shapiro said of the day-to-day existence. "It was very isolated. Very lonely. From the travel to the time in Buffalo, ours was different than most teams. It was an existence that could have presented a lot of opportunity for complaining and making excuses. And it was a good reflection of our team's character."

Added Biggio: "You can make [a situation] as bad as it is or as good as you want. Going into our situation, not being able to play in Toronto and coming to Buffalo, playing on the road for the first couple of weeks, we could have easily looked at it as if, our backs are against the wall, it's okay if we don't win this year, it's kind of a crazy year. The way we took it is we're here for each of us in the locker room and it's shown over the longevity of this long year with injuries and guys going down, guys stepping in and picking it right up. There's just a lot of tight-knit guys here on this team and it's made it a lot of fun."

Fun it was, especially at a time when moments of joy were fleeting amid a global pandemic. The Blue Jays managed to celebrate a postseason berth as castaways in an empty stadium before a crowd of cardboard cut-outs. It was weird and awkward and largely unforeseen, too, save for a relentless young group that believed it was possible, and then made it happen.

8

THE HOLY QUINTET OF BLUE JAYS HOME RUNS

The day after ending the 2016 American League wild-card game with one mighty swing, Edwin Encarnacion stood in a quiet corner of the visitors' locker room at Globe Life Park in Arlington and contemplated what he had just accomplished. A year earlier, he watched from the on-deck circle as Jose Bautista crushed the souls of the Texas Rangers with his celebrated bat-flip home run in Game 5 of the American League Division Series, triggering an oft-blustery debate that's led in recent years to a cultural shift in the sport's celebratory antics. Bautista's rocket had soared its way directly into Toronto Blue Jays lore, alongside Roberto Alomar's drive after Dennis Eckersley's taunts in Game 4 of the 1992 American League Championship Series; Ed Sprague's pinch-hit, two-run shot in Game 2 of the 1992 World Series; and Joe Carter's epic title-clinching swat in Game 6 of the '93 Series versus the Philadelphia Phillies.

Encarnacion's walk-off home run in the 11th inning of a 5–2 win over the Baltimore Orioles qualified him for the club, too. "It's very impressive" to be on that list, he said. "When you get the opportunity to win the game, it's something very special. That's how you want to be remembered, for doing things like that, helping your team win in the playoffs. It's very special for me. I feel proud."

The way those moments are clustered at the franchise's two historical peaks underlines how momentous and enduring significant postseason home runs can be. As former Blue Jays GM Alex Anthopoulos put it: "That's what sports are about. Those are the things that live forever." Bautista's homer created the type of where-were-you-when moment fan bases can wait entire generations to enjoy. In the case of Blue Jays' supporters, there was a two-decade gap on the highlight reel. Up to then, the homers by Alomar, Sprague, and Carter had stood as the club's holy trinity, each creating a pivotal point in the organization's annals. Then came Bautista, and a flip so epic that teammate Ryan Goins said, "On a [scale of] 1 to 10 that's a 27." There may not be a more electric Blue Jays moment—ever. "That's one of those bat flips that has nothing to do with the pitcher, that has nothing to do with the team that we're playing against," said Brett Cecil. "It's just excitement pouring out of Jose."

In that sense, Bautista's home run is a notable complement to Alomar's drive, each borne out of the intensity of ferocious competition. The Sprague and Carter shots were, too, but they didn't spring from the same powder keg of emotions. Sprague gut-punched an Atlanta team on the verge of going up 2–0 in the Fall Classic, and Carter blindsided a Phillies team trying to force a decisive Game 7. Encarnacion's laser put multiple exclamation points on a game that, one way or another, the Blue Jays were poised to win imminently. Context matters.

Bautista's shot capped off one of the wildest innings in postseason history. It started with Rangers second baseman Rougned Odor controversially scoring the go-ahead run in the top half when Russell Martin's throw back to Aaron Sanchez struck Shin-Soo Choo's bat in the box. A crowd of 49,742 erupted into an unruly mob, throwing bottles, cups—anything not bolted down—onto the field when umpires ruled Odor was allowed to advance after initially sending him back to third base. The Blue Jays played on under protest. In the bottom half of the inning, three Texas errors and a fielder's choice tied things up before Sam Dyson threw a 97-mph heater in the wrong spot to Bautista, whose blood runs hot even in the mildest of on-field circumstances. Heading up to the plate, he later wrote on the Players' Tribune website, "my adrenaline wasn't 10-out-of-10, it was 10-million-out-of-10." After dropping the hammer, he looked forward, turned his head to the right, flung his bat into foul territory, and circled the bases. "I can't really remember what was going through my mind, to be quite honest with you," he said afterward. "After I made contact, I didn't plan anything that I did, and so I still don't even know how I did it. I just enjoyed the moment, rounded the bases, and got to the dugout."

Alomar can relate. Trailing 6–1 through seven innings against the Oakland Athletics in 1992, the Blue Jays had rallied for three runs in the eighth when Eckersley finally stopped the bleeding by striking out Sprague. The Hall of Fame closer pumped his fist—par for the course with him—but then enraged the Blue Jays by pointing and staring into the dugout. "We were yelling stuff like you would never believe," said Pat Tabler. "I was making up stuff to yell at him. It was unbelievable."

In the ninth, Devon White led off with a single before Alomar tagged a 2–2 fastball. Immediately his hands shot up, index fingers pointing to the sky as the ball cleared the wall to tie the game and charge up his teammates. "It was like, 'Yes, we're burying these guys and we're going to the World Series,'" said Tabler. The Blue Jays won it 7–6 in 11 innings to take a 3–1 series lead. "My reaction was emotion, I wasn't showing anyone up, I just raised my hands up," said Alomar. "Bautista was emotion, too. When you're into the game in a big game like that, sometimes you do things you normally wouldn't do. I don't think in any way I was trying to disrespect anybody, and in the same way I don't think Bautista was trying to show anyone up."

Regardless of intent, being on the other side of a big home run sucks, and an opponent isn't likely to grant much leeway under the circumstances when emotions are riding high. The teams continued to trade barbs publicly for days afterward. But Eckersley, for his part, didn't fan the flames, saying after the game, "I'm trying to get myself geared up, and if they took it the wrong way, I'm sorry. They got their payback. They can gloat in there while I eat crow. I got mine."

Dyson handled things a little differently. After Bautista rounded the bases, Encarnacion stepped to the plate and with the crowd still roaring, the Blue Jays slugger put his hands up, signalling for people to settle down. The pitcher approached the batter's box, yelled something toward Encarnacion, and both dugouts emptied. "I told him that Jose needs to calm that down, respect the game more. It needs to stop," Dyson later told reporters. "He's a huge role model for the younger generation that's coming up playing this game, and he's doing stuff that kids do in Wiffle Ball games and backyard baseball. It shouldn't be done.... That's unacceptable, regardless of what level you're on.... If you watch his replays throughout the year, I think you'll understand."

The home runs by Sprague and Carter didn't carry quite the same charge. Jeff Reardon appeared more stunned than anything on the mound after Sprague followed Derek Bell's walk by ambushing a first-pitch fastball and ripping it over the wall in left for a 5–4 lead in

Jose Bautista celebrates his seventh-inning, three-run homer in the ALDS with a majestic bat flip.
(Darren Calabrese/The Canadian Press)

1992. Atlanta's closer, an August 30 waiver-trade pickup from Boston, had good success against the Blue Jays during the regular season, allowing one run over 5⅓ innings in four appearances. Sprague, on the other hand, had only 50 plate appearances during the regular season, but was advised by Rance Mulliniks that Reardon would try to get him out with the fastball, so he should be ready for it. He was, and it changed the series. "Without him," said Jack Morris, "who knows what happens?"

The level of excitement for the Blue Jays and their fans multiplied exponentially when Carter connected against the Phillies. The National League champions had survived a season's worth of nervous ninth innings with Mitch Williams, who managed to save 43 games against six blown chances despite 44 walks in 62 innings. But the only thing on Carter's mind as he stepped up to the plate with the Blue Jays down 6–5 and two men on was living out his childhood dream of delivering a World Series–winning hit. Williams had already blown one save in the Series, and Carter was ready to make it two. With the count 2-2 after he swung over a breaking ball, Carter guessed Williams would double up on the off-speed pitch and ended up being late on the fastball. Since that kept him from hooking the pitch foul, it turned out that his timing was perfect. The Phillies slinked off the field as the Blue Jays celebrated. Pat Hentgen went from charting pitches in preparation for a potential Game 7 start straight into party mode. "Clipboard gone, out there jumping in the air," he said, "it was the greatest thrill of my career."

Encarnacion left others feeling similarly about his home run. The wild-card game between the Blue Jays and Orioles is an under-appreciated classic, filled with terrific pitching, tenacious at-bats, and great defensive work. Ezequiel Carrera's RBI single in the fifth inning erased a 2–1 Baltimore lead and things stood there until the 11th, when lefty Brian Duensing began the inning by striking out Carrera. Orioles manager Buck Showalter then replaced him with Ubaldo Jimenez. With lower stakes, that call wouldn't have raised much rancor, since Jimenez to that point had largely given Josh Donaldson, Encarnacion, and Bautista—all due up after Devon Travis—fits that year. In theory, the Orioles could ride him out, build a lead and then bring in Zack

Britton, who had just laid down one of the greatest seasons ever for a closer. New-age thinking frowns on such an approach, but then again, Showalter often frowned on new-age thinking. Regardless, things instantly went haywire. Travis lined the third pitch from Jimenez to left for a base hit and Donaldson did the same to the next offering.

Up came Encarnacion and if ever there was a time for Britton, this was it. Instead, Jimenez stayed on, and 49,934 stood in anticipation of what was about to happen. In his own head, Encarnacion was doing the same thing. Usually, he thought, Jimenez would start him off with a two-seamer away, but he needed to be ready for a fastball, just in case the righty tried to come inside in search of a double-play grounder. In the end, Jimenez did neither, laying in a middle-middle cookie that Encarnacion rocked way out to left-centre field. He'd barely finished his backswing when he dropped the bat, fingers pointed in the air, the dome again shaking in rapture, this time thanks to his swing, with Bautista standing on deck. "I was so emotional—it was crazy," says Encarnacion. "I don't remember what I was thinking. I just wanted to run the bases, score. When Bautista did it, it felt great when he hit that homer and to win the game, that's the best thing I felt. The same happened to my team [on my home run]. It was one game, win or lose and if you lose you go home. Scoring the run to win the game is the best feeling."

One that like those produced by its four predecessors, will long be remembered and revered.

9

CARLOS DELGADO'S
FOUR-HOMER GAME

The four-home run game is perhaps the most difficult single-game personal feat to achieve. Consider that there have been 23 perfect games thrown in big-league history—it goes without saying how much has to fall a pitcher's way for that to happen—yet only 18 times have players gone yard four times in a single contest. Sure, a hitter needs some good fortune to get there too, but it's impossible to fluke your way into this annal of history.

On September 25, 2003, Carlos Delgado didn't need some good fortune; he needed some good medicine. The slugging first baseman, putting the finishing touches on perhaps his most complete offensive season—one that should have landed him the American League MVP Award that eventually went to Alex Rodriguez of the last-place Texas Rangers—reported to the SkyDome feeling sick. He doubted whether he'd be able to take the field against Jorge Sosa and the Tampa Bay Devil Rays. "Sore throat, runny nose, really bad headache—you know, one of those," he recalled. "That was a crazy day. I went out and took batting practice and I took a couple of rounds, I took it in, I went to the trainer's table, I [lay] down, took some medicine, and told the trainer, 'Wake me up at 10 to 7:00.'"

Up from his nap, Delgado decided to play, and once that decision was made, there was no feeling sorry for himself. Even so, as he headed out to first base behind starting pitcher Pete Walker, he was unsure how much he had in him. By the time he stepped up to bat in the first, he was already grasping for ways to be competitive in the box. "I went up there and said [to myself], 'Damn, I don't feel so good,'" said Delgado. "Sometimes you just have to suck it up. The thing I remember from that day is telling myself, 'You don't feel so good. Don't try to do too much. Kind of go back to the basics.' And usually things work out better when you do that. Sometimes you have great batting practice, hitting the ball out of the ballpark, and you think it's going to be a great game. And the next thing you know the game starts and you want to hit it [farther] than you did in batting practice and you have a terrible game. Then sometimes you want to execute, see the ball and do whatever you need to do, and things just flow. Go figure."

He dug into the box in the first after a one-out Frank Catalanotto single and Vernon Wells walk, took a strike, and labelled a meaty 0–1 fastball from Sosa off the glass at the old Windows restaurant in centre field. Often forgotten is that it was also career homer No. 300. As he circled the bases, Delgado made a point of asking for the ball.

His next at-bat came leading off the fourth. This time Sosa fell behind 1–0 and threw a changeup on the outer half that stayed up enough for Delgado to loop the ball just over the wall in right field. "Oh my goodness," broadcaster Rod Black bellowed in his call of the game. "He has got Jorge Sosa's number." The success against Sosa should have been no surprise—Delgado finished his career 14-for-28 with seven home runs against the right-hander. No. 2 of the night also marked the third straight at-bat in which he'd taken Sosa deep.

The Blue Jays led 4–1 at that point, but by the time Delgado's third at-bat arrived, leading off the bottom of the sixth, the Devil Rays had stormed back and were up 6–5. Manager Lou Piniella was taking no chances and summoned lefty Joe Kennedy, who had surrendered only five hits in 36 at-bats to Delgado during his career. "That guy absolutely owned me," said Delgado. Then again, on this night, *nobody* owned him, and he proceeded to flip the script by smacking a flat, waist-high curveball on the outer edge of the plate into the seats in right-centre. It was the only home run Delgado ever hit off Kennedy. "I thought I could never get a hit off this guy," he said. "He hung a curveball and I hit it out. It was one of those days things were working out for me."

But it wasn't as easy for the Blue Jays, who again trailed, this time 8–7, when Delgado dug in leading off the eighth for his fourth at-bat. Lance Carter, who saved 26 games despite a 4.33 ERA in 2003, was on the mound. Delgado insists he had no thoughts about going all-out for a fourth homer. "If I could decide to actually go for a home run and get one I would have hit 1,000," he said. "I just thought, 'I want to get a good pitch and hit it hard.' Whenever I tried to hit a home run, very

THREE-HOMER GAMES

Before his big day against the Devil Rays, Carlos Delgado hit three homers in a game on four separate occasions. Overall, the Blue Jays have had 20 three-homer games in franchise history:

- **Otto Velez** on May 4, 1980, at home off Cleveland's Dan Spillner, Wayne Garland, and Sid Monge
- **Ernie Whitt** on September 14, 1987, at home off Baltimore's Ken Dixon, Mike Griffin, and Tony Arnold
- **George Bell** on April 4, 1988, away off Kansas City's Bret Saberhagen
- **Joe Carter** on August 23, 1993, at home off Cleveland's Albie Lopez (2) and Jose Hernandez
- **Darnell Coles** on July 5, 1994, away off Minnesota's Pat Mahomes and Larry Casian (2)
- **Carlos Delgado** on August 4, 1998, away off Texas' Todd Stottlemyre, Eric Gunderson, and Danny Patterson
- **Carlos Delgado** on August 6, 1999, away off Texas' Rick Helling (2) and Jeff Zimmerman
- **Darrin Fletcher** on August 27, 2000, away off Texas' Rick Helling
- **Carlos Delgado** on April 4, 2001, away off Tampa Bay's Paul Wilson, Doug Creek, and Ken Hill

seldom it worked. You get big, you try to do too much. As a home run hitter, I'm telling you, I was better when I wasn't trying to hit home runs. Same way I used to hit better in bigger ballparks. At the smaller, hitter-friendly ballparks, sometimes you think, 'I'm going to hit it out,' and you change your approach and everything goes to [hell]."

Depending on the situation and who he was facing, Delgado would hunt pitches either by location or type. In a 2–2 count versus Carter, he correctly anticipated changeup, got a cookie that hung right over the heart of the plate, and pummelled it off the top of Windows in centre field. In a rare show of celebration for Delgado, he flung his bat aggressively enough to make Fernando Tatis Jr. blush, but then circled the bases stone-faced, bumping knuckles with Eric Hinske at home plate before turning for the dugout, taking off his helmet, looking up at his teammates celebrating in the dugout, and smiling. He was and

- **Carlos Delgado** on April 20, 2001, away off Kansas City's Mac Suzuki, Tony Cogan, and Roberto Hernandez
- **Chris Woodward** on August 7, 2002, at home off Seattle's Joel Piniero (2) and Kazuhiro Sasaki
- **Vernon Wells** on May 30, 2006, at home off Boston's Josh Beckett (2) and David Riske
- **Frank Thomas** on September 17, 2007, at home off Boston's Tim Wakefield (2) and Kyle Snyder
- **Adam Lind** on September 29, 2009, away off Boston's Clay Buchholz (2) and Takashi Saito
- **John Buck** on April 29, 2010, at home off Oakland's Justin Duchscherer, Jerry Blevins, and Craig Breslow
- **Edwin Encarnacion** on May 21, 2010, away off Arizona's Dan Haren (2) and J.C. Gutierrez
- **Jose Bautista** on May 15, 2011, away off Minnesota's Brian Duensing and Kevin Slowey (2)
- **Edwin Encarnacion** on August 30, 2015, at home off Detroit's Buck Farmer, Guido Knudson, and Alex Wilson
- **Josh Donaldson** on August 28, 2016, at home off Minnesota's Alex Wimmers, Kyle Gibson, and Pat Light
- **Kendrys Morales** on August 31, 2017, away off Baltimore's Jeremy Hellickson and Mychal Givens (2)

remains the only Blue Jays player to accomplish the feat. "My boys gave me a hard time for flipping the bat. I didn't do it on purpose. I was in la-la land," Delgado said. "I hit the first home run, whatever, yeah, second home run, then I get the third home run and after that I don't really remember much. I think the medicine really affected me because I saw every pitch down the middle of the plate."

The Blue Jays tacked on two more runs in the inning and Trever Miller locked things down in the ninth for an 8–6 victory. Everything afterward was a blur for Delgado, who specifically remembers a phone conversation with his dad "that was pretty cool."

"Obviously a lot of joy, a lot of phone calls, a lot of media interviews," he said, "but it seemed like the game was over and the next thing you know, you were at the ballpark the next day for another game. It was so fast, I couldn't even celebrate it."

Of the 18 players to hit four home runs in one game, Delgado is the only one to do it with only four plate appearances. In 2002, former Blue Jays teammate and close friend Shawn Green accomplished the feat by going 6-for-6 with seven RBIs for the Dodgers. That same year, Mike Cameron also had a four-homer game. Then it didn't happen again until Josh Hamilton in 2012, with Scooter Gennett (June 6) and J.D. Martinez (September 4) in 2017 becoming the most recent new members.

"It just kind of happens," said Delgado. "I don't want to minimize it and I don't want to rain on anyone else's parade, but you really can't control it. You can't say, 'I'm going to go out and get four home runs.' Obviously you have to have enough power and talent, but I don't think that automatically makes you a better hitter because you add four home runs to your résumé. Just my opinion. Don't get me wrong, I think it was great, but I don't think it will define you as a hitter."

Given how productive a career he had, it shouldn't. But it did make for a night unlike any other in Blue Jays history, one rarer in baseball than a perfect game, proving a point Delgado has long argued. "I always said hitting is harder than pitching," he said, laughing.

10

FRANCHISE ICON: ROBERTO ALOMAR

The moment Roberto Alomar learned he was traded to the Toronto Blue Jays, the young man—who would become arguably the most complete player ever to suit up for the franchise—didn't know what to think. He was 22, loving life with the San Diego Padres, a first-time All-Star on the cusp of big things. Now, the Puerto Rican had to adapt to another city, in another country, and fill big shoes. "I couldn't believe it in the beginning," he remembered. "I was shocked, so young in my career, San Diego was looking for a second baseman for such a long time. But things happen for a reason. I called my dad [Sandy, a veteran of 15 big-league seasons], and my dad always gave me the right advice. He said, 'You're going to a great city, you're going to a great team, a great organization, and you're going to be playing for a great manager. All you have to do, Robbie, is go out there and play baseball the way you can do it.'"

Alomar did precisely that, beginning a relationship with the Blue Jays and their fans that endures to this day. His five years in Toronto were as electric as they come. He was one of the driving forces behind three American League East titles and two World Series championships. A dynamic athlete, he hit for average and for power. He intimidated opponents with both his speed and base-running instincts. And his defence—man, his defence—was something to behold. Even after an acrimonious split with the Blue Jays, and the ugly spitting incident with umpire John Hirschbeck at the dome as a visitor, his bond with Toronto continued. His No. 12 was the first number retired by the team. He's also the only Hall of Famer enshrined as a Blue Jay. (Roy Halladay's family requested that the right-hander be enshrined without a logo on his cap.) In March 2011, Alomar returned to the team as a special assistant, regularly running camps for kids across the country, among other duties. "I just try to give back to the youth all over Canada some of the knowledge that I learned from this game," he said. "That's really what I'm doing, trying to be as busy as I can be on behalf of the Blue Jays."

Yet it all started with trepidation. Joining him in the move north was Joe Carter, the duo coming in exchange for Fred McGriff and Tony Fernandez, two of the club's most popular players. The public's faith was shaken. Demonstrating the skepticism at the time, Pat Tabler, who signed with the Blue Jays as a free agent the day before the stunner, called Carter, an old teammate. "'I can't believe they traded McGriff and Tony Fernandez,'" he remembers saying. "And Joe goes, 'Tabby, wait 'til you see Robbie Alomar. He's the best second baseman in the National League.'" Tabler couldn't wrap his mind around the claim. He remembered Alomar from his winter ball days, when as a young kid he'd shag balls and take grounders with Sandy. "I said, 'Joe, come on. Ryne Sandberg's over there,'" said Tabler. "He goes, 'He's better than Sandberg.'"

Alomar soon erased any lingering doubts. He slashed .295/.354/.436 with 41 doubles, nine homers, 69 RBIs, and 53 stolen bases in 1991, winning a Gold Glove in the process. The numbers only got better from there, and his popularity soared to the point where companies sought him out for endorsement deals. "Catch the taste," he said famously in one TV ad for concentrated fruit juice. "Right away I got real comfortable," said Alomar. "The fans embraced my game, they loved the way I played, and from that point on it was all me."

What made him so valuable was his ability to deliver whatever the game situation dictated. He could scratch his way on base and swipe a bag with his speed. He could move over a runner, or put the ball in play on a hit-and-run. He could find a gap or put one over the wall. And he could steal hits with his glove.

The best example of that came in Game 4 of the 1992 American League Championship Series against the Oakland Athletics, when his ninth-inning two-run homer off Dennis Eckersley tied the game and led to a victory widely credited with changing the franchise's fortunes. "It got us over the hump where we'd been trying to get for years," said manager Cito Gaston. Alomar ended up being series MVP, carrying the Blue Jays to the first of their two World Series championships.

Alomar's power was, in a sense, sneaky because he didn't display it regularly enough to be considered a power hitter, but he had more than enough pop to hit in a number of different lineup spots. The Blue Jays used him primarily in the two-hole, although batting third for Cleveland in 1999 he hit a career-high 24 home runs with 120 RBIs. "Robbie had all the tools," said Sandy Alomar Jr., his older brother, who caught for 20 big-league seasons. "The one thing that a lot of people don't realize is that he put every tool of his arsenal into play, and his awareness of the game was head over his heels over everybody else. He had that sixth sense for the game, he anticipated very well, and he never went out of his role."

The offensive production he delivered so consistently and spectacularly often overshadowed his work in the field, where he made the spectacular look routine because of his remarkable athleticism and daring creativity. Shovelling ground balls with his glove to the first baseman, tossing behind-the-back to second base, and diving for balls up the middle became commonplace. "I remember sitting in the dugout and they would score a ball an error and I'd think there would be no other second baseman in the league who would have gotten to that and yet he's going to get an error," said Pat Hentgen. "As good as he was offensively, his best asset, to me, was his defence."

Alomar won a Gold Glove in each of his five seasons with the Blue Jays, a franchise record he shares with centre fielder Devon White. Genetics certainly helped (his dad was predominantly a second baseman and shortstop) but his work ethic was relentless. The elder Alomar remembers once driving to the ballpark for a game and being surprised when Roberto, who was supposed to be in school, popped out from under a cover in the back of the family's station wagon, forcing his way into another session of fielding grounders. "I hit a ground ball one time, the ball hit him in the mouth and split his lip," said the father. "He started crying and I said, 'Hey, you want to be in baseball? Take a block of ice, put it on your mouth, stop the bleeding, and start playing.'"

The same determination was on display every time he took the field, although things started to turn after the second World Series title. The Blue Jays were spinning their wheels in 1994, sitting at 55–60

Roberto Alomar makes a leaping throw over the Chicago White Sox's Dan Pasqua in Game 1 of the 1993 ALCS. (John Swart)

when the players' strike hit, leading to the cancellation of the Fall Classic. Things went completely sideways in 1995, despite the surprise April reacquisition of David Cone, who didn't make it through July before he was sent off to the New York Yankees at the trade deadline. Infamously, Alomar wished he had been dealt instead. That off-season, he reunited with Pat Gillick in Baltimore, where he signed a three-year deal with the Orioles.

The same Blue Jays fans who had adored him made him a target for their scorn during subsequent visits. "I believe they didn't really understand what happened," he said. "I think the media made it look like I just left because maybe money. To me it was an opportunity I had with the Baltimore Orioles and Pat to win another championship.... I think the Toronto Blue Jays wanted to take a different direction and they wanted to sign younger guys, and maybe the fans didn't understand that."

The undeniable low point of his career came during his first season with Baltimore, on a visit to Toronto on September 27, 1996. After taking a borderline pitch for strike three, Alomar began arguing with Hirschbeck, spitting in his face after the dispute escalated. The situation deteriorated even further when he later told reporters that the ump was under stress because his eight-year-old son died in 1993 from a rare brain disease known as ALD. When the comment was relayed to him, Hirschbeck tried to challenge Alomar in the Orioles' clubhouse but was restrained at the entrance. Alomar was suspended five days and ordered to pay US $50,000 to an ALD research fund.

The two shook hands at Camden Yards the following April, and Alomar later helped raise money for a foundation started by the Hirschbeck family. When Alomar was inducted to the Hall of Fame in 2011, Hirschbeck called to congratulate him. "John embraced me the same way I embraced him," said Alomar. "When I got in, he phoned me and left a message. It was a great message and, you know, it was like he said, we both moved on and hopefully people can move on and let this episode go."

After the Orioles, Alomar bounced to Cleveland, the Mets, the White Sox, and the Diamondbacks before back problems felled him in the spring of 2005, at training camp with the Tampa Bay Devil Rays.

In his final Grapefruit League game before retirement, manager Lou Piniella pulled him after he committed two errors and struck out in the first inning against the Blue Jays. He fell 276 career hits short of 3,000. "I took a lot of pride in what I did. I just didn't want to be the kind of guy that goes out there and doesn't give 100 percent," said Alomar. "If my body wasn't allowed to play the way Roberto Alomar can play, I wasn't going to play [any] more."

True to his word, he didn't. But he eventually found his way back to the Blue Jays, connecting with the fans who once adored him, through a new role at home in his adopted land, where he belongs.

11

DAVE STIEB'S NO-HITTER

The ball sailed toward right field off the bat of Jerry Browne, and Dave Stieb couldn't watch. On the cusp of finally achieving an accomplishment that had so cruelly eluded him, he thought, "What if?" His past experiences, heartbreaking ones, with no-hit or perfect-game bids in the ninth inning taught him to never take anything for granted. Sure, the ball's trajectory off Browne's bat *suggested* an easy out. But what if a gust of wind happened to blow? What if right fielder Junior Felix lost the ball in the sun? What if there was another punch in the stomach to come?

"Anything can happen," said Stieb, who had indeed learned that the hard way. Maybe if his elbow wasn't barking during that ninth inning in Chicago in 1985, or that weak chopper hadn't taken an unfathomable hop and Fred McGriff had time for one more step in consecutive 1988 starts, or if he hadn't gotten squeezed on the first pitch to Roberto Kelly in 1989, he could have let his guard down. But all that happened, and he didn't need to imagine any other crazy ways for things to go wrong. "I put my hands over my eyes and I heard the crowd cheer and I knew Felix caught it," said Stieb. "I turned and I was like, 'Oh my God, I've got my no-hitter. And this should be my second or third.'"

All those elements made the first and only no-hitter in Blue Jays history through 2020 such a momentous achievement. Every no-no is special and remarkable, but given all the agonizing near-misses Stieb endured before getting there, that September 2, 1990, afternoon at Cleveland Municipal Stadium had extra meaning. It had finally happened, and that offered some closure. "After coming close so many times, that's all I would hear about from people: 'You've come so close. You're going to get a no-hitter,'" said Stieb. "It was almost like I strived to do it for them, just to shut them up and be done with it."

In that sense, the no-hitter was more relief than joyous occasion, and his past with the no-hitter makes it easy to understand why.

THE BIG 50

On August 24, 1985, at Comiskey Park, Stieb took a no-hitter into the ninth inning against the White Sox. Then Rudy Law and Bryan Little hit back-to-back homers to open the frame. Gary Lavelle and Tom Henke had to come in and record the final three outs of a 6–3 win, but what went wrong that day was no mystery. "My arm was killing me," said Stieb. "I had this little thing in my elbow, and if I didn't have a no-hitter going, I would have never gone out for that ninth inning."

Three years and one month later, on September 24, 1988, at Cleveland Municipal Stadium, there was no making sense of what went down. One out away from the no-no, Julio Franco hit a weak chopper

Dave Stieb works in the ninth inning of his September 3, 1990, no-hitter against Cleveland. (Tony Dejak)

to second and as it skipped by to Stieb's left he thought, "I got the no-hitter." But the ball suddenly shot up and over the head of second baseman Manny Lee, and the no-hitter was gone. Everyone was in shock. "It was like, 'I cannot believe that ball took that bounce,'" said Stieb. "Franco should have just fallen down and acted like he pulled his hamstring and let us throw him out because that's a no-hitter. You're out, dude. Give Manny Lee credit; I'd never seen a guy try to jump so high beyond his ability in my life, and it still went over his glove by two feet." And there was still a game to play. Ernie Whitt had to come out to the mound to calm his pitcher. The Blue Jays led Cleveland 1–0 and victory was still far from assured. "He was in disbelief. I was in disbelief," recalled Whitt. "And then it's like, 'Okay, let's gather ourselves up and put this game away and we'll talk about it with a beer in the locker room afterward.'" Stieb got Dave Clark on a fly ball to centre to end it.

Afterward, Stieb's friend and longtime agent Bob Lamonte phoned him and mentioned that he caught the tail end of the game on TV. "He goes, 'I was kind of pissed because I'm supposed to be coming to see your last start in Toronto, and you're going to throw a no-hitter and I'm not there to see it,'" said Stieb. "I said, 'Don't worry, Bob, I'll do it next game.' This is how stupid a perfectionist I am."

True to his word, Stieb diced up the Baltimore Orioles in his next appearance at Exhibition Stadium, and was again an out away from the no-no when Jim Traber's broken-bat flare down the first-base line dropped just beyond McGriff's reach. Heartbreak again. "I'll never forget it. On that mound with two outs in the ninth, I'm like, 'Oh my God, I told Bob I would do this and here I am, it's right in front of me. I could do it right here and that story will go on forever,'" said Stieb. "That would have been so great. But Traber gets a freaking blooper base hit over Fred McGriff and I swear to God when that ball was hit, I looked over at Fred and he just froze. He did not move for probably two seconds. Then he started going back and reached up—Fred's a big guy—and it went four inches over his glove. I went like, 'Are you kidding me? Did I just lose this no-hitter like that, after losing the other one six days ago like that?'"

No joker could kid like that. The two fluke hits kept him from joining Johnny Vander Meer as the only men to throw consecutive no-nos in the big leagues. He was that close to one of the sport's most untouchable records.

A year later, August 4, 1989, at home against the New York Yankees, fate was even more sinister. Stieb retired the game's first 26 batters—unusual for him because he typically would walk a batter or two, even on his better days—when Kelly stepped up. Home-plate umpire Terry Cooney called a borderline first-pitch breaking ball inside for a ball, and Stieb legitimately missed inside for ball two. He and Whitt went breaking ball again on the 2–0 pitch and this time Kelly ripped it to left field for a double. "It was like, 'How am I ever going to get one?'" said Stieb.

The answer came almost exactly 13 months later—fittingly, back in Cleveland. While in his other near-misses, his stuff seemed overwhelming from the outset, that day against Cleveland, it was not. Leadoff man Alex Cole walked to open the bottom of the first but was promptly thrown out trying to steal second against Pat Borders. Stieb issued another walk in the second, with Carlos Baerga also being gunned down. "That really helped me," said Stieb. "I was effectively wild. The biggest thing for me was my slider. I wasn't controlling it that

NO-HIT NEAR MISSES

Aside from Dave Stieb's spoiled no-hitters, the Blue Jays have had five no-hitters spoiled in the ninth inning:
- **Jim Clancy** allowed a leadoff single to Minnesota's Randy Bush at home September 28, 1982
- **David Cone** allowed a one-out single to Texas' Benji Gil at home June 17, 1995
- **Roy Halladay** allowed a two-out homer to Detroit's Bobby Higginson at home September 27, 1998
- **Dustin McGowan** allowed a leadoff single to Colorado's Jeff Baker at home June 24, 2007
- **Brandon Morrow** allowed a two-out single to Tampa Bay's Evan Longoria at home August 8, 2010

well, and I was fortunately throwing it down in the dirt and they were swinging at it."

After that he settled, striking out the side in both the third and sixth innings, and retiring 15 straight batters from then on. "I realized I'm not sticking stuff where I need to, but they're helping me so I'm going to go with the flow," he said. "We got to the sixth inning, no-hitter going. Seventh inning, no-hitter going. Now guys weren't around me, talking to me, and I'm full-blown into this thing."

Ken Phelps opened the eighth with a walk but three fly balls followed and then in the ninth, after pinch-hitters Chris James and Candy Maldonado went down, Stieb walked Cole on four pitches. "I could not throw the guy a strike," he said. Up came Browne, who took a slider inside for ball one, a fastball on the outer half for strike one, and then lofted a fat slider in the air to right. "Those were crappy pitches," said Stieb. "When I threw him that slider, it was right up in the wheelhouse, but I knew he was a little guy and he's not a home run hitter, and it was a crappy pitch for that situation. That's what is weird. I'd lost so many no-hitters on better pitches, and I got the no-hitter on this hanging slider that he hits as hard as he can to Junior Felix."

Once Stieb realized the ball had settled into Felix's glove, he put his right arm up, pointed to the stands, and was quickly surrounded by Borders, Kelly Gruber, David Wells, and the rest of his teammates. They lifted him up in the air, and he smiled through the disbelief, never having to wonder "what if" again.

12

JOSE BAUTISTA'S 54-HOME RUN SEASON

Looking back now, it makes complete sense that Jose Bautista owns the Toronto Blue Jays' single-season home run record of 54, and that he's one of just 27 players to ever break the 50-homer plateau. The six-time All-Star is among the greatest players in franchise history, one destined for a spot on the Rogers Centre's Level of Excellence. Even before adding his signature bat-flip homer to his résumé, he already featured prominently in the club's record books. More importantly, he was a pillar for the organization to build around. Few hitters in team history have dominated the way he did.

Yet before the 2010 season, no one envisioned any of that coming—not even close. Sure, plenty of people in the game noticed the raw tools and athleticism and wondered why the whole was less than the sum of the parts, but suggesting then that the Blue Jays were sitting on a multidimensional superstar would have been grounds for ridicule. After all, Bautista had managed all of 43 home runs in 1,314 at-bats over 400 games before the Pittsburgh Pirates sent him north for journeyman catcher Robinzon Diaz. To many around the game, Bautista was a utility man at best.

Instead, with the help of manager Cito Gaston and hitting coach Dwayne Murphy, Bautista unlocked the power he flashed during his awe-inspiring batting practices—something that had caught the eyes of Gaston and Alex Anthopoulos, at the time the Blue Jays' assistant GM, during the frequent spring games played between the Blue Jays and Pirates. It took a year and a half after he joined the Toronto roster, but in 2010 it all came together. One of the most spectacular offensive seasons in team history followed, highlighted by Bautista's home run No. 50 off Felix Hernandez on September 23, 2010, a first-inning solo shot that Shawn Hill and four relievers made stand up in a 1–0 win. A pair of homers off Baltimore Orioles right-hander Chris Tillman the following day and a multi-homer contest against the Minnesota Twins on September 30 pushed him to 54, seven better

THE BLUE JAYS HOME RUN RECORD

Jose Bautista's 54 still stands as the single-season Blue Jays home run mark. Here's the record's progression over the years:

1977	**Ron Fairly**	19
1978	**John Mayberry**	22
1980	**John Mayberry**	30
1986	**Jesse Barfield**	40
1987	**George Bell**	47
2010	**Jose Bautista**	54

than George Bell's record of 47 in 1987, and 10 more than Carlos Delgado's 44 in 1999. It was as stunning as it was brilliant.

"To be honest, everything after 30 that season was gravy for me," said Bautista. "It was a magical season and an unbelievable year in the sense that I couldn't believe that it kept on happening. I couldn't believe that I kept on getting those pitches. I couldn't believe that I kept connecting and hitting balls out of the park. For me, it felt like I was in a dream. Fifty? When I hit my 30th that year that was the last thought in my mind. Actually, the last thought in my mind was 40. For all I knew, and I went to the All-Star Game that year with 24 home runs, I would have been happy with 25. They just kept coming because they kept pitching me the same way—fastballs in—and I kept hitting them.

"People got me out like that for six years prior to that, and I'm assuming they thought I wasn't going to sustain what I was doing and kept trying to get me out the same way. It wasn't up until the next season that they totally changed their approach where I had to make some adjustments."

Without doubt there was skepticism about Bautista's chances of maintaining his power show over the course of an entire season. Pretty much every year someone rides an unsustainable hot streak to the top of the leaderboard only to fall off as numbers normalize over the grind of 162 games. In May 2010, Bautista shared the top of the American League home run charts with Ty Wigginton, who hit his 12th homer on May 15. Wigginton hit just 10 more over the next 4½ months.

Based on his track record, there was no reason to believe Bautista wouldn't fall off the same way. Only he kept hitting dinger after dinger. Underscoring just how good his year was, consider that Albert Pujols finished second to him in home runs at 42—an incredible 12 back. Behind them, Paul Konerko hit 39, Miguel Cabrera and Adam Dunn 38, and Joey Votto 37. Bautista didn't just beat the field; he blew it away. "That was unbelievable," said teammate and close friend Edwin Encarnacion. "The way he had his timing, the way he was doing it, was something crazy."

No. 17, establishing a new career best, came June 4 against A.J. Burnett. No. 18 followed against the right-hander two innings later. No. 30 came off Alfredo Simon on July 27 and No. 40 came on August 23 off David Robertson, a go-ahead drive in the eighth, in the type of performance that would become part of his signature in the years to come (Darren O'Day should have taken note). In the third inning of that game, Bautista took Ivan Nova deep for No. 39, and in his next at-bat, he had to hit the ground to avoid a pitch up and in from the New York Yankees right-hander, leading to an umpire's warning and the benches clearing. After crushing Robertson's 0–1 fastball to left, Bautista stared angrily at the mound, dropped his bat, and slowly rounded the bases. The Blue Jays won 3–2.

"Given what transpired earlier," Bautista told reporters that night, "I enjoyed it pretty good."

The same goes for his season as a whole.

13

ROY HALLADAY WINS 22 AND THE CY YOUNG

In 2001, the Toronto Blue Jays sent Roy Halladay back to school. What he learned, in part, was to take the pitching mound with the discipline of a disciple in a house of worship, and to treat each outing with the appropriate gravitas. The way he approached a demotion from the big leagues to Single-A and how he embraced some very hard lessons righted a career that had lost its way. Eventually a remarkable resurrection took hold, and the prayers of both an organization desperately trying to save a cornerstone of its roster and a player looking to find his own game were answered in 2003 with a Cy Young Award season.

On the final pitch of the final game of one of the most brilliant seasons ever delivered by a member of the Blue Jays, a man celebrated for his unflinching stoicism unleashed his pent-up emotion. As Jhonny Peralta's grounder to second became the final out of Halladay's franchise-record 22nd win, he fist-pumped, roared, and (gasp!) actually revelled in the moment. "It was almost like being let out of church," Halladay said. "You know you've been good for so long and so patient that you could finally let things go. You knew you were done for the year, so that's exactly what it felt like—after sitting through a really long sermon, you finally get out and you can kind of go nuts."

After reinventing himself physically and, perhaps more important, mentally in 2001, Halladay delivered a brilliant 2002 season, going 19–7 with a 2.93 ERA in a league-best 239⅓ innings over 34 starts. The performance offered validation for all he'd been through, and signalled his emergence as a legitimate front-of-the-rotation starter in the majors. He'd done it. Yet the shock of 2001 never felt far enough away for him to get comfortable. During his revival, a zealous commitment to process became dogma. A burning desire to pursue any little edge possible "never seemed to stop," he later said. And in 2003 he found another gear.

"After that first year of winning 19 games, I felt like that was the kind of pitcher I could be and should be if I continued to work hard and do things the right way," said Halladay. "And I always felt this driving force to continue to prove myself, and show that's what I was about, and to do it consistently. So that [2003] season for me, especially at the start, I felt that there was a lot of emphasis on being able to show the consistency and being able to show it wasn't a fluke to win the 19 games, because I've seen guys that come and go win 19 games. I was really focused on trying to establish myself and not get lazy with it.

"I talked to a lot of people over the winter before that season. Some of the best advice I got was never stop learning, never stop competing, never stop improving. One of my less favourite managers actually made a great point: 'You should never expect to make a team out of spring training until you have at least five years in the big leagues.' The rest of my career I felt like every year I had to make the team, and that's the way I tried to prepare myself. And that kind of became my mantra. I think that I was always going to prepare as well as I could, I was going to give everything I have, and I honestly believed that if I did things the right way, prepared the right way, even though I had no control over the end result, for the most part it would be favourable if I continued to take the right steps."

That belief came in handy early in that 2003 season, when he stumbled out of the gate with a winless April, staring down a 5.13 ERA following a 15–5 win over the Texas Rangers on May 6. Doubt could have very easily set in, especially given his backstory, but Halladay trusted his process, trusted in his work, and proceeded to win his next 11 starts. By the end of that run, a 4–2 win over the Montreal Expos on June 22, in which he allowed two unearned runs in eight innings, his ERA stood at 3.57—even with a seven-run blip against the Boston Red Sox on June 1. Halladay hit the All-Star break at 13–2 with a 3.41 ERA in 153 innings over 21 starts, and he simply kept going from there. The Cy Young talk started to build. Through it all he leaned heavily on Harvey Dorfman, the famed sports psychologist and author of *The Mental ABCs of Pitching*, who was an instrumental figure throughout Halladay's career.

"We talked so much about consistency of outings, consistency of approach, and there was a lot of stuff going on with the Cy Young stuff that I had never had to deal with before," said Halladay. "It was such an absolute mental grind just to keep myself from getting out of my approach, from changing the way I was thinking and doing things. I didn't want to go out and all of a sudden become a different pitcher. So I was really trying to focus on what my strengths were and how I was having success."

Heading into September, Halladay was neck-and-neck in the Cy Young Award race with Esteban Loaiza, the former Blue Jays right-hander who struggled during his time in Toronto but blossomed that season with the Chicago White Sox. The New York Yankees had already run away with the American League East, and by then the wild-card was out of reach as well, so the focus in large part shifted to the pitching chase.

Halladay made six starts that September, going the distance in five. Only a senseless sixth-inning ejection by home-plate umpire Phil Cuzzi on September 22, after Rocco Baldelli was hit by a pitch, prevented it from being a clean sweep. The pièce de resistance came September 6 against the Detroit Tigers, when Halladay threw a 10-inning, three-hit shutout in a 1–0 victory, trading zeroes with Nate Cornejo until Bobby Kielty's pinch-hit RBI single in the bottom of the 10th off Fernando Rodney sealed the deal. Memories of that game are among Halladay's most vivid from that season. "There's nothing I enjoy more than completing a game, and I remember I honestly was hoping we didn't score in the ninth inning. I know that's bad, but I remember thinking, 'Boy, this would be really cool if I could go out there and throw 10 innings.' And after the 10th I was really hoping we would score," he said, laughing.

Perhaps the most amazing part of the entire performance was that he needed only 99 pitches to get it done. "I remember hearing that after the game," he said. "I try to talk to people, especially young pitchers. One of the biggest things that helped my career was learning how to pitch to contact. You know there are so many guys that come up and they're trying to strike guys out right from the first pitch, and they're afraid to have the ball put in play. I started to realize that not only did it help me if they put the ball in play, but the sooner they put the ball in play the better. And usually, the worse of a swing it was. So I really tried to establish myself to where they knew I was going to go after them, and they had to get something early. I wanted to force it down their throat where they had no choice but to swing."

Rarely did that work out well for Halladay's opponents. By season's end, he finished 22–7 with a 3.25 ERA in a career-best 266 innings over 36 starts. He allowed 253 hits and walked only 32 while striking out 204. He induced 476 ground balls, good for 58.4 percent of the balls put in play against him. And he did it in the slugger-rich American League East, holding the Yankees to a 3.22 ERA over five starts and going 2–1 with a 4.76 ERA in six starts against the Red Sox.

"At that time, it was nearly impossible for a pitcher to win a Cy Young Award coming out of the AL East," said Vernon Wells (who had a monster season of his own that year). "For him to be able to do that, it sets him apart from a majority of the people that have won that award. I think that got overlooked a little bit, but that's something special right there."

As Halladay surged down the stretch, Loaiza faded, posting a 5.30 ERA in six September starts. He finished the season at 21–9 with a 2.90 ERA in 226⅓ innings over 34 starts. By the time the Cy Young balloting was revealed November 11, it was no contest: Halladay collected 26 of the 28 first-place votes. The news came at about 4:30 AM local time on the Kohala Coast in Hawaii, where he was on a Nike baseball tour. "Nike made a little video to send back. They had Mimosas for us and stuff, it was pretty cool," he recalled. "I remember doing an interview, sitting outside over the beach doing it, with all the green trees, thinking, 'Man, this is going to be tough to beat.'"

It proved to be. The 266 innings in 2003 took a toll on Halladay. He struggled through shoulder issues in 2004 and pitched through fatigue in 133 innings over 21 starts. "I had to make some major adjustments [to my off-season throwing program] that winter, which I didn't do," he said.

The next year, another brilliant campaign was truncated at 19 starts in July by a Kevin Mench liner that fractured his left fibula. Halladay's second and last Cy Young Award came years later, in 2010—with the Philadelphia Phillies.

His 22 wins remain a single-season franchise record for the Blue Jays. Fittingly, that final victory was far from his prettiest of the season. He allowed four runs on eight hits and a walk in his ninth complete game. He needed 122 pitches to beat Cleveland 5–4, with Peralta's groundout stranding the tying run at second base. Much as he had in his career, Halladay in 2003 overcame adversity, persevered, and found success. And memorably, he allowed himself one emphatic celebration.

"For me," he said, "it was the culmination of the whole season."

14

THE INAUGURAL GAME

On April 7, 1977, snow covered Toronto, so in the minutes before the Blue Jays played their inaugural game against the Chicago White Sox, the field at Exhibition Stadium was not groomed but shovelled. Instead of taking batting practice, visiting infielder Jack Brohamer strapped shin guards to his feet and skied across the diamond, using bats as poles. Other players donned parkas and shivered together in the dugouts. Somehow, despite all that, the game's 1:30 PM start time was delayed by only 18 minutes. Bill Singer's first-pitch fastball to Ralph Garr was a strike. And three hours and 22 minutes later, a local car dealership was ready to offer Doug Ault a free Datsun.

The Blue Jays won 9–5 on that grey and frigid afternoon, and things were as good as they would be for a long time in the expansion franchise's maiden voyage. They won only 53 more times in 1977, finished with a run differential of minus-217, and ended up 45½ games back of the East-champion New York Yankees. Despite all the lows—and there were many—simply getting on the field was an accomplishment, and the inaugural Opening Day, miserable cold and snow and all, epitomized that. "I had tears in my eyes," said Paul Godfrey, the Metro chairman who helped land an expansion team for the city. "It was a monumental day in my life, to see it all happen. I can still picture it today. I was equally as excited [then] as I was watching them win the World Series."

The crowd of 44,649—their largest of the season—bundled up for an extreme taste of life at the lakeside stadium and, like the players often did themselves, the fans found ways to grind through it. They started lining up outside the gates at 10:00 AM despite below-zero temperatures. And the snow only made things worse. Ault was among the players who wondered whether they could play at all. But after such a long buildup, it would have taken much more than a little snow to halt the proceedings. Fortunately the snowfall began to taper off, the temperature warmed enough for some of it to melt, and the grounds crew managed to get the field into playable condition.

Singer, one of the team's few recognizable names as a two-time 20-game winner, ended up walking Garr to open the game, retired Alan Bannister and Jorge Orta, and then served up a two-run shot to Richie Zisk. In between pitches, the Californian scraped out the dirt caking in his cleats. His footing continued to be an issue for the whole outing.

In the bottom of the first, White Sox lefty Ken Brett struck out John Scott and Hector Torres before Ault took a deep breath and walked into the batter's box from the on-deck circle. The 32nd selection in the expansion draft (taken in the turn just before the Blue Jays selected a catching prospect named Ernie Whitt), Ault arrived from the Texas Rangers, where he was blocked at first base by Mike Hargrove. A rare left-handed thrower who hit right-handed, he played 129 games in 1977. In that moment, however, he was just another new guy with promise looking to capitalize on an opportunity. Also, he wanted to simply feel his hands.

"I'm freezing, and I'm asking myself how am I going to even hold a bat, let alone swing it," the late Ault said in a video celebrating the Blue Jays' 10th anniversary. "The first hitter went up and struck out, and that's when I heard my first boos. And I don't mean there were a few people were booing. Everyone was booing. Everybody wanted to see us do [well]. The second hitter got up and he struck out too. And the boos really got loud. I'm on deck thinking, 'My gosh, I'm next. They're booing, they want a hit, they want something to happen.'"

"I take a strike, and then they really started booing," said Ault. "They're thinking, 'Oh man, three strikeouts in a row,' I'm thinking, 'I've got to swing the bat, I've got to do something.'" He went after a low-and-away heater, smacking it over the wall in left centre. Exhibition Stadium erupted. "I've never seen the mood of any fans change like it did at that time. From boos to total cheering," he continued.

The home run instantly gave him a place in franchise history, but the White Sox were leading 4–2 when Ault next came to the plate with Torres on first to open the third. He held his swing on a breaking ball to run the count to 2–1 before turning on the next pitch and poking it down the right-field line to tie things up. At that point he evolved from answer to a trivia question to franchise folk hero. "Everybody thought he was Babe Ruth," said Howard Starkman, the longtime Blue Jays executive who was the club's public relations man at the time.

Canadian Dave McKay's RBI single in the fourth put the Blue Jays ahead for the first time. Later that inning, Ault showed that he was human by grounding into an inning-ending double play with the bases loaded. No matter. Alvis Woods added a two-run homer in the fifth, Ault delivered an RBI single in the eighth that made it 8–5, and Gary Woods capped the scoring with a double-play ball that allowed the final run to score.

With his big day on Opening Day, Ault became an instant sensation. A Datsun dealer approached him soon after to offer him a 280z sports car. He gladly accepted. "Little did I know they plastered my name and BLUE JAYS on the side of it," he said. "Well, I couldn't go anywhere. That was the biggest mistake I made in baseball."

Ault finished the 1977 season with a .245 average, 11 homers, and 64 RBIs over 129 games. It was the only season in which he spent the majority of his time in the majors. After that he played in 54 games in 1978, spent all of 1979 at Triple-A Syracuse, got into 64 big-league games in 1980, and then never played in the majors again. After stints in Japan and Mexico, he served as a manager in the Blue Jays' system, handling Single-A teams at Dunedin, Kinston, and St. Catharines before managing Syracuse. Tragically, he fell on hard times and died in 2004 in what was ruled a suicide. He was 54.

For many, Ault is a mere footnote in Blue Jays lore. But for the team's first generation of fans, his name sparks instant recognition and warm memories of a team in its infancy.

15

FRANCHISE ICON: CITO GASTON

ntering his third full season in the big leagues, Cito Gaston figured that he knew all he needed to know about hitting. The previous season, 1970, he made the National League All-Star team as the centre fielder for the San Diego Padres, batting .318 with 29 homers and 93 RBIs. That put him on the map, and big things were expected from him. Instead, his production went backwards in 1971, as well as during his next three years in San Diego, a slide that prompted the Padres to trade him to Atlanta. The move would eventually lead him to the Toronto Blue Jays, but at the time, it meant he went into the 1975 season as a bench player for the Atlanta. Even that proved advantageous. While there, a rant by general manager Eddie Robinson showed him how wrong his approach at the plate had been, and helped set up his post-playing life. "To be honest, I played six years in the big leagues before I learned how to hit," he lamented years later.

"One day we came off a bad road trip from the West Coast and we always had trouble there," Gaston recalled. "Now, normally you don't have a GM call a meeting, but he had a meeting and he said, 'Do you fucking guys ever look for a pitch?' And I'm in shock, because I've been taught look for a fastball, then adjust, and don't guess. So I raise my hand and say, 'Isn't that guessing?' He said, 'It's not guessing if you're looking for a particular pitch. And don't look for pitches that you can't hit. Why look for a pitch you can't hit? You've got to look for a pitch you can hit. Do it 3 out of 10 times, you're a superstar. You've just got to get it right 3 out of 10 times.' It opened my eyes."

By then, though, Gaston was on the downside of his playing days, and he only was able to apply his newfound knowledge sporadically. He hung on for three more big-league seasons, playing for a rookie manager in Atlanta named Bobby Cox in 1978, and then suited up in Mexico for two years before returning to the Atlanta organization as a minor-league hitting coach. His work there captured Cox's attention, and when Cox was hired to take over as Blue Jays manager following

Cito Gaston wipes away a tear during the Blue Jays 1993 World Series celebration at the SkyDome. (Hans Deryk)

the 1981 season, he invited Gaston to join him as his hitting coach. Gaston accepted, beginning a tremendous career in Toronto during which he'd guide the team to consecutive World Series championships.

Indeed, Gaston's fingerprints are all over many of the franchise's greatest players. "The job Cito did was amazing," said longtime outfielder Lloyd Moseby. "He was the right man for the job. He had a calm demeanour, he was a real positive guy and he tells the truth, which a lot of guys don't do. That's why he's one of my favourite people in the world." Gaston's teachings as hitting coach were instrumental in helping along the development of players including Moseby, Willie Upshaw, George Bell, Jesse Barfield, Tony Fernandez, Kelly Gruber, and Fred McGriff—guys who helped the Jays emerge from their dark expansion days into a golden era.

Rather than force-feeding his philosophies, Gaston initially spent time getting to know his players individually before handing out advice. "When I came, I had to learn more about these guys, and I used to walk around with a little book and keep charts and notes about this guy and that guy, just selling them on what we wanted to do as hitters," said Gaston. "You get a couple of guys first, then you get a couple more, and a couple more, they'd buy into it, and then they'd come back.

"Jesse [Barfield] and I had a special drill we'd run every day—I could have been killed doing it because I'm right in front of him—where I'd throw the ball and make him pull it. He led the league in home runs (40 in 1986) that year."

At the heart of Gaston's approach was Robinson's message: have a plan, hunt for your pitch, lay off the pitcher's pitch. One of Gaston's talents was in picking up the ways opposing pitchers tipped what was coming. He'd sit in the dugout with players, looking for any small edge to exploit, discussing the mental part of the game.

"Gruber bought in," said Gaston. "Gruber was probably one of the most talented guys, as talented as Robbie Alomar. If I told Gruber that he had to hit a breaking ball, he would sit on it and he would hit it. He could hit any pitch that he wanted to. But I had to tell him all the time, 'What do you want to hit? Don't swing at the other stuff unless you got two strikes, then you battle.'"

And what really served Gaston well is that he didn't coach in a one-size-fits-all mode. He let players take what they needed from him and offered more only if they were willing to accept it. "Me and Cito never had a relationship like, 'I want you to do this,'" said Bell. "I'd say, 'Cito, I'm a little bit late on the ball. Watch my swing when I'm coming, what I'm doing,' and he helped me get through the ball a little bit quicker. That was pretty good. We used to come and hit extra batting

CITO'S TOUCH

In the spring of 1989, Lloyd Moseby's mother, Birdo, died and the Toronto Blue Jays centre fielder was crushed. "My mom was everything," he said. "I really didn't even care about baseball anymore. I pretty much quit at that point." Through his first 69 games of the season, he batted .191, quite obviously not himself. Manager Jimy Williams lost faith in him. But Cito Gaston, who took over as manager in mid-May, still believed in Moseby and in August reinstalled him as leadoff hitter. He went on to hit .236 with a .326 on-base percentage the rest of the way as the Blue Jays rallied to win the American League East for the second time. "Cito got me into his office and said, 'Mo, I want you to lead off for me and take us to the house,'" Moseby remembered. "And I did, and I don't know how he called that. I don't know what made him do that, but he just showed me how much he loved me. Despite all of the things I went through that year he never gave up on me. So Cito, he's a very special man to me. He's always been there for me, and even to this day he's one of the most special people that I know." Said Gaston, "I knew he was heavy-hearted. I wanted to let him know I was there for him and I sure was on his side."

Whether it was Moseby or someone else, Gaston made a habit of sticking with struggling players, an approach that was sometimes criticized, even by players in his own clubhouse. But in doing that he drew from his experiences as a player, believing short-term pain often led to long-term gain. "You have to have guys believe in themselves and give them that chance to prove themselves," said Gaston. "I always used to say, 'I'll lose the game today, but I'll win three down the road because I treated that guy really well.' I let him stay out another hitter, I kept playing him. You're building confidence when you do that, and you'll win more games."

practice, and we used to discuss everything over there. And I never got into a slump."

Hyperbole aside, the hitters almost to a man implicitly trusted Gaston, something that proved pivotal early in a 1989 season that was quickly going awry. Cox left the Blue Jays to return to Atlanta following the 1985 season and third-base coach Jimy Williams was promoted to replace him, but his tenure was bumpier than a back-country side road. The biggest blowup was with the plan to move Bell to designated hitter before the 1988 season, a scheme forced upon the reigning American League MVP, who wanted no part of it. A feud ensued, and tensions between Bell and Williams continued to simmer, even after the plan was abandoned. Things went south for the whole team the next year. They opened the season 12–24, and Williams was fired after the Blue Jays lost three straight in Minnesota.

The next morning, Monday, May 15, Gaston received a call from Fran Brown, Pat Gillick's executive assistant, who instructed him to stay at home. "I said, 'Why?' and she said, 'I'm just telling you, stay home,'" recalled Gaston. "Next thing I know I get a knock on the door and it's Paul Beeston and Pat Gillick. They said, 'We just fired Jimy. We want you to take over the team.' I said, 'I really enjoy what I'm doing. It's not too often you go to work and enjoy your work.' Paul just looked at me and said, 'Cito, you in?' So I said, 'Okay.' I lost about 10 pounds those first two weeks managing. I also blame it on the fact it became 24/7 because Paul's a workaholic and Gillick is too. They'd make you one whether you were already or not."

Despite Gaston's initial misgivings, the Blue Jays responded immediately to his promotion to interim manager, winning five of the next six games. While their play improved, Gillick interviewed Lou Piniella, but ultimately balked at the compensatory demands New York Yankees owner George Steinbrenner wanted to allow the fired manager to escape his contract. Unable to land his first choice, Gillick instead removed the interim tag from Gaston on May 31, dubbing him in a news release as "the most appropriate choice."

"We still think we've got a chance to win this division," Gillick added at the time. "We felt this was the easiest transition we could make. Cito knows our players. Over the last two weeks, we think Cito's handled the club very well."

The Blue Jays went through a series of fits and starts from there, winning five straight from June 19 to 23 before dropping nine of their next 11. On July 5, a 5–4 loss to the division-leading Baltimore Orioles dropped them to a season-high 10 games off the pace. A 51–28 flourish followed and carried them all the way to their second division title. Not bad for a guy who didn't want the job.

"When we started to turn things around, I had players come up to me and said, 'Hey, Cito, if they offer it to you, you have to take it,'" said Gaston. "And then the night before they called me in [to remove the interim tag], Gruber said, 'Cito, you have to take this job. All the players want you to be here.' I knew those guys better than I did any other season because once you become the manager they don't come and talk to you like they do as a coach. There's a little bit of distance because you're supposed to be their boss, they don't come around as much, but that year, I had an advantage. I didn't tell them to do any more than what they could do, and I always say 'let the players play, the cream will come to the top.' About a month and a half into it, I got comfortable, and as you go, you get even more comfortable."

Surprisingly, Gaston didn't win the American League Manager of the Year Award, finishing a distant second to Frank Robinson, whose Orioles the Blue Jays chased down for the division title. The slights would continue for Gaston throughout his career. Though his work led the Blue Jays to three consecutive division titles and back-to-back World Series championships, he was never recognized on a national level. There are some who feel that within baseball circles, he never got his due, his managerial work devalued because of the quality teams he was consistently blessed with.

"That's even tougher to manage guys like that because everybody wants to play," said Moseby. "Cito kept the guys going. He did let the players police themselves, because we're men. He would fight for us out there [with] the umpires, he would have meetings when we needed it. Sometimes you have that meeting where you're screaming and hollering but he'd come in and say, 'Hey, take a deep breath. You're

THE MANAGERS

1977–79: Roy Hartsfield—The first manager in team history didn't have much to work with, amassing a 166–318 mark over three seasons of pain.

1980–81: Bobby Mattick—The super scout and player development master took over just as some of the talent he had helped collect began showing up in the majors. He went 104–164 as those players endured their growing pains.

1982–85: Bobby Cox—Helped lead the team out of the basement and to its first American League East championship in 1985, building a 355–292–1 record before returning to Atlanta.

1986–89: Jimy Williams—Promoted after serving as a third-base coach under Cox, he never led strong teams to the postseason. After 12–24 start in 1989, he was fired, posting an overall record of 281–241–1.

1989–97: Cito Gaston—The beloved hitting coach became a popular manager, rescuing the '89 season and eventually leading the Blue Jays to consecutive World Series titles. Posted a 701–652 mark (including the postseason) in his first stint.

1997: Mel Queen—Highly respected pitching coach served as interim manager after Gaston's firing at end of the '97 season, posting a 4–1 record.

1998: Tim Johnson—Former Blue Jays utility infielder had a rocky season despite an 88–74 mark, clashing with popular players and eventually losing credibility over false claims about Army service.

1999–2000: Jim Fregosi—Old-school baseball lifer restored some order after Johnson's firing, finishing with a 167–157 mark.

2001–02: Buck Martinez—Popular former catcher left the broadcast booth and returned to the dugout but oversaw a flawed team that led to GM Gord Ash's firing. Never saw eye-to-eye with J.P. Ricciardi and was fired after a cumulative record of 100–115.

2002–04: Carlos Tosca—Well-respected player developer led a young team that overachieved in 2003 and was then fired when that injury-stung group regressed the following season, posting an overall mark of 191–191.

2004-08: John Gibbons—A former minor-league teammate of Ricciardi's, his first run as manager was marked by run-ins with Shea Hillenbrand and Ted Lilly. Fired with the team spinning its wheels in '08, posting a cumulative 305-305 record.

2008-10: Cito Gaston—Oversaw a strong run in the second half of '08, had a dismal '09, and then retired after a surprising 85-77 season in 2010 under new GM Alex Anthopoulos. Record in his second go was 211-201, and 912-853 overall.

2011-12: John Farrell—Longtime Red Sox coach cut his teeth running the dugout in Toronto, but twice asked to return to Boston when the manager spot there opened up. After his second season ended in controversy, he was traded with pitcher David Carpenter for infielder Mike Aviles after posting a 154-170 record.

2013-18: John Gibbons—A surprise hire after Anthopoulos pulled off a pair of blockbuster deals, he oversaw a messy first season but eventually led the team to an American League East title in 2015 and a wild-card in 2016. Was 488-484 in his second stint and finished at 793-789 overall.

2019-2020: Charlie Montoyo—Joined Blue Jays after 22 years in the Rays organization, 18 of them in the minors, with stops at every level. Led the team through the ugly bottom of the Mark Shapiro/ Ross Atkins rebuild in his first season before guiding club to the 2020 playoffs, leaving him at 99-123 through his first two years.

doing fine,' and we'd go 'Damn, we suck, Cito. What are you talking about?' But that was just him. He was an uplifter."

Even amid all the success, he was consistently second-guessed in some corners of the media, his tactics questioned. After Gaston left as manager in 1997, he didn't get another managing job until 2008, when the Blue Jays brought him back to replace John Gibbons. He remained in the role through the 2010 season, when he retired from the dugout and took a consultant role with the organization.

"Since I've had a lot of time to think about it, I always figured if you couldn't be manager of the year when you were 12-24 and [then ultimately] win your division, you're never going to win it," said

Gaston. "I don't know what happened there. I was a little disappointed I didn't win it.... I wasn't even offered an interview for four years to have a manager's job. I don't know if people thought poorly of me, or somebody said something about me or what. I'm not sure."

The closest Gaston came to another job was with the Chicago White Sox for the 2004 season. General manager Ken Williams, who played for him on the Blue Jays, wanted to hire Gaston but was overruled by owner Jerry Reinsdorf. He opted to bring back former White Sox infielder Ozzie Guillen, who led the team to a World Series title in 2005. Years later, Gaston was standing by the batting cage in Chicago when an errant ball struck Reinsdorf on the leg. "He turned around and looked at me like I threw the ball at him," said Gaston. "So I walked over and said, 'Hey, Jerry, I didn't throw that ball at you.' Then he started explaining. He said, 'Hey, Cito, you know what? We had to make a tough choice and we went with Ozzie.' I said, 'Hey, he won you a World Series, but I would have won it in the first year.' And I turned around and walked away."

Another missed opportunity for Gaston came after the 1999 season, when he interviewed with both Cleveland and Milwaukee. Sensing he was going to get the Cleveland job, he withdrew from the Brewers process only to watch Charlie Manuel get hired instead. He turned down some teams in the years that followed when he felt he was being used to fill the minority interview requirements.

Aside from a brief stint as Blue Jays hitting coach in 2000 and '01, Gaston was out of the game until president Paul Godfrey and GM J.P. Ricciardi brought him back with the team in dire straits in 2008. Gaston led the team to a 51–37 finish that season, oversaw a 75–87 mess in 2009 in which some players in a rotten clubhouse nearly revolted, and finished up his career with an unexpectedly strong 85–77 campaign in 2010, when the Blue Jays hit a club-record 257 home runs.

"I think people respect the way I manage," he said. "I certainly didn't try to embarrass the other team, and a lot of times I had coaches who wanted to embarrass the other team but I wouldn't let them do it. Coming back the last two and a half years here, I've had guys come up to me from other teams and say, 'We know why you turned it around.

Not only was it your managing, you took the handcuffs off, you let them swing the bats.'"

Ultimately, that was Gaston's greatest strength, his touch with hitters. One of his final gifts to the Blue Jays was the guidance he and hitting coach Dwayne Murphy provided to Jose Bautista, helping the slugger funnel his raw power into elite-level production. It is just another part of his lengthy legacy.

"The good thing about Cito? Players liked to play for him," said Alfredo Griffin. "He never raised his voice against you. He just quietly puts his hand on your shoulder and said, 'Hey, man, you messed up.' And you don't say anything, just make sure you don't make that mistake again. He doesn't yell at you like Bobby Cox. Two different managers. I love them both, but Cito was a different type of man, plus he had a veteran team where everyone knew what they were supposed to do. And when you have a team like that, you become a great manager."

16

THE REIGN OF ALEX ANTHOPOULOS

When the Toronto Blue Jays celebrated clinching a playoff berth on September 26, 2015, Alex Anthopoulos remained on the fringes during the champagne toast that led to an impromptu shake-and-spray session. Afterward, a few players told him he should have addressed the group, that it was important. He told them he didn't feel right taking centre stage, that it was their clubhouse, their party. But four days later, when the Blue Jays clinched the American League East in Baltimore, manager John Gibbons didn't let him off the hook.

The Blue Jays secured their first division title since 1993 in the first game of a doubleheader. Though some players sat in the dugout with "travellers" mugs during the nightcap, the party had to wait for the conclusion of the second game. It couldn't end fast enough. Once it did, everyone strapped on goggles, grabbed bottles, and gathered in the centre of the clubhouse. "Okay, Alex is going to say something," Gibbons announced, dragging his GM into the circle. "Everyone's got their bottles," Anthopoulos remembered, "and you could just tell no one wanted to wait for anything. I didn't plan anything, it was last minute, so I'm there, and I see everybody, and I'm not going to get into the, 'Hey, I'm proud of you guys, this and that.' These guys are ready to explode, I have five seconds because these guys can't wait to go nuts." Gazing upon the championship team he had assembled, he shouted, "Un-fucking-believable year." Then, mayhem.

The moment, recorded by LaTroy Hawkins via cell-phone camera and posted to Instagram, revealed Anthopoulos in a manner the public had never before seen. Clad in the ski goggles that have become a staple of boozy postseason soakfests, he delivered his concise message and then hopped around the room as the champagne corks and alcohol streams rocketed around him. Generally disciplined and buttoned-down, his unfettered exuberance on that night released six years-worth of pressure built up from the relentless grinding it took to reach that point. No one could blame the master of the 3:00 AM email for wanting to scream, shout, and let it all out.

Twenty-nine days later, he was gone. Stunning his adoring fan base, Anthopoulos walked away from a five-year contract extension worth $10 million, which was offered just as he was on the verge of leaving. Knowing all along that he was likely at the end, he made sure to savour every second on his way out the door. Anthopoulos explained his decision to leave by citing concerns over the "fit" with incoming president and CEO Mark Shapiro, a comment open to interpretation. So too was this: the five-year offer came not from Shapiro, the man to whom Anthopoulos would report, but from two Rogers Communications executives—Edward Rogers, the Blue Jays chairman and Rogers deputy chair, and Rick Brace, president of the company's Media Business Unit at the time.

Then things got ugly. Fans who in April and May had clamoured for Anthopoulos' firing turned virulently against Shapiro and ownership, even though the outgoing GM handled things with his usual diplomacy. His repeated use of "fit" became one final addition to the Blue Jays' lexicon of loaded words, the way payroll "parameters" and "boundaries" once sparked divisive debate. Years later, after completing the teardown of Anthopoulos' playoff teams at the 2019 trade deadline, Ross Atkins, his successor as GM, added another entry when he boasted the team "turned 14 years of control into 42 years of control."

Though everyone has moved on—Anthopoulos is president, baseball operations and general manager for Atlanta, while the Blue Jays returned to the postseason in 2020—there's never been a full public airing of exactly why things played out the way they did.

The only thing certain when the news dropped October 29 was that the wild reign of an executive dubbed the "ninja GM" was over. A mere 32 years old at the time, Anthopoulos had been hired by then-president and CEO Paul Beeston on the penultimate day of the 2009 season to replace the fired J.P. Ricciardi. Anthopoulos inherited an awful team with a tire-fire clubhouse and a barren farm system. As a cruel bonus, iconic ace Roy Halladay wanted out, refusing to waste his last good years with a rebuilding team in the American League East.

TORONTO BLUE JAYS

Over the six years that followed, Anthopoulos turned around the franchise, rebuilding its scouting staff, resetting the draft philosophy, re-entering the Latin American market, and restructuring player development operations. He manipulated the old free-agent compensation rules to build a cache of draft picks. When Marco Scutaro walked, the Blue Jays plucked Aaron Sanchez and Justin Nicolino as draft reparations. Similarly, Rod Barajas turned into Asher

General manager Alex Anthopoulos talks to reporters during the 2009 GM meetings in Chicago. (M. Spencer Green)

Wojciechowski; Scott Downs into Daniel Norris and Jacob Anderson; Kevin Gregg into Dwight Smith Jr.; Miguel Olivo into Kevin Comer; John Buck into Joe Musgrove; Frank Francisco into Matt Smoral; Jon Rauch into Mitch Nay; and Jose Molina into Tyler Gonzales. The GM gambled on high-talent underachievers in trades for Brandon Morrow, Yunel Escobar, and Colby Rasmus, and when he saw that approach wasn't working, began to make character a bigger priority. That led to perhaps his signature trade: The theft of Josh Donaldson from the Oakland Athletics. The other contender for that honour was dumping $81 million of the $86 million Vernon Wells was owed onto the Los Angeles Angels. Under pressure from above to change the conversation around the team, Anthopoulos pulled off the uncharacteristic blockbusters with the Marlins and Mets that blew up in 2013. Contract extensions for Jose Bautista and Edwin Encarnacion worked out brilliantly; extensions for Ricky Romero and Morrow did not. He pulled off one of the greatest trade-deadline buildups ever in 2015. And that's just for starters. "He hit the ground running that first day and never went to sleep, I'm convinced," said Beeston.

There never was a dull or idle moment, and Anthopoulos did it all with an earnestness and style that fit the market. His backstory also made him easy for fans to relate to. He grew up in Montreal, the son of a Greek immigrant who earned an engineering degree before starting a successful heating-and-ventilation company. The youngest of three boys, he played bass in the brothers' basement band growing up. As a teenager, a friend with season tickets to the Montreal Expos introduced him to baseball and he fell in love with the game. Still, music was his primary focus through high school until his days at McMaster University, where he studied business and became obsessed with sports through his circle of friends.

Exactly 10 days from his 21st birthday, his father died unexpectedly of a heart attack. That changed everything. He and his brothers took over the family business after the funeral—Anthopoulos tried to run it while in Hamilton, completing his third-year studies—but they quickly realized they hated it. And his father's sudden death made Anthopoulos realize the worst thing he could do was spend his life at a job he hated. He wanted to work in baseball, and after the family business was sold, he phoned then–Expos general manager Jim Beattie. Anxiety forced him to hang up before Beattie answered, but he mustered the nerve to call back. This time, he told Beattie he would work for free doing anything the organization needed. The Expos brought him in to sort fan mail, and later gave him a $7-an-hour job copying game notes in the public relations department. But he used the access he had to ask questions of anyone who would listen, eventually working his way into the team's scouting department. Over time his responsibilities increased, and in 2003 he joined the Blue Jays as a scouting coordinator. Ricciardi soon took notice, and by the end of the 2005 season Anthopoulos was an assistant general manager. At the same time, he fostered a close relationship with Beeston by constantly asking questions. Impressed, Beeston at one point turned to then–scouting director Jon Lalonde and asked, "Where the fuck did he come from?"

"It was quite obvious this guy was unique. I sensed that the first day I met him," Beeston added. "I hadn't seen something like this in a long, long time, in business, forget baseball."

Once he was named general manager, Anthopoulos operated with the same tenacity and determination. In December 2010, when the Blue Jays acquired Brett Lawrie from Milwaukee for Shaun Marcum, Brewers GM Doug Melvin noted that "with Alex, there's a lot of phone calls."

The first season under Anthopoulos ended with an unexpected 85–77 record and plenty of optimism. He hired John Farrell, the Boston Red Sox pitching coach, to replace the retiring Cito Gaston after the season, but the Blue Jays slipped to 81–81 in 2011 while integrating some younger players. Afterward the Red Sox called to see if they could hire Farrell back, a request Beeston rejected. Farrell returned in 2012, and the season showed promise until starters Morrow, Kyle Drabek, and Drew Hutchison were injured over a four-game span in June. Things went off the rails with more injuries in July, a 9–19 August was among the worst months in franchise history, and steady leaks out of Boston about Farrell made for a thoroughly miserable season. Compounding matters was Escobar taking the field with a homophobic slur scrawled on his eye-black patches in August, while Omar Vizquel ripped the Blue Jays coaching staff in September. The 73–89 mess and subsequent trade of Farrell to Boston paved the way for the Marlins and Mets blockbusters and the return of John Gibbons as manager ahead of the 2013 season, though at 74–88 it didn't end much better.

The bumpy road continued through 2014. Undermined by some key injuries in August and the lack of significant reinforcements at the trade deadline, when Anthopoulos was at his payroll limit, the Blue Jays finished 83–79. Then in December news broke of the club's attempts to replace Beeston. Kenny Williams and Dan Duquette, the two candidates whose names were leaked, had strong baseball backgrounds. Anthopoulos took note of that. But heading into his contract year, he decided to do things his way. First, he signed Russell Martin to the richest free-agent contract in team history at $82 million over five years. Then he traded for Donaldson and Marco Estrada. Each added a needed dose of character to the clubhouse. At the deadline he acquired Troy Tulowitzki, David Price, Ben Revere, Mark Lowe, and Hawkins. The team surged into the postseason.

Meanwhile, an intriguing story was unfolding in the shadows. As the search for a new president ran its course, Anthopoulos wasn't among those considered for the role, in part because Beeston never gave him the chance to meaningfully interact with ownership. Rogers executives didn't know what they had in him until it was too late. Another Rogers miscalculation was that Shapiro would be good for Anthopoulos, when it turned out their approaches and outlooks for the franchise were widely divergent. Anthopoulos led a tenacious but free-flowing and loose front office. On one occasion, he jokingly challenged assistant GM Andrew Tinnish, then–analytics head Joe Sheehan, and analyst Jason Pare to literally stand on a table to prove how much they wanted him to sign first baseman Justin Smoak. They did, and Anthopoulos signed the player. Shapiro, meanwhile, is more system-and-process oriented, with decision-making a more collaborative effort, involving input from multiple departments. That was a big change from Beeston, who basically made sure the numbers worked and then took them up the Rogers ladder.

Ultimately, Anthopoulos stayed true to his word that he cared more about work environment than salary, and he walked away from life-changing money. Few have such courage in their convictions. In the process he probably did everyone, including himself, a favour by not simply taking the payday and operating in an environment that would surely have become dysfunctional over time.

About 30 minutes into the wild celebration that followed the Blue Jays' 6–3 victory over the Texas Rangers in Game 5 of the ALDS, Dioner Navarro and Anthopoulos embraced. "Hey, I've got something for you," the backup catcher said, reaching into his back pocket. "I saved this ball for you. It's the game ball from the last out." Anthopoulos was stunned. "For that guy to think about me—we'd just won the craziest game in Blue Jays history—and to keep the ball, it meant a lot," he said. "It's one of the most heartfelt gestures from a player I've ever gotten. It sounds cheesy to say it, but I was really moved." Said Navarro: "I just thought he needed to have it after all the hard work he did to bring in players that made the team better, and all the moves and changes that ultimately made the team make it to the playoffs after a long time. So the ball was a little something to show our gratitude."

Anthopoulos had the ball authenticated. It sits on a mantel at his home alongside the framed second-base bag from the night of the American League East clinch in Baltimore, and his Executive of the Year Award, which came from his peers. "Winning the division was most gratifying because it was such an emotional roller coaster getting to that point," said Anthopoulos. "It was so much fun. August, September. The chase was unbelievable."

So too was the end of his reign with the Blue Jays.

17

THE EXECUTIVES

They went out to celebrate. Jack Morris and the Toronto Blue Jays had just completed a $10.85 million, two-year deal and team president Paul Beeston was giving his new right-hander the full George Steinbrenner–style wining-and-dining experience. Morris remembered, "Nobody had ever done it with me, so we had a nice dinner here in Toronto, toasted a couple glasses of champagne, and at the end of the evening Paul grabbed his glass and said, 'I've got to get going, but before I go I want to propose a toast.' We look at him and he said, 'To Jack Morris, the newest member of the Toronto Blue Jays. May you never know how much more I was willing to spend on you.' To this day, I just laugh about that, because more than likely there was some truth in it."

The moment is vintage Beeston—who even after successful negotiations made sure his bargaining partners never felt they had the upper hand. An accountant by training, the eccentric and often sockless raconteur leveraged his people skills as much as he did his talent with numbers from the moment he was hired as the first Blue Jays employee May 10, 1976, until his retirement following the 2015 season. His run with the team was interrupted from 1997 to 2002 when he served as Major League Baseball's chief operating officer, but even then he still watched over the team from afar. When Paul Godfrey's contract expired following the 2008 season, Beeston returned as team president. Almost everything of note in franchise history happened under his watch. "The only constant in the world is change and I think it's probably appropriate," Beeston told radio host Jeff Blair of Sportsnet 590 The Fan upon his departure in 2015. "I am a Blue Jay, my loyalties are not transferable, I'm not for sale to any other team, and quite frankly I'm leaving here very, very pleased that the foundation is here."

That foundation, the one he handed off to new president and CEO Mark Shapiro, in many ways traces back to franchise's birth.

Many of the business models put in place by Peter Bavasi, the club's first general manager, and later refined by Beeston, "are still operating here from a business point of view," said Howard Starkman, a longtime executive who was among the team's first hires. But the most important structure, the one that worked so effectively during the club's golden era, didn't really lock into place until the fall of 1981. Beeston, the executive vice president of baseball operations at the time, grew tired of clashing with the micromanaging Bavasi and threatened to resign, hinting that general manager Pat Gillick would do the same. Peter Hardy, the chairman of Labatt and also vice chair of the club's board, didn't let it happen. "They reviewed the thing and they basically ended up letting Bavasi go," said Starkman. "After that they had Paul running the business and Pat running the baseball, and Hardy was the one they [each] answered to."

Hardy took over as CEO and gave Beeston and Gillick the latitude to do as they saw fit, serving as the funnel between the club and ownership. "You try to put the decision making down as low as possible," he once said. "Define the job functions and job responsibilities and authorities so people know what they can do and what is expected of them."

In many ways Beeston's business acumen was shaped by his relationship with Hardy, whose savvy earned him a strong voice in the commissioner's office. Famously, a 1985 feature in *Sports Illustrated* titled "The Dream Team" named Hardy baseball's best executive. Little wonder that Beeston described him as "my mentor in business and how you handled things."

The Blue Jays promoted Beeston three times in the subsequent years, first to executive vice president, business in 1984; next to president and chief operating officer in 1989; and finally adding CEO to his title in 1991. During that time he operated under the principle of "no surprises," constantly keeping his bosses apprised of what was happening, and building up enough trust to get an easy yes when he came asking for financial approvals. That approach served him and the team well under the ownerships of Labatt, Interbrew S.A., and Rogers Communications Inc. As he put it during a 2013 interview, "The sale begins at the time of the sale. If I'm a car salesman and I sell you a car,

I'm selling you the second car the minute you walk out the door. I'm keeping you. I'm going to treat you well, with integrity, with honesty, make sure that if your car comes in it gets to a mechanic, because I'm selling you that second [expletive] car. When I came back here, the sale began at the time of the sale. It doesn't stop. It's making sure these guys knew what you're all about, and making sure they understand the philosophy of what you're doing."

Still, while Beeston remained consistent in his practices, everything else changed around him. Hardy retired in 1990. Gillick left the team after the 1994 season, with assistant Gord Ash succeeding him. Interbrew purchased Labatt and inherited the team in 1995. Peter Widdrington, the longtime Labatt president and Blue Jays board member, left his role as board chairman in 1996. Finally, amid attempts to sell the club in 1997, Beeston left for Major League Baseball.

The Blue Jays were largely rudderless afterward until Rogers purchased the team in September 2001. Sam Pollock, the wildly successful general manager of the NHL's Montreal Canadiens during the 1960s and '70s, replaced Beeston as CEO. He'd been serving as the club's chairman and team director and was a brilliant executive. But the organization wasn't the same. "It wasn't a question of support, it was probably [that] you didn't know who to turn to because the club was in a little bit of flux," said Ash. "Sam Pollock was a tremendous asset to me from a learning point of view, and obviously having success with the Montreal Canadiens and being able to think two and three steps ahead. And he was a great ally to have and a great sounding board, so I can't complain on that front. [But] when Paul left, that was a void that never fully got replaced because he had great perspective and great ability to ask the right questions—did you think about this, and what about that? You missed that voice of reason.... I don't think any excuses are needed, but it was a difficult time. The club was for sale, there was no long-term plan, and in this business you better have a long-term plan or you're going to be in trouble."

Once Rogers took over, Godfrey was installed as president and CEO, and while he had a plan, it changed multiple times as the Blue Jays got rocked by the combination of an underachieving team and a weak Canadian dollar. "You've got to remember the big thing that really hurts a Canadian baseball team is the dollar differential," he said. During Godfrey's seven seasons, he negotiated SkyDome's purchase and pushed the payroll near $100 million in 2008, but the Blue Jays never even sniffed the playoffs (their best showing was a second-place finish in 2006... 10 games behind the Yankees).

Beeston initially returned on an interim basis in October 2008 and spent a year trying to find a permanent replacement before taking the job himself. That came after he fired general manager J.P. Ricciardi on the penultimate day of the 2009 season and hired Alex Anthopoulos to replace him. A rebuild followed. In the ensuing years, Beeston trimmed down the business side of the organization and tried to operate the team under his own terms, within the Rogers corporate structure. "This is not [expletive] rocket science, trust me on this one, but it's tough for people to get in their minds," said Beeston. "We don't have receivables and we don't have inventory, the toughest things you have to manage. We win, we draw; we draw, we make money; we make money, we reinvest back in the team; we reinvest back in the team, we're going to have long-term sustainability. It is not rocket science—but don't lose the trust of the fans."

Beeston's final season was preceded by controversy, when attempts to hire Ken Williams from the Chicago White Sox and Dan Duquette from the Baltimore Orioles were leaked to the media in December 2014. Talks on compensation with the Orioles dragged into January before failing over their demands for top prospects Jeff Hoffman, Max Pentecost, and Mitch Nay. They were cut off January 25 and the next day, January 26, Beeston was given a one-year extension.

His final season was a brilliant one, with the Blue Jays winning the American League East for the first time since 1993 and advancing to the American League Championship Series. After the team's Game 6 elimination in Kansas City, he popped into manager John Gibbons' office and joked about negotiating a contract extension with pending free agent Marco Estrada, saying there's no way he'd give the pitcher a suite on the road.

"The first word that comes to mind is loyalty. Paul's a loyal guy," said Pat Hentgen. "I've never actually worked with Paul day in and day out in the front office, but I can tell you from a player's standpoint, we always admired him. We always respected him and how he was a loose personality. He made you feel at ease. At times, he could make you feel uncomfortable, but he always did it on purpose, to see how you would react."

Adds George Bell, "It's like when you build a building and you have a strong foundation—Paul is that for this organization. He loved the game, he loved the players, he loved the people around him. He's a true Blue Jay."

18

MARK SHAPIRO AND THE REMAKING OF THE BLUE JAYS

In the summer of 1989, Mark Shapiro graduated with a history degree from Princeton University, and no firm idea of what to do with it. Many of his classmates departed campus set on their next steps, heading off to high-paying jobs on Wall Street, or elsewhere in corporate America. Several of his high school friends, meanwhile, were returning home to Baltimore and beginning their lives there. Neither option really appealed to Shapiro, who at that time was searching not only for his own identity, but also a different path from the others. So, he and childhood friend Mitch Kaplan decided to check out of the rat race. They piled into an old Oldsmobile 98 that belonged to Shapiro's father, Ron, and set out on a road trip, the journey being the destination. They started in Baltimore with a tent, two sleeping bags, a camping stove, and a cooler, showering in lakes or by dousing themselves with water in jugs, as they weaved back and forth through the United States and Canada. "Thank God there was no social media, particularly from Montreal," Shapiro said, laughing. Kaplan, an outdoorsy type, pushed his friend into strenuous hikes, light mountain climbing, even caving. A week in Montana and the journey through the Rockies up to Alberta were among the highlights. Once they hit Vancouver, they turned south for good, picking up the Pacific Coast Highway and taking it all the way down to San Diego. A detour to Sin City proved fateful, but not for obvious reasons. "The car broke down just outside Vegas," Shapiro lamented. "Had to get the freaking transmission redone."

Pricey repair aside, the trip proved formative for Shapiro on a personal, if not a professional level. To that point, his summers had been filled playing baseball and training for football, particularly during the four years at Princeton, where he was a centre and offensive tackle for the Tigers. Suddenly, he had the gift of both freedom and time. "That was my first chance to reflect a little bit, and my first chance to see North America in a way that I never could have imagined seeing it, pushing the boundaries of my comfort and flexibility. It was incredible," he said. "Mitch pushed me to do things that I would never have normally done, which was pretty cool."

Pushing boundaries eventually became a theme for Shapiro professionally, too, eventually bringing him back to Canada to undertake a near total overhaul of the Toronto Blue Jays. His tenure as president and CEO of the club has spanned the spectrum of the baseball executive experience. There was the hurricane of tumult and emotion that swept through upon his arrival on November 2, 2015. The devastation of a teardown at the big-league level alongside a simultaneous organizational recalibration. And the renewed hope and optimism inherent to a team on the rise. The passage of time and an exciting young core have eased the turbulence of his early days, which was fuelled in large measure by the disconnect between him and Alex Anthopoulos that led the former GM to leave after building an American League East winner in 2015. Even still, Shapiro remains a polarizing figure.

Some of the rancour is simply part and parcel of sitting at the helm of a professional sports franchise. But some of it is also reflective of the ongoing tug-of-war in baseball between traditionalists and those driving the game's data-driven evolution. Shapiro has long been at the forefront of change, starting with his revolutionary work in Cleveland's player development system early in his career, and he's continued to employ cutting-edge business practices to a change-resistant industry at every step since. His influence in the game—he's one of commissioner Rob Manfred's close confidantes—and devotion to practices viewed as unorthodox make him a poster boy for the disaffected. His philosophies and the manner in which he describes them can be a turnoff to fans used to seeing the game the way it's always been, and outright threatening to those in the industry content to do things the way they've always been done.

"People tend to be fearful of what they don't understand," Shapiro said of the sport's lingering internal struggle. "That's why the biggest competitive advantage is not analytics, it's not tools and resources, it's not smart people. The biggest competitive advantage is culture. When you have a culture that's truly open-minded, when you have a culture that's not at all based upon credit or blame, when you have a culture that really is not based on one leader or one person, but just an obsessive collective focus on getting to the right answer and the best answer, you're going to beat people.

"Look at the teams that are playing in the playoffs year after year, not that cycle in there occasionally," he continued. "Tampa—no ego. Houston was just really smart, not focused on that one guy or one person. The L.A. Dodgers, even though they have resources, that's what they're doing. Theo Epstein [formerly president of baseball operations for the Chicago Cubs], wherever he is, that's what he's doing. Brian Cashman [GM of the New York Yankees] has adjusted, in a big way, towards doing all those things. Cleveland is obviously built on that premise. Those are the teams that are there. The teams that are fighting it are not the teams winning. They might win occasionally. But they are not the teams winning year after year. You can't argue with it. You'll become like a dinosaur, or you'll become extinct. Sooner or later you need to understand that you have to adapt. I'm not making decisions the way I made decisions in 2002. It's very different now."

No doubt, as is the journey Shapiro has taken from the one he started out on. The eldest of four children, he bonded over baseball with his father, Ron, a prominent and influential player agent based in Baltimore, whose clients included Brooks Robinson, Jim Palmer, Eddie Murray, Cal Ripken Jr., and Kirby Puckett. The access to some of the sport's biggest and brightest stars fed Shapiro's passion for the game. But as he grew into a 6'2", 260-pound high schooler, he excelled on the gridiron, "a by-product of my-pear shaped body," he quipped. Football offered "an incredible vehicle out of the insecurities of adolescence," he added, and unbeknownst to him at the time, "the determination, the perseverance, the toughness, the grit played into the values and attributes that now I know were a core skill-set for me."

Still, baseball always held sway in his heart and when he floated the idea of following in his dad's footsteps and becoming a player agent, the elder Shapiro wasn't having it. Ron's father, also named Mark, emigrated to the United States from Ukraine, which at the time was under Russian rule. After arriving at Ellis Island, he found work loading plumbing equipment onto a truck, quickly moved into sales, and eventually started his own plumbing supply company. Lacking a high school degree, he instilled education as a priority for his children. Ron graduated cum laude from Harvard Law School, while his brother completed medical school. That mentality filtered down once Ron had his own family, so that was one part of his reluctance to support Shapiro's aspirations in baseball. The other was that he didn't see a real route into the industry for his son. The agent business was beginning to change at that point, moving from simply advocating on a player's behalf to servicing a variety of needs in an increasingly cut-throat environment, all while recruiting ever-younger talent to keep the pipeline going. The opportunities were similarly limited on the club side. Doors to the executive offices were then still largely closed to those who hadn't played some type of pro ball, or who didn't have direct ties to the powerbrokers who ran the sport. "There wasn't a clear path for me to a front office executive role," said Shapiro.

Instead, he envisioned himself working in non-profit property development. On the advice of some leaders in the field, he decided to get experience on the for-profit side first. To that end, as Shapiro and Kaplan were winding through their six-week road trip, he made loose plans to meet with the CEO of Ahmanson, a Southern California property development company based in Orange County, that was starting a new management training program. Unsure of when he'd arrive, he promised to notify the CEO when they had reached Northern California and was able to firm up a date. Shapiro had a suit in the back of the car, but "you can imagine what I looked like" upon arrival. He crashed at a friend's place, showered, and immediately went for the interview. "He loved the story of what I was doing so much," said Shapiro, "I got the job."

The CEO had developed the program himself based on the way he had wanted to be trained out of school. Shapiro was the first person hired and he hated the entire experience. "I felt such a disconnect with the people that I worked for in that business," he explained. The following spring, he joined his father for a spring training tour and met with several baseball executives, including Joe McIlvaine, who was assistant GM of the New York Mets; Jim Beattie, who was the player development director for the Seattle Mariners; and John Hart, who was

Cleveland's director of baseball operations. "Like any 22-year-old kid," he said, "I was like, I want to do that." After the trip, he promptly wrote a cover letter and mailed résumés to each of the 26 clubs that existed at the time. Only McIlvaine responded, and what Shapiro thought was the opportunity of a lifetime was little more than a courtesy chat. "It wasn't exactly a positive that my dad was an agent," said Shapiro. "Even though he was so respected, he was still the other side, so people were questioning my intention. Was I coming in to learn and just go back and be an agent?"

Undeterred, Shapiro kept pushing, even after he moved across the country in 1991 to New York, where he began work as an analyst for a retail company. He was there about five months when Dan O'Dowd, then the director of player development in Cleveland, called out of the blue. The club, coming off a 105-loss season, had an entry-level position with no title and O'Dowd invited him to fly into Cleveland for an interview. "We wanted to create diversity of thought, people that would just look at the game differently than the way that we would based upon our path," said O'Dowd. "We were looking for people that, quite honestly, were intelligent, that could process thoughts quickly, could problem solve. And that were creative thinkers."

Shapiro jumped at the opportunity, even as his visions of glamour met the gloomy realities of dilapidated Municipal Stadium. "It was hilarious, man," Shapiro recalled. "I'm going up a narrow staircase that was lopsided, sitting in [now GM] John Hart's office, a space heater by his desk because it's so drafty. Fake plastic plant. Missing ceiling tiles." Yet Hart's vision for the organization was as inspiring as the surroundings were depressing. A young core of players was coming. A move to Jacobs Field was two years away. Leveraged properly, they would transform the franchise. Shapiro was sold on the plan before he left. Once he landed back in New York, a message with a job offer awaited on his answering machine. He eagerly signed up for a 40 percent pay cut and a dingy cubicle, and three months later, rented a small U-Haul truck, loaded up his belongings with his younger brother David, and just as the calendar flipped to 1992, began his new life as a baseball executive.

Hart and O'Dowd immediately put Shapiro to work, almost exclusively on the big-league side to start. He did background work, picked up players from the airport, pulled game reports from fax machines and organized them. But Hart also had him do some analysis for Cleveland's innovative plan to sign their pre-arbitration eligible players to multi-year contracts. "No one had ever done that before," said Shapiro. Thirteen players ended up signing that spring, guaranteeing cost-certainty for the club and financial security for the player. Others did the same down the road. Agreements with Carlos Baerga, Albert Belle, Sandy Alomar Jr., Jim Thome, Kenny Lofton, and Charles Nagy saved the team millions. Agreements with Alex Cole, Mark Whiten, Glenallen Hill, Jack Armstrong, and Scott Scudder did not.

After a year as a jack of all trades, O'Dowd called Shapiro into his office and told him that while the work he was doing was valuable, he needed to establish a core skill-set and a foundation. The solution was a transition to player development. "I felt like Mark was going to end up being a high-level executive in the game, he just innately had those characteristics," said O'Dowd. "And I'm a big believer, to this day, that the greatest training for a future GM or president is to run a player-development system because you get pulled in a million different directions. Every day you have another fire that you're putting out. You're managing a diverse group of personalities and people, and you have to become proficient in organizing, and attention to detail in running a world-class process."

Once he moved into the new role, a light bulb turned on. "Man, it was just immediate," said Shapiro. "Like, this was what I was meant to be doing." The transition marked a pivotal point of his career, allowing him to holistically reimagine the way players were groomed. He applied not only the lessons he learned from the stars he grew up around thanks to his dad, but also his own experiences playing football at Princeton. "Like, how would I want to be involved in the process of being developed? How would I want to be talked to by a coach? What's the best possible way to develop players?" said Shapiro. "After a very short period of time, I had ideas about how to change the development system and John Hart was just like, 'Yeah. I got your back. Do it.'"

O'Dowd encouraged him to break from traditional moulds, too—an organizational tenet was to ask why are things done the way they are—and that's what Shapiro did. He individualized development plans for each player, increased the emphasis on strength and conditioning training, and built up resources to help with the mental side of competition. Johnny Goryl, a veteran in Cleveland's player development system, took Shapiro under his wing. Other key influences were Mark Newman, the longtime Yankees player development executive; Karl Kuehl, who co-wrote *The Mental Game of Baseball* with Harvey Dorfman; Rick Peterson, at the time a pitching coach in the White Sox organization who'd eventually be among the first big-league coaches to embrace biomechanics; and Charlie Maher, a sports psychologist hired to help build a system-wide framework for development.

"We were basically just throwing bats and balls out and providing guys a chance to play, conventionally training only one side of the athlete," said Shapiro. "We could define that this guy can't focus, but we weren't ever prescriptive in giving him a way to focus. We could say, this guy's struggling with anxiety, but we never gave him a way to handle the anxiety. John and Dan supported everything and encouraged me at a level that I didn't understand at 25, 26 years old. I look back and I'm like, 'Holy shit, I can't believe those guys empowered me to that level.'"

Three years after losing 105 games, Cleveland went 100–44 in the strike-shortened '95 season and won the first of five straight American League Central titles. Promoted to director of minor-league operations in 1994, Shapiro suddenly became one of baseball's top executive prospects. He turned down an offer from the New York Yankees to be an assistant GM one year, and the next got offers from the Oakland Athletics, Colorado Rockies, and Florida Marlins. Hart asked him to stay and made him an assistant GM in 1999, after the Rockies hired O'Dowd as GM.

By that point, however, as ownership of the team shifted from the Jacobs family to Larry Dolan in 2000, trouble loomed on the horizon.

The roster was aging and expensive. Cleveland's economy was being decimated by the departure of Fortune 500 companies. The NFL's Browns had just returned to the city. In 2003, the Cavaliers would draft LeBron James and take centre stage in the market. Hart left after the 2001 season, when the team won its sixth division crown in seven years but faced the storm of fundamental threats. On his way out the door, he told Dolan that Shapiro should be his replacement and the owner agreed to the succession plan. Shapiro, though, knew what was coming and wanted to ensure he had the runway needed to execute his plan. He asked Dolan and his son Paul, at the time the team's vice president and general counsel, if they knew why he was in line to be the next GM. "Larry was really honest and said no," said Shapiro. "I said, 'Is it just because John told you?' He said, 'Largely, yes.' And I said, 'Well, I don't want the job then. I want to interview for the job. Because there are going to be tough times. If you don't know why I'm the guy, then you're going to question when we go through tough times why I have that job. And it's going to be hard to stay the course and be hard to buy into the plan.'"

They agreed to an interview, and Shapiro prepared a 100-page document outlining his strategy, core values, and plan to rebuild the club. He was hired November 1, 2001. "It's easy to get the job when you're the only guy getting interviewed," Shapiro laughed. "It was a good way to set the tone going in. Larry and Paul were new to the game. It was an opportunity to inform them of this is the way I think we have to do things. That evolved a lot because I was even unaware of what was going to happen and how we had to evolve."

Shapiro, all of 34 at the time, immediately began tearing down the club. A month into the job, he traded away Roberto Alomar. Lofton and Juan Gonzalez left as free agents. Bartolo Colon and Chuck Finley were dealt in June, reliever Ricardo Rincon in July. Much as he would be in Toronto 14 years later, he was vilified in Cleveland. The club nosedived, losing 88 games in his first year in charge, and after the beloved Thome left for the Philadelphia Phillies, 94 in the second. The payroll went from roughly $92 million in 2001 to $79 million the next season and $48.5 million the year after.

But behind the scenes, the entire operation was being updated. Future GMs Josh Byrnes, Chris Antonetti, Ben Cherington, Neal Huntington, Mike Hazen, Ross Atkins, and Mike Chernoff were in the early stages of their careers. They pushed forward into analytics as the industry began waking up to the market inefficiencies that data could reveal. And a new core of talent was being amassed and developed. "We couldn't operate as a big-market team any longer and we needed to try to find better ways of doing things," said Shapiro. "Oakland was already pushing the envelope. There were different, isolated people out there. Theo Epstein was just starting the job in Boston. We brought in a lot of really bright, talented people that were starting to push that envelope, and pushed me, as well. It was more creating a culture at that point that was open-minded and focused on finding new opportunities to get better."

In 2005, Cleveland won 93 games and Shapiro was voted *Sporting News'* Executive of the Year. After a step back in 2006, he bagged the honour again in 2007 when his team won the American League Central and fell one win short of reaching the World Series. The following July, the model of constant renewal the franchise still employs came to the fore when ace CC Sabathia was traded to the Milwaukee Brewers for prospects. In the summer of 2009, the same happened with Cliff Lee and Victor Martinez. Shapiro's son Caden was so angry about the last one that the following Halloween, he dressed up as Martinez and as they went trick-or-treating, pointed out to strangers that his dad had made the trade. No matter, Jake Westbrook followed the others out the door in 2010. Michael Brantley, Corey Kluber, Carlos Carrasco, and Justin Masterson, core parts of Cleveland's next playoff teams, were among the players to come back in return.

The next stage in Shapiro's evolution came after an organizational restructuring pushed him up to president following the 2010 season. The switch left him in charge of the club's business side while Antonetti, promoted to GM, ran baseball operations. Though the two continued to work closely, eventually they became more focused on their differing duties. Once a strategic rebranding and a major stadium renovation were completed ahead of the 2015 season, Shapiro began feeling like he'd hit a ceiling. An offer to serve as Princeton's athletic director tempted him, and though he turned it down, exploring the opportunity left him, for the first time, more open to leaving. "It was largely a built-out organization, incredibly talented," said Shapiro. "I was largely like an adviser.... Once I had learned the business side and built out and hired and put things in place, I realized I liked some things on the business side but that the baseball side is still what fuels me."

That combination made him exactly what Blue Jays wanted as they searched for a president to replace the retiring Paul Beeston. The previous winter, their search went public when requests for permission to speak with Kenny Williams, the White Sox's executive vice president, and Dan Duquette, the Baltimore GM, leaked. Williams was denied permission to pursue the job, while Duquette's candidacy collapsed when Orioles owner Peter Angelos sought then top prospects Jeff Hoffman, Max Pentecost, and Mitch Nay as compensation. The Blue Jays brought Beeston back for one final season, buying time to find a candidate with a background in both baseball and business. Anthopoulos' contract was also up after 2015, positioning the club to clean house if things went poorly.

Quietly, the search went on as the Blue Jays floated through the first half of the season playing .500 ball. Major League Baseball supplied a list of names that included Ned Colletti, Sam Kennedy, and Shapiro. When Dave Dombrowski abruptly parted with the Detroit Tigers after the trade deadline, the Blue Jays brought brought him in for a conversation. But he was always headed to the rival Boston Red Sox and a reunion with owner John W. Henry, whom he worked for with the Marlins. Shapiro had by then become a focal point, anyway, impressing with his structured and disciplined framework for the business. His hiring was announced on August 31, handing him control of the club once the season was over. "He's very well-respected around baseball, from the commissioner's office to the other teams," Blue Jays chairman Edward Rogers (who is also deputy chairman at parent company Rogers Communications Inc.) said in 2015. "Obviously Rogers is not only a baseball company, and I think having leaders that are well ingrained and know what they're doing gives us confidence."

For Shapiro, the opportunity "fit a lot of different things that were important to me. The role here is different from every other major-league team. The person that is president of this team largely acts on a day-to-day basis as an owner, from the Major League Baseball perspective. In Cleveland, I went to owners' meetings, but Paul Dolan represented the team. Paul Beeston represented the Blue Jays. When the meeting of 30 happens at every owners meeting, I'm in that room now. So it's exposure. I sit on different committees that I couldn't sit on in Cleveland, because Paul took up most of those opportunities. My opportunity to learn, my opportunity to expand on an MLB level was much greater here. That's one thing. Two, I felt like there was an opportunity here to build upon what had been done, but still modernize systems that largely had not been invested in or committed to."

Moving to Toronto from Cleveland had a great deal of appeal, too, giving his teenaged kids a chance to grow up in an international and diverse metropolis rather than in a small-pond city. Before taking the job, the family visited to check out different neighbourhoods, trying to envision what their life would be like. The more liberal environment in Canada better meshed with Shapiro's social leanings, too, especially as the United States took a rightward tilt. And he saw significant upside in what the Blue Jays could become again. "I felt like we can build a sustainable championship team here in this market if we build out those systems and a strong foundation and the culture," said Shapiro.

But as the 2015 Blue Jays moved steadily toward an American League East championship, ending a playoff drought stretching back to 1993, the ground shifted. Rather than inheriting a flawed team ripe for a rebuild—like the Cleveland team he first took over—there was suddenly a championship-calibre core that revitalized a dormant fan base. Anthopoulos was positioned to be a coveted free agent, revered for finally building a winner. Bringing him back seemed like a no-brainer, but there was a total disconnect between the two men. Citing vague concerns about the "right fit," Anthopoulos turned down a five-year extension worth $10 million that included an opt-out after the first year. Blue Jays fans were apoplectic.

Shapiro ended up wearing the entire mess and his introductory news conference turned into a defence of what had happened, prompting Edward Rogers to make rare public comments on the matter. "We really wanted Alex to lead the Jays into the future and tried very hard to do that, and we were sincere in our efforts and we couldn't come to something that was of his satisfaction," he said. "Just reading a lot of the press, there was a notion that in his renewal offer, somehow his job had changed. His job had not changed at all. His direct manager will change, but his breadth of scope and responsibility had not changed. We had full confidence in him."

In hindsight, Anthopoulos did everyone a favour by preventing the situation from becoming paralyzingly dysfunctional. Still, the fallout loomed over every decision the Blue Jays made for the next few years, the push toward modernization winning over some fans, others embittered by the potential alternative reality had Anthopoulos continued onward.

Undaunted, Shapiro executed his plan with the same determination he pushed through with in Cleveland. Atkins came over from Cleveland as his general manager and they tweaked around the edges of the roster to help the Blue Jays win a wild-card in 2016, as the organization underwent a swift and stunning rewiring. The franchise essentially operated on parallel tracks, the big-league team left to mostly run as it had, while the player development, scouting, analytics and business operations were methodically overhauled. "That was just good business," said Shapiro. "I was fighting to keep the major-league payroll high, fighting to keep investing in the team, but it was a tough one because it wasn't a balanced team. Your best players were all your oldest players, which is really tough. Usually if that's the case, you're heading towards a cliff. But even with that, I felt like based on upon the success of '15, what it meant to the country and the city, there really was no alternative. The alternative was blow it up. That's why we kept on trying to ride it as long as we objectively felt like there was a chance."

The high-profile departures of Edwin Encarnacion after the 2016 season, Jose Bautista following 2017, Josh Donaldson late in the '18 campaign, and Marcus Stroman at the trade deadline in '19 coincided with the downturn and sped the turnover. A core of young players centred around Vladimir Guerrero Jr., Bo Bichette, Cavan Biggio, Lourdes Gurriel Jr., Danny Jansen, and Nate Pearson rose through the ranks beneath them, their transitions turning some of the public tide. An off-season highlighted by the signing of ace Hyun-Jin Ryu to an $80-million, four-year deal in December 2019 created faith that Shapiro's Blue Jays could take big swings when the time was right.

"Part of the plan from Day 1 and part of the understanding has been that there will be a time that we need to outspend, outpace revenue with spending on players," Shapiro said at the close of the 2019 season. "When? They'll rely on us... to say, 'Okay, we are close enough to a contending team that we need to go out and spend on players now that supplement this core.' We'll have the flexibility to do that starting this off-season, because when you're young, by nature your payroll goes down, but I think the key is as we start to mature, and guys start to get in their prime, they're going to become more expensive, we need to make sure we A, keep those players in place and B, we add the necessary pieces at the right time."

A return to the postseason amid the chaos of the 2020 pandemic season followed, and has the potential to be a springboard into a brighter future. The signing of George Springer to a franchise-record $150-million, six-year deal in January 2020 was the latest step toward that path. Whether the Blue Jays get there depends on Shapiro, back behind the wheel of a vehicle he made all his own, cruising down the road of opportunity and possibility.

19

DOME SWEET HOME

There is no romanticizing old Exhibition Stadium, the utilitarian-at-best first home of the Toronto Blue Jays, aptly and unaffectionately dubbed the "Mistake by the Lake" by many who frequented the dump. It was bitterly cold. Many seats faced the wrong way or had obstructed views. And the seagulls—those annoying, screeching seagulls—overran the stands. The place was a means to an end, no more, a site sufficient for those working to land a baseball team for the city to be able to say they had a place to play. Even though it was a decrepit football stadium being awkwardly retrofitted, Paul Godfrey knew he needed at least that much in his back pocket.

In 1969, when he was a member of the North York municipal council, he paid his own way to baseball's winter meetings in Bal Harbour, Florida, to stump for a team in Toronto. Frank Lane, a special assistant to the general manager with the Baltimore Orioles at the time, shared a drink with the kid full of chutzpah, and directed him to plead his case directly to commissioner Bowie Kuhn. Godfrey did just that, telling Kuhn that Toronto deserved a team. "He said, 'Well, where would you play?'" recalled Godfrey. "I said, 'Sir, if you give us a team, I'll make sure the city council builds you a stadium.' He looked down at me—he was about six foot five, a big, tall man—put his hand on my shoulder, and said, 'Son, let me tell you the way baseball works. First you build a stadium and then we'll consider giving you a team. When that stadium is ready, you come and see me.'" That's how the baseball incarnation of Exhibition Stadium was born.

Godfrey's vision all along, however, was for a domed stadium. Given the unpredictable weather in Toronto, a roof made sense, and he was among a group of young, conservative politicians during that period with grand ambitions to develop the city into a world-class destination. Along with landing a baseball team and building a convention centre, a dome was one of his goals. Still, Exhibition Stadium helped land the Blue Jays, and talk of a proper facility died

Toronto fan Doug Allen, dressed as a gorilla, holds up a flag in the top deck of the SkyDome as he celebrates the first baseball game played there on June 5, 1989. (Hans Deryk)

down for a while until the 1982 Grey Cup, infamously known as the "Rain Bowl" because of its miserable weather conditions, was played. The concourses were overrun, the concessions ran out of hot drinks, and the washrooms were so full that some men urinated in the sinks. Ontario premier Bill Davis attended the game and was sufficiently appalled, creating an opportunity for Godfrey to approach him, much as he had when seeking provincial money for the Ex renovations during the 1973 Grey Cup. Privately, they decided enough was enough. A few months later Davis declared a dome for the city "inevitable." So too were the convoluted behind-the-scenes machinations that followed. Six-and-a-half years and $572 million later, SkyDome, now known as Rogers Centre, opened both its roof and its doors. It was awe-inspiring. "Moving there," said longtime manager Cito Gaston, "was like moving into a palace."

SkyDome changed everything. The Blue Jays went from the worst facility in baseball to arguably the best, a technological marvel with a four-panelled, retractable roof that made it the first venue of its kind. The bitter winds, fog, and rainouts that were staples of life at Exhibition Stadium disappeared. Rain or shine, the game always started on time. And the place gleamed. "There was a wow factor," said catcher Ernie Whitt. "It was just a beautiful structure, and with the dome open, you had the CN Tower right there looking over you." The clubhouse was the first of the luxurious lounges standard at big-league parks today, with ample space and plush leather couches for players to kick back on. Other building features included a hotel with rooms that overlooked the field, multiple restaurants, a health club, luxury suites, and upgraded concessions. "It was strange because you'd have 50,000 people in the seats but it was very quiet because everyone was looking around at everything and not actually what was happening on the field," said Whitt. "It seemed like for the first month the game was secondary. The priority was 'look at this beautiful stadium.'"

More important, the dome changed the business for the Blue Jays, spiking the capacity in the stands while concurrently creating scores of new revenue streams. Though the SkyDome wasn't ready for baseball until June 5, 1989, the club's total attendance soared to 3,375,883, an increase of nearly 800,000 fans from 1988. That number climbed to 3,885,284 in 1990 before the Blue Jays became the first big-league team to break the 4 million mark in attendance in 1991, with 4,001,527. They did that again in both '92 and '93, when the club record of 4,057,947 was established; the attendance still ranks sixth in baseball history. Unsurprisingly, in both those seasons, the Blue Jays ran the game's biggest payrolls as a result.

Hard times followed both on and off the field for the Blue Jays, and the SkyDome suffered as a result. The average game attendance dipped by 10,000 fans to 39,257 in 1995, after the strike-shortened '94 campaign, and season attendance bottomed out at 1,495,482 fans in 2010 with some peaks and valleys in between. The multisport-stadium fad came to an end when the Baltimore Orioles opened Camden Yards in 1992, and as more and more retro ballparks transformed the fan experience in other cities, public adoration of SkyDome faded.

A distaste for the place arose as the bills added up. At the project's inception, the plan was for the municipal and provincial governments to supply $30 million apiece. The federal government donated land, while a consortium of 30 companies contributed another $150 million. The province agreed to cover any shortfalls, and there ended up being plenty, with the debt load on the building eventually exceeding $300 million. By 1991 the province, which owned the building, decided to sell SkyDome to ease the burden on taxpayers. After 2½ years of negotiations, it was sold to a group called Stadium Acquisition Inc. for $150 million in March 1994. By November 1998, the building was in bankruptcy protection and the following April another consortium called Sportsco International, in which former Blue Jays general manager Pat Gillick was a partner, completed a court-supervised purchase for $80 million. Sportsco fared no better. In 2004 Godfrey, named president and CEO after Rogers Communications Inc. bought the club in September 2000, negotiated the dome's purchase for $25 million. "People said, 'Hold on a second, how could you buy a $572 million building for $25 million?'" said Godfrey. "My answer at the time was it's not even worth $25 million because there's only one buyer for it, and it doesn't turn out a cash flow by itself."

A MULTIPURPOSE HOME

The SkyDome/Rogers Centre has served as the venue for everything from big-name concerts by bands such as the Rolling Stones to NBA games and monster truck rallies. It's also hosted two major baseball events outside of the regular season and postseason:

1991 All-Star Game: Behind game MVP Cal Ripken Jr., who hit a three-run homer in the third inning off Dennis Martinez, the American League defeated the National League 4–2 in the Midsummer Classic. Blue Jays manager Cito Gaston served as a coach on Tony La Russa's AL staff.

2009 World Baseball Classic: The Canadians hosted Pool C first-round action in the second edition of the international event, with Canada losing both its games—6–5 to the United States and a 6–2 stunner to heavy underdog Italy. The US and Venezuela advanced to the second round.

By that time, ownership of the SkyDome became vital for the Blue Jays, since they took flack for many of the aging building's shortcomings but had no authority to do anything about it. The purchase resolved that problem, while also giving the team control over all the revenues generated by the facility. A series of upgrades have since helped modernize Rogers Centre, as it was renamed in 2005, and a wider redevelopment of the building, along with the adjacent area was being planned behind the scenes when the pandemic hit. Some details leaked late in 2020 and the notion of an entirely new, baseball-only stadium, akin to the ones that are now industry standard, captivated the imagination of fans. But with momentum stalled and significant regulatory hurdles to clear, a new home to replace their largely unloved utilitarian venue remained more vision than reality. "I really get irritated when people say, 'It's not a real stadium, it should be open air,'" says Godfrey. "This was for the community... and the taxes it generates more than paid for the stadium. The public just hears the final price, they forget that it creates jobs, there's sales tax on all the parts, and it stimulates the economy."

For the foreseeable future, at least, Rogers Centre will remain dome sweet home for the Blue Jays.

20

FRANCHISE ICON: GEORGE BELL

A lot of stories about George Bell start with the star outfielder being mad about something. Often he was angry at the media or, occasionally, fans. Once he urged those critical of him to "kiss my purple butt." Sometimes he'd have it out with general manager Pat Gillick or, more frequently, manager Jimy Williams, or even both at the same time. That's what happened in the spring of 1988, when he was unhappy about the ill-fated plan to move him from left field to DH after an MVP campaign. And opponents, particularly the Boston Red Sox, made him see red, especially when he felt pitchers were taking liberties by pegging him and his teammates with pitches a little too often. Bell's legendary 1985 karate kick to Bruce Kison's midsection was the response to one such incident. "I stopped that shit," he said with a smirk.

"I was very competitive. I don't like to get beat," Bell continued. "I'm not a fighter. Off the field, I never fought anybody, but on the field I'd do it. I was mean. On the field I was mean. People think I'm a mean guy. I'm not mean at all."

Well, people who watched or competed against him will contest that assertion, as that frothing intensity marked a tremendous 12-year career and helped make him one of the inaugural members of the Toronto Blue Jays' Level of Excellence. Indeed, Bell is a towering figure in franchise history, and was at the heart of the club's emergence from expansion doormat to perennial power. Loved or loathed, he was always respected and feared, in large measure for his ability, but also because of the ferocity with which he utilized it.

"Let me tell you about George's personality," said Cito Gaston, who developed a strong bond with Bell as his hitting coach before managing him. "He's a good guy. He just wanted to seem like he was angry all the time. But if George liked you, George would die with you. If you're in a foxhole, you want George at your back.... But George, he didn't take any shit. He'd go to the mound, he'd fight you, and he didn't care."

Longtime Blue Jays catcher Ernie Whitt, who calls Bell one of the best teammates he ever played with, said, "That man, all he ever wanted to do was win. I know he had a hard time with the media, sometimes he was misunderstood, but the bottom line is that he wanted to win. He wanted his teammates to play hard and win, and as a player you respect that."

The fire in Bell came from his father, who instilled in all four of his boys the aggressive manner they took onto the field. Bell was the eldest and the most talented, although Jose, Ronaldo, and Juan also made it to pro ball (only Juan reached the majors, appearing in 329 games). The foursome often played on the same team growing up, with local coaches in San Pedro de Macoris, Dominican Republic, fighting to get them on their team. Bell described himself as "shy" growing up, a persona that changed once the game started.

"My dad taught us when you play a game, especially baseball, there's intimidation," said Bell. "People try and intimidate you and you have to play with a lot of intensity, and we grew up like that.... I came over from the Dominican [Republic] taught to respect people. But in this game, if you don't stand up for yourself, and you'll see many players who will let you know what I'm saying, they really try and get you off [your game]. They're trying to get you in a way where you can never concentrate again. I didn't let that happen."

By age 15, Bell began to attract scouts, and his profile only grew from there. He worked out for Atlanta, who ultimately didn't sign him. A session with Philadelphia followed and at age 17, he signed for $4,500 with the Phillies in 1978. After 17 hours of travel, he made his rookie-ball debut that year in Helena, Montana, where to say he was a fish out of water would be a gross understatement. His first thought as he surveyed his new surroundings was, "I don't know anything."

A year later Bell hit 22 homers with 102 RBIs and an .895 OPS over 130 games at Single-A Spartanburg but played only 22 games at Double-A Reading the next season, prompting the Phillies to leave him unprotected in the Rule 5 draft. Gillick scooped him up on December 8, 1980. A Rule 5 pick must remain on the big-league roster for the

George Bell points at Royals' pitcher Bud Black after Bell was hit by a pitch in the sixth inning of a 1985 playoff game in Toronto. (Gene Puskar)

full season and in 1981, Bell appeared in 60 games, batting .233 with five homers. He spent all of 1982 and most of '83 at Triple-A Syracuse before emerging in 1984 with 26 homers, 87 RBIs, and an .824 OPS.

"In school we talked about Canada, but not Toronto," Bell said of his acclimation to his new surroundings. "I knew about the Blue Jays because Alfredo Griffin and Damaso Garcia were playing for the team. When I came here, I didn't know there was a piece of land so beautiful like Canada. That was amazing. I was happy to be here. I was proud to come to the organization and I stayed long enough to build my career here."

Bell's infamous altercation with Kison came on June 23, 1985, after he was hit high on the left arm with one out in the fourth inning. The Blue Jays were a team on the rise, in first place in the American League East at the time en route to their first division title. Kison had narrowly missed Whitt's head in the second inning before Bell became the fourth batter hit by the Boston Red Sox in the series at Exhibition Stadium.

"We were all getting beaten up by pitchers trying to intimidate us and I said, 'I don't want to take that,'" remembered Bell. "Having emotion on the field, that shows your teammates and the opposing team that there's nothing wrong with going out and playing with a lot of intensity in the game, and I did."

A wild melee ensued once Bell kicked Kison. Bell turned to swing at catcher Rich Gedman as both benches emptied, some trying to calm things down, others getting in on the action. Blue Jays bullpen coach John Sullivan wrestled Kison to the ground and then got kicked in the face by Red Sox first baseman Bill Buckner, who later told reporters, "I told him to get off and he ignored me, so I got him off."

Bell was the only player ejected and was later suspended two games. Whitt exacted some revenge of his own on Kison by hitting a grand slam in the sixth inning that settled an 8–1 victory. Whitt repeatedly stared out at the mound on his way around the bases. "Bruce Kison had a reputation of headhunting, and there was always a big battle between us and Boston," he said.

Buckner later labelled Bell baseball's "dirtiest player," but that reputation didn't hinder Bell's ascent to stardom. At times he seemed slump-proof, with a low-maintenance swing that rarely required significant intervention from Gaston. He didn't do much guessing at the plate and rarely was he cheated on a swing. He also had a knack for shortening his stroke with two strikes and hitting the ball up the middle or to the opposite field. "I don't consider myself a smart hitter, but to be in the big leagues to have a lot of success you have to be smart," Bell said. "I consider myself not a genius, but smart enough to set up the pitchers sometimes. Sometimes the pitcher's going to tip when he's going to throw a fastball, a breaking ball, a changeup, and you don't miss those opportunities. You go out and try to do the best you can. I had quick hands, and when you have quick hands you can stay back and still hit the ball pretty good. One thing you've got to do is recognize what you're hitting. If you're looking breaking ball and he throws the fastball and the fastball is middle-out, you still have a chance to hit the fastball to right field."

In 1987 that approach led to his best season, when Bell batted .308 with 47 homers, 134 RBIs, and an OPS of .957. He beat Alan Trammell of the Detroit Tigers for American League MVP honours. But that was cold comfort, since the Blue Jays lost their final seven games of the season to finish two games back of the Tigers and out of the playoffs despite 96 wins. "That's one thing that really hurt me," said Bell.

Another thing that hurt was the way Gillick and Williams moved him to designated hitter so prospect Sil Campusano could play left field on an everyday basis the following spring. Bell said when the matter came up during his contract talks between seasons, he made it clear, "I ain't going to play no DH. I could probably play DH in a day game after a night game, but I want to play in the outfield to keep me ready." He said he was assured the DH proposal would be scrapped, but the plan leaked out in the media before spring camp opened. So he arrived in Dunedin, Florida, angry, refusing to DH in one Grapefruit League game. "In that time, being a DH was not a job. You've got to be an everyday player," said Bell. "I would feel like I was stuck in the garbage."

Nonetheless, the reigning MVP started the 1988 season at DH, clubbing an Opening Day–record three home runs off Kansas City Royals ace Bret Saberhagen in a 5–3 victory. He lined out to deep left field in his only other at-bat. "I almost hit four home runs because I was mad. I was really pissed," said Bell. Two weeks later the Blue Jays abandoned the whole scheme and moved Bell back to left field.

"You know what? I'll just say it like this and I won't say any more: It probably could have been handled a bit better, explained to him a little bit better," said Gaston, who was still hitting coach at the time. "Just don't spring it on him, explain it and see if you can get him to understand what you're trying to do."

Though Bell remained productive, the relationship between him and the team had changed irreparably. He put up solid seasons in

1988, '89, and '90, but after the Blue Jays finished two games out in 1990, Gillick decided to shake up the club. That off-season, he pulled off the blockbuster for Roberto Alomar and Joe Carter that sent Tony Fernandez and Fred McGriff to San Diego, and also acquired Devon White. Bell was offered a one-year deal—as DH only. "It was time to go," he realized.

"Even Paul Beeston told me, 'It's better to go [to] the free-agent market,'" remembers Bell. "We were all trying to win since 1985, and nothing came up because most of the time we didn't make the right trades and stuff like that. They traded some players, brought in some new players, new faces, and everything changed."

Bell signed a $9.8 million, three-year deal with the Chicago Cubs, finished out his deal with the Chicago White Sox after being traded for Ken Patterson and a promising outfielder named Sammy Sosa, and then called it a career.

"Sometimes it's just time to go, and you know, I was not mad. I was sad," said Bell. "I built my career [in Toronto], I came over here when I was very young, and when I was 30 years old I had to go. So that's okay."

Despite the awkward ending, Bell's career with the Blue Jays was far more than just okay. He returned in 1996 to find his place on the Level of Excellence that rings the Rogers Centre, an honour as lasting as the mark he left upon a franchise on the make.

21

ALFREDO GRIFFIN SHARES ROOKIE OF THE YEAR

The first few years of any expansion franchise's existence tend to be difficult. There's excitement locally about simply having a team, to be sure, but more often than not what happens on the field of play offers little to feel good about. Fans simply have to hope that the immediate pain eventually leads to long-term gain. So it was for the Blue Jays in 1977, '78, and '79, when they lost 107, 102, and 109 games, respectively, the only triple-digit-loss seasons in club history. For coaches, executives, and fans alike, a lot of patience was needed.

That's what made Alfredo Griffin's emergence as a cornerstone shortstop so important for the Blue Jays and their fans. After so many losses, they needed a win—any win—and Griffin really gave them that. While Pat Gillick meticulously put in place the pieces that would eventually lead the Blue Jays to 11 years of competitive and contending baseball, Griffin offered some immediate validation, something to give people reason to think things would one day turn around. Griffin was named American League Rookie of the Year in 1979, a prize he shared with Minnesota Twins third baseman John Castino, and fans finally had a lasting achievement to celebrate.

Griffin signed with Cleveland in August 1973 as an amateur free agent and worked his way up through their system relatively quickly, getting cups of coffee with Cleveland in 1976, '77, and '78 by the time he was 20. But after finishing the 1978 season at Triple-A Portland, he became a target for the Blue Jays, who had scouted him in the minors and taken a liking to him. Gillick acquired Griffin and Phil Lansford from Cleveland on December 5 for Victor Cruz, a reliever they'd picked up from the St. Louis Cardinals a year earlier with Tom Underwood for Pete Vuckovich. Though Vuckovich went on to win a Cy Young Award with Milwaukee in 1982, Gillick had picked up an everyday shortstop with upside.

1979 AL Rookie of the Year Alfredo Griffin.

Griffin took a simpler outlook on the trade. "I really didn't know anything about Toronto," he said. "The only thing I knew is that my teammates and the people who know baseball thought it was good for me, because it was the beginning of the expansion for the Jays, and I had a better chance [to play] there than in Cleveland, so I was really excited about it."

He broke camp as the everyday shortstop and leadoff man, but that quickly ebbed as he struggled at the plate. He collected two hits in his second game, then didn't get another until five games later. Hit No. 4 didn't come for another five games. Two weeks into the season he was batting 4-for-49—or .082—as the Blue Jays headed to Texas for three games with the Rangers. In Arlington on April 23, he remembers hitting coach Bobby Doer pulling him aside. "He said, 'Listen, son, today's the last chance you have to stay in the big leagues. You have to start hitting from today,'" Griffin recalled.

Jarred, Griffin spoke to teammate and fellow Dominican Rico Carty, who urged him to speak with Rangers outfielder Al Oliver. He agreed. Oliver sternly told him, "'Listen to me, you're going to hit my way,'" recalled Griffin. "He got a little rubber knob, put it on my bat and told me, 'Grab the bat from there. Choke up whether it's two strikes, no strikes, choke up all the time. Just make contact, look for the fastball. And when you get a fastball make sure you hit it hard somewhere. If they throw you a slider and you're out in front, forget it, but just look for the fastball. Don't be looking for changeups. You can't hit it. You don't know how to hit the changeup.'" Oliver also told Griffin, a switch-hitter, to raise his front leg, regardless of which side of the plate he was batting from. "Make sure the ball's close to you, and you swing when it's close to you," Oliver told him. "That's your timing. You can't time with your head, you've got to time with your leg." Griffin took heed immediately. "I started doing that, I went on an eight-game hitting streak, and that was it."

On May 8, a three-hit night pushed his batting average up to .200 for the first time all season. By the end of the month he was up to .278 with a .353 on-base percentage, quickly becoming precisely the type of player the Blue Jays envisioned him to be.

THE AWARD WINNERS

On November 19, 2015, when Josh Donaldson was named the American League's Most Valuable Player, he became the eighth member of the Blue Jays to win a major award. The honour roll:

MVP Award

1987	George Bell	.308/.352/.605, 47 home runs, 134 RBIs
2015	Josh Donaldson	.297/.371/.568, 41 home runs, 123 RBIs

Cy Young Award

1996	Pat Hentgen	20-10, 3.22 ERA, 265⅔ IP, 177 SO
1997	Roger Clemens	21-7, 2.05 ERA, 264 IP, 292 SO
1998	Roger Clemens	20-6, 2.65 ERA, 234⅔ IP, 271 SO
2003	Roy Halladay	22-7, 3.25 ERA, 266 IP, 204 SO

Manager of the Year

1985	Bobby Cox	99-62, AL East title

Rookie of the Year

1979	Alfredo Griffin	.287/.333/.364, 2 HR, 31 RBIs
2002	Eric Hinske	.279/.365/.481, 24 home runs, 84 RBIs

While his offence stabilized, his defence fluctuated. Griffin's range and plus-arm tantalized, but he was raw, recklessly charging balls and making wild throws. He finished the season with 36 errors. "Luis Gomez was the shortstop here, a good defender with good hands, and he told me to calm down," said Griffin. "He said, 'You don't have to try and get every ground ball. Balls are going to come hard to you. Playing on turf is not the same as playing on grass, so you cannot charge every ground ball.' So I was able to define when a ball was hit hard to me or hit slow, and that helped me. It helped me take my time to read the runner, whether he's fast or not fast, and I went from there." Support came from his coaches, as well, who "told me I make a lot of plays where other shortstops weren't able to get there, and that was the cause of me making a lot of errors, and I was fine. They said, keep playing the way I played, don't change my aggressiveness, and it paid off, really."

Griffin finished the 1979 season with a batting average of .287, on-base percentage of .333, and slugging percentage of .364, all career highs. He became a fan favourite and remained the starting shortstop through the 1984 season, when the emergence of Tony Fernandez allowed Gillick to try to address the club's need for bullpen help. He sent Griffin, Dave Collins, and cash to the Oakland Athletics for reliever Bill Caudill. Eventually, Griffin returned and was part of both World Series teams.

"I was grateful that Paul Beeston brought me back and said, 'Listen, I want you to be part of this team. This team has a chance to win. You're someone that's showed me you have the courage and know how to play the game the right way,'" said Griffin. "So I was a big part of that."

Fitting closure for one of the franchise's first stars.

22

THE 10-HOMER GAME

The most prolific single-game home run outburst by a team in big-league history came without warning. There were no brisk winds whipping in from Lake Ontario to suggest the ball might be flying more than usual at Exhibition Stadium on the night of September 14, 1987, no particular hot stretch anyone was riding to indicate something big might be coming. "I don't think there was even any gust," said Ernie Whitt. "Just a normal day."

But it wasn't; far from it. The Toronto Blue Jays launched a record 10 home runs against the Baltimore Orioles in an 18–3 victory that day. Whitt, the Blue Jays' beloved pull-hitting catcher, went deep a career-best three times. George Bell and Rance Mulliniks hit two each, and Lloyd Moseby, Rob Ducey, and Fred McGriff topped off the night. The Orioles needed six pitchers to survive the onslaught, and five of them surrendered a long ball, four of them giving up multiple dingers. "It was just unbelievable," said Cito Gaston, hitting coach at the time. "I was certainly happy because it was one of those games where you could sit back and relax and just let the guys go."

They got started early, when Whitt led off the second inning by taking Ken Dixon deep to open the scoring. Jesse Barfield followed with a double before Mulliniks ripped his first of the night. Two outs later, Dixon walked Nelson Liriano, then gave up Moseby's 23rd of the year. Down 5–0 against a strong Jim Clancy, Dixon and the Orioles were done right then and there. The Blue Jays, on the other hand, were just getting started.

A Mike Hart solo shot to open the third put Baltimore on the board, but in the bottom of the frame Bell led off against Eric Bell with his 44th homer of the season, and two outs later Mulliniks hit his 10th, for one of only three multihomer games in his 16-year career. Whitt's second and the Blue Jays' sixth homer came in the fifth off Mike Griffin, while in the sixth, Mike Kinnunen served up Bell's 45th.

Blue Jays manager Jimy Williams started subbing out his regulars at that point, but that didn't stop the bombardment. Ducey of Cambridge, Ontario, a well-regarded prospect at the time, launched the first home run of his career off Kinnunen, a three-run drive that pushed the lead to 14–2 and gave the Blue Jays a major-league-record-tying eight homers in the game. Manny Lee and Lou Thornton, in for Tony Fernandez and Bell, followed with singles and promptly scored when Whitt capped off his night by giving the Blue Jays sole possession of the record, taking Tony Arnold deep for his 17th of the season.

"Well, at that point in time you don't really think about it," Whitt said of the historic element. "You know that you're winning the ballgame, and that everything came together for us as a team."

The Blue Jays still had more in them, with McGriff leading off the eighth against Arnold with his 19th. An Upshaw fly-out and Liriano single later, Jack O'Connor took over and became the only Orioles pitcher to emerge from the contest unscathed, retiring Ducey and Lee to end the frame.

Tom Henke worked around a pair of singles to finish things off in the ninth, and it was to the Orioles' good fortune that they didn't have to pitch another inning. The Blue Jays scored in all but one of their eight turns at the plate, going deep in six of them and, most significantly, securing a spot in the record books along the way.

"Tonight was an embarrassing ballgame," Orioles manager Cal Ripken Sr. told reporters afterward. "I'm not the only one who's embarrassed. Everyone in that clubhouse is embarrassed."

Across the diamond there was elation, and awe at what was accomplished. "It was a crazy night," said Whitt. "One of those games I had once in my career where I hit the ball hard three times."

23

THE 10-RUN COMEBACK

Let's be real. Even though we'd all like to believe that, as Yogi Berra said, "It ain't over till it's over," when a baseball game gets one-sided, it's usually really over. Comebacks from big deficits are rare, in part because over the grind of 162 games, players can't go all-out every day. It's not that the effort isn't there, or that they don't care, but typically the fight isn't quite the same. On occasion players, or a team, do actually pack it in, but by and large, what happens is simple and logical self-preservation within the context of a marathon season. All of this explains why comeback victories—especially from big deficits—are so special. They're rare, tremendously exciting, and for the players on the winning side, they feel pretty damn good.

The greatest comeback in Toronto Blue Jays history—rallying from 10–0 down in the seventh inning to beat the Boston Red Sox 13–11 in 12 innings at Fenway Park on June 4, 1989—started out innocuously. Boston pitcher Mike Smithson had allowed just four hits and a walk through the first six frames but opened the seventh by issuing walks to Lloyd Moseby and Ernie Whitt. Unimpressed, Red Sox manager Joe Morgan brought in Bob Stanley, who after walking Rance Mulliniks to load the bases, induced a double-play ball out of Nelson Liriano that scored one run. Stanley surrendered an RBI double to Junior Felix before escaping the jam. The Sox led 10–2 with six outs to go.

But the Blue Jays kept coming. One-out singles by George Bell, Fred McGriff, and Moseby in the eighth scored two runs. One out later, Mulliniks doubled in another run. And after Rob Murphy took over from Stanley, a Liriano grounder through the right side made it a 10–6 game. That lead still should have been plenty of breathing room for the Red Sox. It wasn't.

Tony Fernandez opened the ninth with an infield single off Murphy and that prompted Morgan to bring in closer Lee Smith. Kelly Gruber greeted him with a walk before Bell's RBI double made it a three-run game. After McGriff struck out, Moseby walked to load the bases for Whitt, who turned on a 2–1 fastball and ripped it over the wall in the right-field corner, his arms in the air as the ball cleared the wall. A 10–0 deficit had become an 11–10 lead.

"Sweet, just sweet," Whitt told reporters after the game. "All I wanted was a base hit to keep the momentum going."

The Red Sox, however, didn't wilt. With Tom Henke starting his second inning of work in the bottom of the ninth, Nick Esasky led off with a walk, was sacrificed to second by Rich Gedman, and promptly cashed in when Jody Reed singled to right. Henke issued a two-out intentional walk to Wade Boggs before giving way to David Wells. The big left-hander engaged in a riveting 17-pitch duel with pinch-hitter Marty Barrett, who eventually bounced out to third base to end the frame.

The game remained tied until the 12th, when Tom Lawless opened the inning with a single, then advanced to second on a Liriano bunt. That set the stage for Junior Felix, the rookie right fielder called up after Jesse Barfield was traded to the New York Yankees for Al Leiter on April 30. Felix turned on Dennis Lamp's first pitch and clubbed it over the wall in right centre, once again putting the Blue Jays out in front.

This time Duane Ward, in his third inning of work, mowed down the Red Sox 1-2-3 in the bottom of the 12th to secure the victory and complete a three-game sweep. The collapse was the biggest in Red Sox history—three times previously they'd blown nine-run leads. For the Blue Jays, the rally fell two runs short of the biggest in baseball history. (On June 8, 1911, the Detroit Tigers came from 12 runs down to beat the Chicago White Sox, while the Philadelphia Athletics did the same thing against the team in Cleveland on June 15, 1925. Cleveland turned the tables in 2001, coming back from 14–2 down to beat the Seattle Mariners—winners of a big-league-record-tying 116 games that season—15-14 in 11 innings.)

Little wonder that manager Cito Gaston describes the comeback as his favourite regular-season win. "That was unbelievable," he said with a smile.

OTHER NOTABLE COMEBACKS

The Blue Jays have managed quite a few big comebacks over the years. Here are some of the other top rallies:

April 27, 2003: Down 7-0 in the second inning and 8-1 after six, the Blue Jays scored six times in the bottom of the ninth to beat the Kansas City Royals 10-9. An Angel Berroa error allowed Dave Berg to score the winning run.

June 5, 2007: Led by a two-run Vernon Wells double and Aaron Hill's bases-loaded walk off Tim Corcoran to win it, the Blue Jays scored six times in the bottom of the ninth to beat the Tampa Bay Devil Rays 12-11.

June 20, 2014: Down 8-0 in the third inning, the Blue Jays completed the second-largest comeback in team history by scoring five runs in the top of the ninth inning to beat the Cincinnati Reds 14-9 at the Great American Ballpark. The Jays torched Reds closer Aroldis Chapman for four runs in just ⅔ of an inning, including Erik Kratz's go-ahead RBI double. An RBI single from Melky Cabrera padded the lead and was later followed by Edwin Encarnacion's three-run moon shot, his second three-run homer of the night.

July 30, 2017: Down 10-4 in their final at-bat, the Blue Jays completed the biggest rally from a ninth-inning deficit in club history to beat the Los Angeles Angels 11-10. A two-run homer by Kevin Pillar got things started, and a Russell Martin RBI single further tightened things before Steve Pearce hit a walk-off grand slam, his second game-winning granny in a span of four games.

Sept. 20, 2018: Down 8-2 in the ninth, the Blue Jays matched their comeback from six runs down the previous summer in a 9-8 win over the Tampa Bay Rays. Rowdy Tellez started this one with an RBI double, Danny Jansen's three-run homer put his team in range, and Lourdes Gurriel Jr.'s two-run drive knotted things up, before Justin Smoak immediately followed with a solo shot to end it.

Twenty-six years and eight days later, the Blue Jays pulled off another huge comeback at Fenway Park, rallying from an 8–1 third-inning deficit for a 13–10 victory. The date was June 12, 2015, and the win was the Blue Jays' ninth in what finished as an 11-game win streak. Afterward Blue Jays manager John Gibbons repeated his oft-stated refrain: no lead feels safe, and no game feels out of reach at Fenway Park. "It's really tough to explain that game," he said, "but it was a hell of a win."

24

BUCK MARTINEZ'S BROKEN-LEG DOUBLE PLAY

Since the implementation of Rule 7.13 prior to the 2014 season, blocking the plate has become a lost art. Designed to avoid frightening collisions like the one that broke the leg of San Francisco Giants superstar Buster Posey in 2011—an injury that was the catalyst for change—the rule forces catchers to provide base runners with a lane to the plate and prevents runners from drilling catchers in the hopes of jarring the ball loose. Despite some hitches, the goal has been achieved.

Had the rule been in place July 9, 1985, a play that arguably displayed more tenacity, toughness, and determination than any other in Blue Jays history would never have happened. In the bottom of the third in what finished as a 9-4, 13-inning victory over the Seattle Mariners, Buck Martinez helped complete Major League Baseball's only 9-2-7-2 double play ever. What's more, he accomplished the second out despite suffering a broken right leg and dislocated ankle on the first. Hours later, at the Seattle hospital where he was laid up, a visiting Bobby Mattick told Martinez, "That's the greatest play I've ever seen." And to think, he wasn't even supposed to play that day.

Martinez, a strong game-caller and defensive backstop, was grinding pretty hard midway through that season, carrying a .165 average as the right-handed half of a catching platoon with Ernie Whitt. It wasn't his day to play, but manager Bobby Cox called him early in the morning and said, "You're catching tonight. We're calling up a kid who's going to make his [Blue Jays] debut, and I want you to catch him." The kid was 28-year-old Tom Filer, a right-hander who'd go on to a 7–0 record in 11 games that year, and the Mariners were pressuring him early that night in the Kingdome. The game was scoreless in the second inning when Harold Reynolds flew out to right fielder Jesse Barfield, who threw out a tagging Wayne Presley at home to end the frame. "Jesse threw it the right side of home plate, and I dove back over home plate to tag Presley sliding home before he got there," said Martinez. "When we came off the field, everybody was high-fiving Jesse and said way to go, and I said, 'Jesse, throw it on the other side of the plate next time.'"

The risk of injury at the plate never concerned Martinez, and contact didn't bother him. Blocking home wasn't merely a point of pride, it was a crucial part of the job description. "That's just the way we were taught. You save the run," said Martinez. "For me, blocking the plate was like hitting a home run. I positioned myself to block the plate, and if I get the ball that would be nice." He laughs at the last part, but he employed far more technique than that. As a matter of course, he would plant his right foot on the upper left corner of home plate to give himself a point of reference if he needed to move to receive a throw, knowing exactly how many steps were needed to get back to the same spot. He also tried to drift along the baseline, rather than in or out, on throws to his left, keeping himself in the runner's path. "I'm just in the way. I don't [brace for contact] until I catch the ball," Martinez explained. "Then you become aggressive. You try to hit him before he hits you, and you always try to get lower than the guy coming at you." Sometimes there's no time for that, like in that fateful third inning July 9, 1985.

Phil Bradley singled to open the inning and after an Alvin Davis fly-out, a Filer balk advanced him to second base. Up came Gorman Thomas, who sent a single to right field. Unwisely, the Mariners decided to test Barfield's right arm again. This time, Barfield's throw was exactly where Martinez wanted it to be, to his left, and the catcher hardly had to move. The only problem was that Bradley and the ball arrived at nearly the same time, the Mariners outfielder driving right into Martinez's shoulder and bowling him over. But his right foot remained anchored in the dirt as the rest of him came tumbling down. "It went numb immediately," he remembered. Remarkably, he held on to the ball, and Bradley was called out.

The play, however, didn't stop. Thomas headed to second on the throw and then turned for third after the collision, and as Filer ran from the backstop where he was backing up the play to home to check on his catcher, Martinez slung the ball from the ground to Garth Iorg, but instead sent it to left field. Thomas turned for home as George Bell chased the ball down and delivered a perfect one-hopper to Martinez, who while sitting up, made the catch and tagged out his former Milwaukee Brewers teammate. "I don't think he could have hit me," said Martinez. "Everyone in the ballpark knew I was hurt. He was tiptoeing around me. I don't think he thought I could tag him because I was incapacitated. I was in control of everything I was trying to do, I just couldn't get up. I knew exactly what I was doing."

The out in hand, Martinez collapsed to the ground, Thomas walked away with his head down, and teammates and medical personnel quickly surrounded the plate. "I was tired," Martinez remembered. "The adrenaline started to wear off and I thought, 'Well, I'm hurt,' but I didn't feel pain. I remember Bobby Cox came out and he said, 'Looks like it's just dislocated. I think you'll be okay.' He was trying to be light. He knew I was hurt, but he added something to the effect of, 'If you can handle the pain you can play tomorrow, because it's not going to hurt your speed.' We were having a laugh. He knew I was done right there. It's the only time I ever got hurt blocking the plate."

Martinez was strapped to a stretcher—Bell insisted on helping to carry him off the field—and when he got to the clubhouse, plans were made to take him to hospital. Since the game was still ongoing, trainer Tommy Craig was told to stay back and another clubhouse staffer was sent to ride with Martinez in the ambulance. "Craig then has one of the all-time lines of my whole career. He said, 'Damn, Buckie, they sent a janitor guy with you to the hospital,'" Martinez said laughing. "I went in the ambulance—my sister-in-law was there for the first time, she had never seen me play before, she gives me a kiss on the gurney, and Howie Starkman goes, 'Don't take that picture!' to the photographers there. He didn't know who it was. He thought it was just some broad."

Martinez was still in his baby-blue Blue Jays uniform when the doctor entered his hospital room, intern in tow. He began explaining the nature of the injury and then turned to the intern and said, "When you have an injury like this, you put the heel in this hand and place your other hand on top of his instep and you jerk like this. I came up off the bed about a foot and everybody went, 'Are you okay?' He was putting the ankle back in place without me knowing it."

Back at the Kingdome, Bell's grand slam in the 13th inning off Ed Vande Berg helped settle a 9–4 victory over the Mariners. The coaching staff visited Martinez afterward, and once they left he found himself in major discomfort, prompting him to try and shift around in his bed. His leg was in traction and he had to raise himself up, "but the weights went down and caught on the bottom of the bed. So now I'm about six inches off the bed and I can't reach the call button, and I just started laughing. I go, 'Well, this is just a [expletive] up day!'"

A few days later he returned home to Kansas City and went for a follow-up with his old doctor on the Royals. The ankle was coming along, but he still was experiencing major pain in his leg below the knee. It turned out there was a fracture the doctors in Seattle had missed—the recovery was going to take longer than expected.

Martinez spent the rest of the summer home in Kansas City while the Blue Jays went on to win the American League East. "It was heartbreaking to not be part of it," he said. But with that one play, he demonstrated the determination and resolve his team came to embody.

25

FRANCHISE ICON: ROY HALLADAY

Roy Halladay sat inside a bathroom stall, door locked, waiting. There aren't many places for players to be alone inside the crowded and decrepit clubhouse at the Englebert Baseball Complex in Dunedin, Florida, and the toilet is just about the only place to get some privacy. Halladay needed space, having been told moments earlier that the Toronto Blue Jays are not only optioning him to the minors, they're sending him all the way back down to Single-A Dunedin. Shame overwhelmed him. During the conversation with general manager Gord Ash, assistant GM Tim McCleary, and manager Buck Martinez, Halladay felt like he was hovering above himself, watching events play out below. Upon his arrival that morning, he noticed that Ash and the coaching staff, chatting at the picnic table outside the locker room door, hushed up as he walked by. And even though Tim Hewes, the club's employee assistance program director, gave him a heads up that the demotion was coming, the news still left him in total shock. Was he actually that bad? The thought of seeing his teammates, of having to explain things, was too daunting, so he sat in the stall and waited until everyone left before he changed and went home.

It's those agonizing moments during the spring of 2001, ones he relived in sweaty-brow nightmares for months afterward, that kick-started Halladay's transformation from athlete in crisis to arguably the best pitcher in club history. "I was just... I was so embarrassed," said Halladay. "Having to make the phone calls home and having to tell them, 'Yeah, I'm going to A ball,' and stuff like that. When you're right in the centre of it and everybody around you is expecting you to be the next Roger Clemens and you have to explain what's going on, that's pretty rough. A lot of that was extremely motivating for me later in my career."

What happened afterward is a testament to Halladay's exceptional will, determination, and mental strength, a process helped along by access to the right people and a dash of serendipity. The move was remarkably risky for the Blue Jays—taking an elite young pitcher long projected as a franchise cornerstone and trying to rebuild him, even though he'd enjoyed some success in the big leagues. More than a decade later they tried it again with Ricky Romero, who for different reasons went from All-Star to A ball. Felled in part by wear and tear to both knees, Romero never recovered. Halladay did, more than living up to the lofty expectations placed on him from the moment he was chosen 17th overall in the 1995 Draft.

"As an athlete and as a person, those [difficult] times are far more valuable than the best of times," said longtime teammate Vernon Wells. "Being able to go to what you think at the time is the worst place and to come back from that really gives you the strength to take on anything the game throws at you. You kind of embrace those moments, because they truly define who you become as an athlete and as a person. You get to search who you are and think, 'What am I trying to do here? Am I going to take this time to improve and be the best person I can be? Or am I going to let the situation get me down and start making excuses and sulk?' We can all see that he used that time as a very valuable lesson to get better not only on the field but off the field."

Halladay did just that, although the transformation didn't happen overnight. The Blue Jays gave him a few days to reset himself and he spent a couple of days relaxing at home with his wife, Brandy. They lived in a second-floor unit of a townhouse in Clearwater, Florida, at the time, and at one point he quipped that if they lived in a taller building he'd jump, but since they were on the second floor, jumping would only leave him with a broken leg—and then he'd still have to report to the complex. Halladay thought the quip was pretty clever, but Brandy did not. She left the house and ended up browsing around a bookstore, where she randomly noticed a copy of *The Mental Game of Baseball* by renowned sports psychologist Harvey Dorfman. "It was the only copy sitting there on the end [of the shelf]," Halladay said. "Somebody must have just stuck it back there. It caught her eye so she picked it up and brought it home. And within the first day of reading it, I felt like the book was written about me."

A couple of things stood out to him immediately. One was how powerful a positive mental approach could be—and that was pivotal given Halladay's propensity to be hard on himself. The second was how impactful a targeted work ethic can be—making sure each exercise or training session is done with a specific purpose in mind, instead of simply working for the sake of working, commonly referred to as "eyewash." The more he thought about things, the more he realized just how wrong his entire mind-set had been. Ultimately, he committed himself fully to the process, but on his terms, which was perhaps his most important takeaway from the book. "Up until that point I was always very concerned with what parents thought, what coaches thought, what scouts thought, and was always kind of seeking that approval," Halladay said. "Once I decided I was going to do this for myself and pour everything into it, if I ended up walking away, I could do that with my head high. If I cashed it in and moped, and didn't give everything I had to try and make a better situation, I felt like it was a complete waste and something I would regret for a long time."

Reinvigorated, Halladay attacked the plan to rebuild himself with gusto. The physical end of it was straightforward—drop his arm slot a touch in order to gain more movement on his overpowering-but-straight fastball. Working with Mel Queen, a roving minor league instructor at the time, he threw nine bullpens in 10 days, learning to sink and cut the ball in the devastating manner that would put bees in the hands of countless big-league hitters. His focus shifted from strikeouts to inducing weak, early contact. The results were nearly instantaneous. But Queen broke him down mentally, too. "As far as baseball-wise, I told him he was pretty naive and stupid, and that's got to change," the late Queen told the *Toronto Star* in 2003. "I verbally abused him pretty hard that first week. A lot of guys wouldn't have taken it. A lot of guys would have walked away. A lot of guys would have punched me." That's why getting and keeping his mind right was far more challenging than the physical end of the process.

"It took me a good two months to where I really believed it," Halladay said. Still, the feeling of his combined work on both fronts "was like supreme confidence," he remembered. "And the first time

I went out in a game and threw like that, it was just a completely different feeling."

In 13 games at Dunedin he allowed 10 runs in 22⅔ innings before moving up to Double-A Tennessee, where he allowed only eight earned runs in 34 innings over five starts. After two strong outings at Triple-A Syracuse—he allowed five earned runs in 14 innings—he was back in the big leagues, and the plan seemed to have come together brilliantly.

After the 2001 season, Ash was fired and J.P. Ricciardi was hired from the Oakland Athletics as his replacement. The Blue Jays were hemorrhaging money at that point and Ricciardi's mandate was to cut payroll, rebuild with youth, and win on the cheap. Halladay was going to be central to that effort. During one of their initial conversations, he asked Ricciardi if he and Dorfman had crossed paths in Oakland, since the Athletics had employed the sports psychologist for a long time. "He said, 'Yeah, of course. He's a good friend of mine,'" remembered Halladay. "I said, 'Do you mind if I talk to him?' He said no problem, and set it up, and he actually had him come out a couple of different times that season." From then on, the two spoke regularly until Dorfman's death in 2011.

In 2002, Halladay went 19–7 with a 2.93 ERA in 34 starts. The next year, he won a franchise-record 22 games and the AL Cy Young Award. Injuries hampered him in 2004 and 2005, but from 2006 to 2009, he went 69–33 with a 3.11 ERA in 129 games. Everything he did was Hall of Fame calibre.

"I liked to get to the ballpark early, but normally he was already there, sitting at his locker reading his notes and the mental book that he liked to read for information that day," said John McDonald, the gifted shortstop who often played behind Halladay. "He had a way of raising my level of awareness, and I felt like if I could get near a ball, I was getting an out for him. That was a great feeling for me and for a lot of the guys on the team. It was just the level of excellence he exuded, the whole package of it.... You felt like you were playing with the best pitcher in the world."

Even more impressive is that he dominated despite pitching in the small ballparks and against the ERA-inflating lineups of the American League East. Then again, if you were to design the perfect pitcher for the division you'd come up with Halladay: good command in the bottom of the strike zone, movement on his pitches in both directions, no fear.

"I learned really quickly after those first couple of years that for me the key was base runners," he said. "I wasn't going to allow walks. I wanted to keep the ball on the ground because there is no letup and there is no spot where you can afford to walk two or three guys and still be able to get out of an inning. It was really important to start attacking guys. That was the best chance of getting through those lineups."

The shame is that all those great seasons Halladay threw went to waste, submarined by the Blue Jays' inability to put together a good enough team to knock off the New York Yankees or Boston Red Sox. The competitive window that opened for the 2006–08 seasons—when the likes of A.J. Burnett, B.J. Ryan, Troy Glaus, Lyle Overbay, Bengie Molina, Scott Rolen, and Frank Thomas were all added—only multiplied the frustration. And when Paul Beeston returned as Blue Jays president after the 2008 season, replacing Paul Godfrey, the team began navel-gazing. Its core was aging. The farm system was thin. Injuries to Shaun Marcum and Dustin McGowan, along with Burnett's opt-out to sign with the Yankees, decimated the pitching staff. There was no way to buy the team out of its mess.

So in the spring of 2009, Ricciardi approached Halladay and said, "'I just don't feel like it's something that's going to happen in your window of opportunity,'" the pitcher remembered. "Then he said, 'If we have the chance to send you to a winner, should I consider it?'"

"That was tough for me, because I felt like we were always going to try and win in Toronto, but it was hard bringing players in at that point," said Halladay, who controlled the process with a full no-trade clause. "So I told him, 'Yeah, if you get something that gives me a chance to pitch in the playoffs, I would do it, but for no other reason. I don't want to be traded. I know you guys would love to cut salary and all that, but I would rather stay here and play here rather than go somewhere that has an outside shot.'"

A surprisingly strong start to the 2009 season put those thoughts on hold, but reality set in during an 0–9 road trip from May 19 to 26, and things went south in a hurry. By July, Ricciardi was essentially conducting a public auction for Halladay, hoping that by dangling the game's best pitcher in the media, players and fans would pressure teams into anteing up big. The weeks through the trade deadline turned into a gong show, with near-daily updates on where the various suitors, led by the Philadelphia Phillies, stood. Halladay hated the attention, but did all the team asked of him. "That was extremely tough," he said.

The Blue Jays were holding out for Kyle Drabek and Domonic Brown, two prospects the Phillies didn't want to part with. When it became apparent neither side would budge, the Phillies changed course and acquired Cliff Lee from Cleveland for a package that

ROY THE MAN

Under a searing sun burning through a partially cloudy sky, Brandy Halladay took the dais at the Clark Sports Center's rolling grounds on July 20, 2019, and spoke about husband Roy's posthumous induction to the Hall of Fame. Lingering grief from his death, at a mere 40 years old, in the crash of his light-sport aircraft on November 7, 2017, was omnipresent among the gathering of baseball's illuminati in Cooperstown, New York. So too were revelations of the demons he'd fought while becoming, arguably, his generation's best pitcher. Repeatedly, Brandy wiped away tears, saying poignantly that the speech wasn't hers to give.

"I think that Roy would want people to know that people aren't perfect," Brandy told a crowd estimated at 55,000. "We are all imperfect and flawed in one way or another. We all struggle, but with hard work, humility, and dedication, imperfect people can still have perfect moments."

The National Transportation Safety Board's investigation into the crash opened a window into the toll performing at such a high level took on Halladay, as well as the struggles he hid. An autopsy found amphetamines, zolpidem (a sleep medication more commonly known as Ambien), morphine, fluoxetine (an anti-depressant better known as Prozac), and baclofen (a muscle relaxant) in his blood.

Pain had been a constant for Halladay in the latter part of his career. Ongoing back problems forced him into retirement. He had included Carlos Carrasco. Halladay pitched in Seattle on July 29. He remembered feeling "relieved because I didn't have to answer any more questions, or even think about it. If it happened, it happened, or if it didn't, it didn't," and then watched the trade deadline pass as Rolen was traded to the Cincinnati Reds and he stayed put.

Halladay quietly finished out another brilliant season as a near-mutiny against manager Cito Gaston brewed in the clubhouse. The pitcher toiled away professionally amid the dysfunction. In what turned out to be his final start for the Blue Jays, Halladay threw a shutout at Fenway Park and hit David Ortiz, retaliation for Adam Lind being pegged the previous night by Jonathan Papelbon. Halladay was a consummate teammate to the end of his time with Toronto.

shoulder surgery in May 2013, but the real issues were two pars fractures, an eroded disk between the L-4 and L-5, and a pinched nerve. His father, Harry Leroy Jr., told NTSB investigators his son suffered from anxiety and depression and was concerned that he was abusing prescription medications. He had been to rehabilitation for substance abuse at least twice, according to the NTSB's final report.

Flying had long been a passion father, a career military and commercial air pilot, and son shared. Halladay's Icon A5 amphibious, light-sport aircraft was his pride and joy. But he had a tendency to push boundaries in the cockpit. His dad worried "that his son did not appreciate the dangers involved with flying," according to the NTSB's record of conversation with him. He flew erratically before the fatal crash into the Gulf of Mexico.

The troubling details of his death and the time leading up to it helped contextualize Brandy's words from what should have been the pinnacle moment of Halladay's illustrious career. "These men who are up here doing these outstanding things, they're still real people. They still have feelings, they still have families, they still struggle," she said. "So many of the guys I've known in my life through baseball, they work so hard to hide that. I know Roy did. And Roy struggled, a lot. Sometimes it's hard to present the image that you know everybody wants to see. It's also hard to be judged by the image people expect of you. It's a perception and an idea and I think it's important that we don't sensationalize or idealize what a baseball player is, but really look at the man and the human that's doing such an amazing thing."

The Blue Jays fired Ricciardi on the penultimate day of the season and replaced him with Alex Anthopoulos, who was charged with starting another rebuild. He and Beeston went to visit Halladay at home a couple of weeks later to try and salvage the relationship and see if he'd consider staying. He wouldn't. "They weren't prepared to make me a long-term offer, but they said they would if that's what it needed," said Halladay. "My question was still the same: 'What are we going to do moving forward?' And they still felt we were a couple years away. I had seen guys get hurt and never come back, and I had a pretty good run and wasn't sure when that was going to end, and I was starting to get nervous. I didn't know how many years I had. I was thinking maybe one, maybe two, or I could get lucky and play eight more. But I definitely felt like my window was short, so at that point I told them I think we should push this if we're still going in the same direction as the organization. I said as much as I want to be here, if [the playoffs are] not going to be a possibility, then I need to make the best decision I can for myself and give myself a chance."

At the winter meetings that December, the groundwork for a three-team deal that would send Lee to the Seattle Mariners, Halladay to the Phillies, and prospects to the Blue Jays was laid out. It was completed a few days later, on December 16. Drabek and catcher Travis d'Arnaud were headed to Toronto, while outfielder Michael Taylor was immediately flipped to the Oakland Athletics for first baseman Brett Wallace. With that, Halladay's spectacular career in Toronto was over.

"I was kind of relieved I didn't get traded mid-year," said Halladay. "I mean, the [Phillies] had pretty much clinched a playoff spot by the trade deadline that year, they were just bulking up for the postseason and to me that just wouldn't have felt right.... I wanted it to be a team of quality people but I didn't want to be on a superstar team that had all these multimillion-dollar players. I wanted to be on a hardworking team, and that's what it was in Philly. Now, it turned into a team of multimillion-dollar players, but at first it was an incredible experience to walk in, just noticing that difference immediately was like, 'Wow.' You know, the confidence and all that was just awesome."

Halladay pitched four seasons with the Phillies before his body finally gave out on him. He made five postseason starts, never advancing beyond the National League Championship Series, but throwing a no-hitter against the Cincinnati Reds in the 2010 division series. He became nearly as beloved in Philadelphia as he had been in Toronto.

On July 2, 2011, he returned to Toronto to face the Blue Jays. He was given numerous standing ovations by an adoring crowd. "I was honestly not sure how I was going to be received," said Halladay. "A lot of people say 'thank you' and 'we appreciate you,' but when you come in and play their team, they may not appreciate you as much—especially after you're winning that game, then you're really expecting them to not like you. But you know, the standing ovation at the start of the game is something I'll never forget. I was standing out there, throwing my warm-up pitches completely torn [between] acknowledging the fans and feeling like I was being disrespectful to my current team. I battled that for 10 minutes, I didn't know what to do, so I didn't do anything in hopes that I could do it after the game, and it worked out that way. Walking off that last inning when they were standing, being able to tip my hat, that was pretty cool. As an opposing player, to go somewhere like that and have that support behind you was pretty incredible."

That's why, when Halladay retired after the 2013 season, he did so only after signing a one-day contract to walk away as a member of the Blue Jays. It was a no-brainer for him. "I always felt like I was a Blue Jay, I just felt that I had this unique opportunity for a couple years to have a chance to chase a dream," he said. "But I felt my roots and everything I had become and everybody that helped me become that were all in Toronto. So it wasn't like I had to sit down and make a decision, it was honestly the way I thought of myself."

26

THE MARLINS AND METS BLOCKBUSTERS

Mark Buehrle's first reaction when he learned of his trade from the Miami Marlins to the Toronto Blue Jays? "You've got to be shitting me," is what he remembers thinking, "because Toronto and New York are the two places I said I'd never sign and play." Perspectives, however, can change over time. Much as the bigger-picture outlook on the blockbuster deals with the Marlins and New York Mets struck by Alex Anthopoulos in the winter of 2012 has evolved, so too have Buehrle's feelings. "The trade probably worked out way better than I imagined," he said. "And obviously knowing now what I didn't know then, I'm glad to get out of Miami and that organization. The way they treat people, I wish I would have known that going into it, because I wouldn't have signed there.... Being [in Toronto], I've called free agents, Alex [Anthopoulos] had me call a couple guys, and I've told them the story and said, 'Listen, if I was a free agent looking for a deal and they were offering it to me, I'd heavily consider signing back in Toronto because of what I know.'"

The Blue Jays, all these years later, are by and large similarly satisfied. The two franchise-altering deals helped the 2015 team end a playoff drought that dated back to 1993, and led to another trip to the American League Championship Series in 2016. Granted, they won the American League East two years later than expected, and it took a lot more wheeling and dealing to make it happen, but those trades definitively shifted the Blue Jays from being an organization deferring to the future to one playing for the present. The mistake was in viewing those transactions as finishing moves, rather than the building blocks they turned out to be. "Every off-season it happens when there's a free-agent signing—I mean everyone thought Washington was going to win [in 2015] because they signed Max Scherzer," said Buehrle. "That's why I said it doesn't matter what teams do in the off-season. You still have to go out there and play, you have to gel together, you can't have too many superstars where everyone's trying to get their own numbers instead of trying to win as a team. You've got to be careful what you trade for."

Wise words, but few could bring themselves to look at things that way on November 13, 2012, when word first leaked about the 12-player swap bringing Buehrle, Jose Reyes, Josh Johnson, Emilio Bonifacio, and John Buck to the Blue Jays for Henderson Alvarez, Yunel Escobar, Adeiny Hechavarria, Jeff Mathis, Anthony DeSclafani, Jake Marisnick, and Justin Nicolino. In terms of volume, star power, and financial commitments, the trade, which was completed six days later, dwarfed any other in Blue Jays history. It was timed perfectly to wash away the misery of a scandal-tinged 2012 campaign. Lowlights included Escobar's homophobic slur, Omar Vizquel publicly trashing the coaching staff, and manager John Farrell skirting rumours of a return to the Boston Red Sox until a trade was finally arranged. Each incident posed a significant threat to team morale and consumer confidence. Factor in the injuries that torpedoed what looked to be a promising season, and the Blue Jays took it in the pants in every way imaginable. Anthopoulos was under pressure from above to make something happen, and fast.

The Marlins stunner flipped the script. Buehrle—blindsided one season into a $58 million, four-year deal he signed as a free agent in Miami—and Johnson bolstered a rotation set to include Ricky Romero, Brandon Morrow, and J.A. Happ. Reyes, also one season into a free-agent contract signed with the Marlins, was the dynamic shortstop and leadoff hitter the team had dreamed of for years. Bonifacio's defensive versatility and speed set him up as a weapon. Buck gave Anthopoulos enough catching depth to make another deal. Mixed in with Jose Bautista, Edwin Encarnacion, Brett Lawrie, Adam Lind, and Casey Janssen, the American League East looked like a slam dunk.

That sense of imminence only amplified on December 17, when the Blue Jays added reigning National League Cy Young Award winner R.A. Dickey, along with catchers Josh Thole and Mike Nickeas, from the Mets. The price was a pair of gilt-edged prospects in Noah Syndergaard and Travis d'Arnaud, plus a young farmhand named Wuilmer Becerra. Dickey's acquisition was met with more trepidation because of the well-founded fears about what Syndergaard and d'Arnaud might eventually become. But with a rotation suddenly so deep that optioning Happ to Triple-A Buffalo was a real possibility, a trip to the playoffs turned into an article of faith. As spring training opened in 2013, Jose Bautista echoed that feeling when he said, "The sky is the limit for us because I know how many good players we have. I've been on other teams where I felt like we've had a chance to go to the playoffs and contend, but we haven't for whatever reason. This is by far the best team I've played on. I just don't see where it can go bad for us. Because of those reasons I think we should and we could be in the playoffs and the World Series."

Amid the brazenness, warning signs were ignored or flat-out missed. The Blue Jays had little organizational depth, especially on the pitching end. Johnson's elbow was seemingly being held together by chewing gum and masking tape; he'd undergo ligament-replacement surgery a year later. Reyes' durability, always an issue, was complicated further as his skills began to erode, a decline that would accelerate alarmingly after he ripped up his ankle in April. Bonifacio's game was a mess, and he was gone by August. And many of the assumptions about the existing roster—that J.P. Arencibia was a big-league catcher, Romero would bounce back, Morrow could stay healthy, Lawrie was set to emerge—collapsed. The Blue Jays finished 74–88, last in the East, and while Buehrle and Dickey each logged solid 200-inning seasons, that wasn't nearly enough to avert disaster.

In 2014 the Blue Jays returned largely intact, but important changes emerged. The steady Dioner Navarro provided a big upgrade from Arencibia, Drew Hutchison returned from elbow surgery to bolster the rotation, and Marcus Stroman came up in May and gave the team a jolt. The Blue Jays spent 61 days in first place before unravelling. They landed at 83–79, 13 games back of the division-champion Baltimore Orioles. Buehrle and Dickey again logged 200-inning seasons, while Reyes' range quietly became a real concern.

Meanwhile, in Miami and New York, Alvarez appeared in his first All-Star Game and posted a 2.65 ERA in 187 innings; Hechevarria dazzled at shortstop; Marisnick became a useful fourth outfielder;

DeSclafani showed some promise in 13 appearances; d'Arnaud posted a .718 OPS in 108 games; and Syndergaard and Nicolino continued to develop in the minors. All the prospect capital the Blue Jays had surrendered was turning into present-day value, but they didn't have a playoff spot to show for it.

Then in 2015, they got there, although ending the drought required the off-season acquisitions of Josh Donaldson, Russell Martin, and Marco Estrada plus the trade-deadline pickups of Troy Tulowitzki (with Reyes part of the package heading the other way), David Price, Ben Revere, Mark Lowe, and LaTroy Hawkins. Buehrle was instrumental in holding down the fort until the reinforcements arrived. Dickey recovered from yet another slow start with a strong surge to the finish line, helping the Blue Jays overtake the New York Yankees.

"The clubhouse wasn't the best the first two years," said Buehrle. "There were some guys who were in for a while, where I don't know if they were comfortable. When we brought Donaldson and Martin in, it was just outside guys coming in that made the culture different and I feel that made everything better, and the guys we brought at the deadline magnified what we did this off-season.... I just feel like everybody's together more. Half the team is there playing video games. Guys are busting each other's balls more and having fun with it. Just joking around and not taking it too serious, having more fun over the course of the year, and of course winning helps that. When you're winning, everyone can get away with joking around and having fun. When you're losing, if a guy missed a stretch, if a guy's not out there shagging [fly balls], it just gets blown up. If you're winning and a guy does that, that's like, 'Who gives a shit? We're winning, it doesn't matter.'"

That's probably the prism through which to view the trades as well. Syndergaard looked like an ace in the making while d'Arnaud was calm and in charge behind the plate as the Mets surged to the 2015 World Series, but without Dickey's 214⅓ innings, the Blue Jays wouldn't have made the playoffs. He logged another 169.2 frames during the wild-card season of 2016. Over his four seasons in Toronto, the knuckleballer went 49–52 with a 4.05 ERA while logging 824⅓ innings over 131 games, all but one a start. He didn't miss a single outing. He pitched through injury. He pitched on short rest when called upon. Yet none of it will ever be good enough because of who he was traded for.

"I think that's been a tough thing with my experience as a Blue Jay, I think that the anticipation and expectation for myself and probably from the fans' point of view was, 'Why didn't this guy win another Cy Young? That's why we got him,' which I completely understand," said Dickey. "Mentally it's been a hard thing to wade into and walk with for three years, because you never want to be the disappointment. So you've got to keep convincing yourself that you're having good years and putting up numbers that are respectable numbers in the AL East. And who knows how your numbers would translate in the NL in the years that you were over here. That's really been the toughest thing for me. You want to be worth it, you want to be worth the trade, you want to be worth the expectation, you want to live up to the expectation. And more times than not you don't—that's just the nature of the beast."

Buehrle, meanwhile, posted a 40–28 mark with a 3.78 ERA in 604⅓ innings over 97 starts with the Blue Jays. The fearless lefty with commendable guts and guile was the only remnant of the Marlins deal left when the Blue Jays clinched the American League East in 2015. Like Dickey, he made the adjustments needed in baseball's toughest division on pitchers. "There was a reason why I signed with a National League team," Buehrle said. "I've had some bad numbers against the AL East in my career. In my mind I said, 'I'm going to the National League, where I'm facing a pitcher instead of a DH all the time. Knowing I'm on the back end of my career, I'm not in the prime of my career anymore, I'm going to go wherever I think it's easier to pitch.' So when I got traded I thought, 'Great, I'm going from, to me, one of the easier divisions and the easier league to one of the hardest ones because of the teams I'm facing.' It's a little more satisfying, not thinking I would pitch this good and have ERAs this good. But it's a team effort, and we're scoring runs and playing defence behind me. I need all that."

Similarly, the Blue Jays needed all that from Buehrle and Dickey to find success. Their arrival opened a competitive window for the team, one that eventually brought a big reward. Maybe they would have ended up in a similar place had they kept all the kids and waited for their arrivals. Or maybe not. Regardless, if that's the price for the exhilaration of the 2015–16 seasons, it sure felt like one that made sense to pay.

27

FRANCHISE ICON: JOSE BAUTISTA

Two-plus years removed from his last game in the major leagues, Jose Bautista is busy making up for lost time at home. He's relishing more daily involvement with his three daughters, driving them to school, taking them to activities afterwards, attending school functions, hanging out with other parents at playdates and birthday parties. Just regular stuff he so often missed while tearing through opponents on a baseball field. "Even with things that happened in the off-season, you've got the blinders on when you're an active major-league player," explained Bautista. "You're always thinking about how to get better, training, recovery, practice. Your mind is always thinking about the game. Not having that in the background has allowed me to fully disconnect from the competitiveness of the sport, the pressure and the attention that comes along with it, get out of the limelight and be a normal father. It's been refreshing in a lot of ways. I'm really able to enjoy it."

The contrast of Bautista, everyday dad, with Bautista, indomitable slugger, is somewhat jarring. On the field he was a giant, an overwhelming force who wielded his bat with the ruthlessness of a Tolkien Nazgul and the prudence of a Fortune 500 accountant. His body of work with the Toronto Blue Jays is rivalled only by Carlos Delgado. His impact can be measured alongside Roberto Alomar and Joe Carter. His bat-flip homer against the Texas Rangers in 2015 is the Carter-World-Series moment for a new generation. His revenge homers after being thrown at, or amidst on-field feuds, are legend. The Blue Jays' revival over the past decade traces directly back to his unexpected emergence as a superstar. He is without question among the most important figures in team history.

"The Blue Jays had a ton of success in the '80s and early '90s, and Jose, for me, represented their next phase of team success," said former Blue Jays general manager Alex Anthopoulos, who led Bautista's acquisition as assistant GM in 2008. "He was the superstar

Toronto hadn't had in a while, and he became the straw that stirred the drink. He gave us an edge. He gave us a swagger. Obviously, an incredibly smart and committed player. He was every bit a superstar on all levels and a guy that just relished the moment on the big stage."

Without doubt, but now that the curtain is down and the lights are dimmed, Bautista insists he is at peace with the likely end of his playing days. While he wasn't yet ready to use the word "retirement" as 2021 dawned, he conceded he's more looking forward to his next career than back at his last one. Finance, perhaps. Working in a front office. Player representation. Consulting. Maybe even TV. "Those are all things I'm open to," he said. "And I have started to get somewhat excited about all those things that might come my way." Coaching might be a consideration but the demands would separate him from his family for too long. "All three of my daughters are at an age that I'd like to be around a little more unless I absolutely need to be away," he said. "I wouldn't pull the trigger on an opportunity that required me to be away from home for an extended period."

That's understandable, given how consuming it was for him to deliver 15 years of high-octane play in the majors. Bautista left nothing to chance in his career, especially once he joined the Blue Jays and with the help of Cito Gaston and Dwayne Murphy, made an adjustment in his timing mechanism that unlocked his power potential. He took deep dives into usage patterns and heat maps long before they became standard fare on baseball websites. He was into yoga and stretching before Lululemon made it trendy. He prioritized nutrition before eating healthy was in vogue as an advantage. He took a business-minded approach to his body, viewing it as a proprietary asset to leverage in the market. "I knew at all points what I was up against and what I had to do to remain competitive and get the best out of myself," he said. "That's just a decision you make to be the best you can be and be an ultimate competitor. Quite frankly, that's how you can truly say you left it all out there and you gave it all you had. I'm glad I did it that way."

It's also why he believed he could remain productive into his forties, an anomalous class of player that disappeared from the sport when drug testing reduced the rampant use of performance-enhancing substances. Reality struck in 2017, his final season with the Blue Jays, when at 36 his fearsome bat speed slowed. His numbers deteriorated to a .203/.308/.366 batting line, and his .674 OPS was the lowest of his career. The next year, Anthopoulos brought him to Atlanta for a 12-game look, the Mets grabbed him afterwards, and he closed out the year with the Phillies. He finished with a .727 OPS, thanks to a 40-point jump in on-base percentage, showing he still had something to offer. But his late thirties dip coincided with an industry shift away from veteran players and toward youth, so opportunity dried up. He didn't play in 2019 and planned to suit up for the Dominican Republic in qualifying play for the 2020 Tokyo Olympics before COVID-19 shut down the world. "I've seen how the market has changed," said Bautista. "With my lack of performance, the youth movement really working out for everybody, and all these bright new young stars coming into the game, the timing wasn't great for me towards the end. I recognize and accept that."

* * *

Acceptance isn't easy for athletes with the type of unwavering ambition that powered Bautista. Throughout his career, his cauldron of emotion made him a lightning rod for everyone from teammates to opponents to umpires to the chattering classes in the game and media to fans. The Pittsburgh Pirates described it as his kryptonite when he was a prospect in their farm system. Proof of that came in 2003 when he was in high-A and missed most of the season because he broke his hand punching a garbage can after a strikeout.

At the big-league level, his disdain for umpires became regular fodder for critics, especially when on the second day of the 2013 season, he infamously said, "Sometimes I have trouble more than other players dealing with my production being affected by somebody else's mediocrity." Hot-take media would scold him time and again for not being professional, even though sometimes he was simply uttering truths people didn't want to hear. A classic example came on April 22, 2015, when Baltimore Orioles rookie Jason Garcia threw a fastball behind Bautista, who responded three pitches later by lining a home run to left. He watched it go before tossing his bat, then slow-trotted around the bases, exchanging words with defenders along the way. During the changeover between innings, Adam Jones yelled over at him that the celebration was bush league, essentially blaming Bautista for being angry about getting thrown at. "What I thought was bush league, or whatever adjective he used to describe the play, was throwing behind me," Bautista said afterward. "That was the bush league move, not me doing what I did."

He was 100 percent right. Yet he always seemed to be on the stand getting cross-examined like Col. Nathan Jessop in *A Few Good Men*, shouting, "You can't handle the truth," at a public sphere that usually couldn't. As a result, a media machine that tends to lazily cast public figures into comfortable moulds kept framing Bautista in tired tropes. He was a hothead. Selfish. Immature. A poor leader hurting his team. Because he didn't suffer fools, reporters that threw clichéd narratives at him would emerge from interviews and scrums and complain about his contrarianism. Those who took the time to really listen, however, understood that Bautista simply demanded the same precision of thought from inquisitors that he delivered in his usually insightful replies. The discord was all a by-product of his on-field vim.

"I could have been better at some aspects of that, especially dealing with some of the calls by umpires and maybe some other stuff," he said. "I never meant any disrespect. I just got so competitive at times that it was hard for me to control on certain days, or when stuff kind of accumulated. I wish I would have been better at that, for sure. It would have made my life a little bit easier in that sense. All those things play into the perception, too, of others on your persona. Maybe people start assuming that you're a certain type of person because you're always upset about maybe an umpire's calls, or something like that. What can I say? I wish I would have been better at that. But in some other ways, when the moment was big, it just seemed like it brought me to a place of some sort of focus. Would I have been able to do that if I was so calm in demeanour like Adam Lind? I don't know. I never sat back and questioned those things. I was just trying to manage as I went."

Few players were as opposite to Bautista in demeanour as Lind, the longtime Blue Jays first baseman nicknamed Sleepy by his teammates.

"In some ways, I wouldn't say envy, but I wish I would have had a little bit of that in me at times," said Bautista. "In baseball, when you let some things affect you too much, it can be a negative. I feel like at times I let stuff linger for a little too long, was too hard on myself at different times. In the general sense, it ended up working out. But I could have saved myself a couple of moments of elevated blood pressure, for sure."

* * *

Whether a more subdued version of Bautista would have been the same player is intriguing, as are his post-career reflections. While in uniform, he certainly felt differently. During the 2013 season, for instance, he said, "If I don't have that [emotion], I'm not the same player." Regardless, his hybrid of George Bell's raging pit bull and Delgado's steady genius served as the foundation for the Blue Jays during his decade with the club. That his emergence was a happy accident—"a superstar player fell in our laps," said Anthopoulos—forced the team to accelerate rebuild plans and made the franchise's return to relevance all the more remarkable.

"That was good fortune on our end," said Anthopoulos. "I don't want to speak for Theo Epstein and the Boston Red Sox, but it's like when they got David Ortiz and he emerged to be unbelievable. How do you react? How do you handle that? Edwin Encarnacion with us was the same way. You change course, because it's hard to find those guys."

The acquisitions of both Bautista and Encarnacion trace back to Scott Rolen. In August 2008, the third baseman was hurt and Anthopoulos was scouring the waiver wire for a stopgap when Bautista popped up on revocable waivers. Under new GM Neal Huntington, the Pirates had decided to turn the page at the hot corner and promoted rising prospect Andy LaRoche, leaving Bautista buried in Triple-A. Playing for five different managers in his five seasons with Pittsburgh, he was never able to get untracked. The coaching staff's insistence he take the first pitch and try to hit the ball to the opposite field ran contrary to his pull-instincts. "I just didn't fit their model or what they're looking for, specifically," said Bautista, who added that when it came to specifics, "all I can do is guess and speculate, just like you could, because I never got a straight answer." Gaston, the Blue Jays manager at the time, had seen Bautista at spring training a number of times and liked his pop. Anthopoulos did, too, and asked then GM J.P. Ricciardi if he could put in a claim. The Pirates wanted a player back. They settled on catching prospect Robinzon Diaz. The deal was done on August 21, 2008.

The next year, when Rolen requested a trade, Ricciardi found a taker in the Cincinnati Reds, who offered up a pair of young arms the Blue Jays liked in Zach Stewart and Josh Roenicke. To make the money work, though, the Reds insisted on including Encarnacion in the deal. Reluctantly, Ricciardi said yes. Unbeknownst to any of them, the franchise's trajectory had been dramatically altered.

In the 11 months between the two deals, Bautista had worked steadily on his transformation. Gaston and hitting coaches Murphy and Gene Tenace turned him loose. If you get a pitch to drive, they told him, go ahead and pull it. But they also drilled into him that he was starting the load in his swing too late, and that he needed to speed up his timing mechanism. With the Pirates, he'd used a toe tap as his trigger. With the Blue Jays, he gradually incorporated his trademark leg kick.

On the surface, the adjustment sounded simple. It was anything but. "The way that I would compare it would be if somebody tells you to brush your teeth with your left hand and not your right hand, you're going to be awkward, it's going to be slower, you're not going to have the same motor control," explained Bautista. "So it takes a little bit of time to adapt."

A turning point came early in the 2009 season, when during a conversation in the weight room, Murphy stood Bautista in front of a mirror and showed him how his body should work. For years, coaches had preached to Bautista to get his foot down earlier. Murphy and Gaston reframed it by telling him to get started on his load earlier, and to be in better control as he transferred his weight through the ball. "I never looked at it in that way before," said Bautista. "I used to start my load as the pitcher was releasing the ball. They made me understand that I needed to start my load when the pitcher was basically taking the ball out of the glove. That would give me more time, if I was loading slow and under control, to then get my foot down when it needed to be down, instead of having to accelerate the second half of my swing, and play catch up with the ball because I started late to begin with. That's what they made me realize more than anything."

Though a light bulb went on, there was no single eureka moment. Bautista and Murphy spent hours in the cage building the muscle memory to make the new leg-kick trigger easily repeatable. Undoing years of habit left him feeling awkward at the plate. Still, there was promise. "What he saw was the ball just jumping off his bat," said Murphy. "Jose's a smart player. I just showed him what his shoulders do, and what they should do, why he didn't pull the ball, why he was so late."

Sporadic playing time made testing the transition difficult, but not facing pressure to produce consistently gave him the space to trust in the process. The Rolen trade on July 31 and the surprise departure of Alex Rios on an August 10 waiver claim to the Chicago White Sox opened a pathway to regular at-bats. From September 5 to October 4, Bautista hit 10 homers, four doubles, and two triples, with 21 RBIs in 27 games. Putting faith in September stats can be a fool's errand, but in this case, there was a fundamental change to support the sudden surge. "I 100 percent felt different," said Bautista. "I felt more confident because I had more time to react and see the ball, and attack it, as opposed to feeling like, oh, crap, the ball is on top of me, I've got to make contact and instinctively speed everything up, hoping for the best. I just felt like I had more time to react. It may not seem like a lot, but even a split second can make a huge difference for a hitter."

Everything came together during a breakout 2010, when he became the first Blue Jays player to break the 50-homer plateau and finished the year with 54. He matched his previous career-high of 16 on May 30. He surpassed it with a two-homer effort against the Yankees on June 4. No. 30 came on July 27, and No. 40 less than a month later on August 23 in the first of a series of signature performances. Bautista homered in the third inning and then, on the first pitch of the sixth inning, sent a ball into the fifth deck of the dome, but foul. Ivan Nova zipped a fastball up and in on the next pitch, drawing a warning from home-plate umpire Jerry Meals and harsh words from Bautista that prompted the benches to empty. That at-bat ended in a flyout to deep centre, but in the eighth, Bautista hammered an 0-1 fastball from David Robertson over the wall in left and took 28 seconds to circle the bases. "Given what had transpired earlier, I enjoyed it pretty good," he said afterwards. On September 17, he broke Bell's club record of 47 homers, and six days later, No. 50 came against Felix Hernandez in a 1-0 win over the Seattle Mariners. Two homers on September 30 pushed his total to 54, still the team record.

Despite trading Hall of Famer Roy Halladay the previous winter, the Blue Jays unexpectedly finished at 85–77. The plan had been to keep accumulating assets and await the arrival of a boffo 2010 draft class. Bautista, with only one year of club control remaining, forced a rethink. "You're at a crossroads," said Anthopoulos. "You have a year of control. Trade-wise, a lot of people are skeptical. Is the performance a mirage? People are using the Brady Anderson example [the former Orioles outfielder had an outlier 50-homer season in 1996, but averaged 19 over 162 games throughout a 15-year career]. So you're limited with what you can get for him in trade because of the uncertainty, the little control, the increasing salary through arbitration. So it was a really tough decision. Do we trade him? Do we ride it out for a year? Or do we build around him?"

The Blue Jays were on the verge of riding it out with Bautista but mere minutes before a February 18 arbitration hearing, they agreed to a US$65-million, five-year extension—a massive bet that the 2010 season wasn't an aberration. When news broke, a few prominent agents called Anthopoulos and asked, in all seriousness, if he'd lost his mind. The talk-show circuit roasted the contract. Anthopoulos often said that nobody had made more guaranteed money off a single season in the game's history. "It was scary," he said. "When we did the contract, it was swallow hard and gulp. You believe in it. Your process was sound. But even if all those things are in line, it's still $65 million and a lot of years. I remember on my daily drive to the ball park in

Dunedin two or three days after the fact just thinking, did we do the right thing, did we make a mistake? You can't help it when there's an avalanche of criticism and second guessing."

Bautista immediately validated the decision with perhaps his most complete season, delivering career-bests in average (.302), on-base percentage (.447), slugging (.608), OPS (1.056), and walks (132) in 2011. He finished third in MVP voting, despite his team's 81–81 finish in a transitional year under new manager John Farrell. He received a then-record number of All-Star Game votes, pushing the Blue Jays into the national baseball consciousness. Not only was the 2010 breakout for real, but he was also firmly among the game's elite. "I always felt like I could do more than my first four or five years in the big leagues," he said. "But I never felt like I'd made it. I never kicked my feet up or thought about it or tried to feel comfortable and complacent. I just kept showing up, kept putting in the work, and kept trying to win and get better. That's just how it went."

* * *

Bautista's success was not without elements of redemption. His career path was atypical in many ways, especially for a player from the Dominican Republic. Born to parents Americo, who ran a poultry farm, and Sandra, an accountant for a large conglomerate, Bautista was raised in a middle-class Santo Domingo home where the emphasis was on education rather than baseball. He and brother Luis attended a private school. Bautista excelled at math and the sciences, and he mastered English through his classwork and American TV shows. A condition of being allowed to play in the multiple baseball leagues that filled his evenings and weekends was the maintenance of his grades. That's why when he was 16, as his contemporaries in the Dominican began signing professional contracts, the possibility "wasn't even a thought in my house," he said. "I wouldn't even dare to bring it up."

Even after he graduated from high school in 1998, Bautista could only pursue baseball while continuing his studies. He trained at the New York Yankees' academy while taking business classes at Pontificia Universidad Catolica Madre Y Maestra. He rejected an offer to sign for $5,000 and later turned down $60,000 from the Arizona

Diamondbacks, understanding that the level of investment a team made in a player determines the scope of his opportunity. It was an early sign of his business acumen.

In the spring of 1999, he took another shot at getting noticed, attending a prospect showcase in St. Petersburg, Florida, that included Prince Fielder. The Cincinnati Reds were impressed, invited him to work out at their complex in the Dominican and eventually offered him $300,000. But before Bautista could accept, the Reds pulled the deal after Carl Linder replaced Marge Schott as owner. Frustrated, he considered giving up on baseball, but a serendipitous chain of events brought Bautista to Chipola Junior College in Marianna, Florida, where he'd end up on a big-league pathway.

Bautista landed there with the help of Rafael Perez, whose father ran one of the youth leagues he had played in, and Juan Peralta, who is now director of the Reds' academy in the Dominican. Both were graduates of a program called the Latin Athletes Education Fund, created by American businessman Don Odermann, which connected qualified students to partial or full scholarships in American colleges, and provided money to cover shortfalls for other necessities. To pay forward their good fortune, Perez and Peralta kept an eye out for potential candidates, and both had been keeping tabs on Bautista. Once the Reds deal fell through, Peralta pitched Bautista to Jeff Johnson, the head coach at Chipola, who offered a full scholarship. Five days later, he was off to Florida, with support from Odermann.

During his first season there, the Pirates selected Bautista in the 20th round of the 2000 draft. The following May, they bought him out of a scholarship at the University of South Carolina—he had planned to study finance—with a $500,000 signing bonus. Though his baseball dreams had finally become reality, Bautista never surrendered on the education piece. During the 2013 and 2014 seasons, he completed an undergrad degree from the University of South Florida.

Even once he'd experienced success and found financial security, Bautista took nothing for granted. The way the baseball industry commodified players hit home after he broke his hand in 2003. The Pirates left him exposed for the Rule 5 draft and Baltimore claimed him, which led to both his big-league debut and a development-stunting four months through the transaction wire spin-cycle. The ride took him from the Orioles to the Tampa Bay Devil Rays to the Kansas City Royals to the New York Mets and then finally back to the Pirates. While he finished the year in Pittsburgh, getting only 96 plate appearances over 64 games split between four teams meant his progress was minimal.

As if all that upheaval wasn't disruptive enough, Bautista would be managed by four different men in the next five years with the Pirates, each with different plans for him. While the consistency of message he got from Gaston and Murphy in Toronto was pivotal, so too was their faith in him.

"I do think you end up in places and cross paths with people for a reason and that's how it worked out for me," said Bautista. "There are 50 different things that I can point out over the course of my life that are not identical and are not as impactful as [his work with Gaston and Murphy], but had a similar outcome. How I ended up going from the Dominican being enrolled in a college to getting a scholarship for junior college; how I got picked out of junior college as a 20th-rounder but got offered second-round money to not go to South Carolina; how I got Rule 5'd after breaking my hand in A-ball. Those things just happened, I ended where I ended up, and I kept going."

* * *

Of course, Bautista didn't simply wait to end up on the right path. There's no chance he would have experienced the type of success he did if he'd been passive. "The thing you have to understand about Jose," Jeff Manto, his hitting coach in Pittsburgh, told *Sports Illustrated* in 2011, "is that this guy had to succeed. He had some kind of will. Every at-bat mattered. Every pitch mattered. If anything, he wanted success too much." During the 2012–14 seasons, that insatiable hunger made him a focal point for the growing discontent about the Blue Jays' collective struggles.

Invariably, those conversations started with his emotional displays on the field and ended in archetypal sports-talk chatter about his leadership. A handful of blow-ups with umpires that led to untimely ejections kept the news cycle well fed. Opponents took umbrage with his behaviour, John Danks memorably saying that Bautista "was out there acting like a clown" because the slugger slammed his bat to the ground after a pop-up. Some teammates quietly complained that while he was everything you could ask for between the lines, they had hoped for more from him in the clubhouse. Anyone looking for easy answers to a problem found one in Bautista.

"I always had trouble with the word leadership because they're all so different," said John Gibbons, who returned as Blue Jays manager in 2013 and ran the club during Bautista's final five years in Toronto. "A lot of times with teams that don't meet expectations, they pin the leadership on somebody, when in reality you didn't have enough talent. That's the way I feel. If you've got a good team and everybody picks each other up, they play hard together and use their talents, you've got a lot of leaders. So that was definitely unfair to him. But a lot of people disliked Jose because they didn't understand him. They didn't know the real guy, anyway. He got a bum rap."

The criticisms became sharper when a wrist injury cut short his 2012 season, and a hip issue prematurely ended his 2013. He delivered another brilliant season in 2014, but a dysfunctional clubhouse, a few key injuries, and wider organizational issues undermined what could have been a playoff team. Critically, the Blue Jays didn't make any deadline adds that summer, as Anthopoulos had his hands tied financially. Bautista, who in the spring was among the players willing to defer salary so the team could sign Ervin Santana, a plan that ultimately fell through, joined veteran closer Casey Janssen in calling out the club's inactivity. "It's a little disappointing that we somehow weren't able to get anything done, but everybody around us that's in contention—and even some teams that aren't in contention, like the Red Sox—somehow figured it out," said Bautista. "We could've used a little boost, just like some of the other teams that went out and got some additions. It's not that you don't feel your team is good enough; it's just that everybody does that at the deadline, figures out a way to improve the roster. We just somehow didn't."

In hindsight, Bautista now points to those comments as a specific situation he wished he'd handled differently. "The message... was accurate, but I came off maybe angry or demanding," he said. "That's not how I felt and not what I wanted to portray. I should have been a little bit more sensitive instead of being so stern with some of my comments at times."

The critiques of his leadership, meanwhile, he described as simply part of the territory.

"Did I take some of it personally at times and thought about it maybe more than I should have? Yeah, I think we're all victim to that," he said. "I think we all want to be the best we can be and sometimes we all feel like the criticism is not fair or not warranted and unjust. But that's part of being a leader. I tried to internalize that as much as I could and not let it come out. Sometimes I was positive. Sometimes I was a little bit negative because I think it does affect you in some way or another. But I was just a horse with blinders on."

* * *

Then came 2015 and everything changed. The arrivals of Josh Donaldson and Russell Martin finally gave Bautista a legitimate supporting cast beyond Encarnacion. Even as the Blue Jays lingered at .500, it wasn't on him or the offence, which was obliterating opposition pitching. Once Anthopoulos plugged the holes at the trade deadline, the team took off. Suddenly, as Gibbons said, they had a lot of leaders, and the narrative turned, Bautista's emotion only a talking point relative to how it effectively helped fuel the team's swagger.

An expression of the respect for him in the clubhouse came amid the celebration in Baltimore on September 30, when the Blue Jays clinched the American League East. As Bautista spoke to a small group of reporters, Donaldson approached, put an arm around him, and congratulated him on his 40th homer. Then he turned away for a moment before returning to tell the scrum that, "This guy is the man, right here." Bautista smiled. "No, you're the man," he replied. Donaldson, the AL MVP that season, insisted on the final word. "This is the man!" he bellowed before walking off.

The reframing of Bautista's Blue Jays tenure was cemented with his bat-flip homer in Game 5 of the division series against Texas. A convincing case can be made that there's no moment more emotionally charged than that one in franchise history, which makes his role in it fitting.

Everything about it was quintessentially Bautista. It followed a wild top of the seventh in which a freak play—Martin's return throw to the mound struck Shin-Soo Choo's bat, allowing Rougned Odor to score—turned the dome into a tinderbox. A series of Elvis Andrus errors in the bottom half set up the tying run and left two on with two outs for Bautista. He glared out at Sam Dyson like a starved lion stalking a zebra. He ripped through a 1-1 fastball like a a predator tearing into its prey. As the ball sizzled toward the left-field stands, he tossed his bat with utter disdain for the vanquished. The building literally shook as he tore around the bases and then rampaged through the dugout, high-fiving teammates with enough force to dislocate a shoulder. "As soon as I made contact, everything became a blur," he said. "I was fully immersed in the moment."

The opportunity for Bautista to shine on such a grand stage finally allowed fans to properly contextualize how special a player they were watching. Even though the homer didn't clinch a championship, because of the 21-year playoff drought, because of the circumstances of that bonkers seventh inning, it didn't matter. New generations of Blue Jays fans who weren't around for the World Series years finally had their own enduring memory. "He represented Toronto and Canada with pride," said Anthopoulos. "It meant something to him. It's rare when you have guys that it's really that important to them. Some guys are good players and they give everything they have to the organization. But there's a whole other layer of player where they're a part of the organization and they care deeply about it, no matter what. Carlos Delgado, Roy Halladay, and Pat Hentgen were the same way. That's special, and when you have superstars that are that way, they deserve the moment in the postseason."

* * *

Had the Blue Jays managed to pull out Game 6 of the 2015 American League Championship Series against the Kansas City Royals to stave off elimination, the majesty of his performance that night would only have added to his lore. He homered twice, including a game-tying, two-run drive in the eighth inning, but was left standing on deck when a Donaldson grounder became the season's final out. So instead, Bautista's next bit of masterpiece theatre came at the beginning of camp next spring, when off-season extension talks came up during his first meeting with media at camp.

The ground had shifted seismically for the Blue Jays after that final out in Kansas City. Mark Shapiro took over from Paul Beeston as president and CEO and Anthopoulos chose to leave rather than work under the new boss. Ross Atkins became GM. The way the team ran began to change. Before the Blue Jays gathered in Dunedin for camp, Bautista and the new front office had a get-to-know-you meeting. His pending free agency after the 2016 season came up. He said he was asked what it would take for him to sign an extension. At a subsequent meeting the weekend the NBA All-Star Game was played in Toronto, he delivered his demand and that was that.

"There's no negotiation, I told them what I wanted," he told a throng of media outside the spring clubhouse. "They either meet it or it is what it is." That was the tip of the iceberg. He rejected the notion of a hometown discount, saying (justly) that he'd already provided the club with one by vastly outperforming the deal he signed with Anthopoulos. He defended his worth and his impact to the bottom line of team owner Rogers Communications Inc. He made clear he'd drawn a line in the sand. "I'm not going to sit here and try to bargain for a couple dollars," he added.

Riveting as it all was, the performance exposed a schism that both sides might have avoided had they approached the situation differently. Bautista said at first, their initial conversation centred around the team, the clubhouse, and the addition of a high-performance department. "One thing led to another and next thing you know what we're talking about my particular situation," he said. "Maybe that led to me thinking [about the negotiation] in the way that it did, and getting too involved. I wish I would have been less involved. That's the way I would have rather gone about it."

Shapiro, meanwhile, had been on his heels from the day he took over because of Anthopoulos' stunning departure. Fans blamed him for the split and were wary of his plans for the team, which had several holes that needed plugging. Bautista's pending free agency "seemed like one of the many circumstances we were thrust into that was a challenge at that time," said Shapiro. "If everything else hadn't been so unexpected and so much different than what I had thought, I might have thought differently about that."

How differently and what that would have changed will always be conjecture. Shapiro and Atkins were concerned about the age of the roster. Bautista was 35, in search of a payday, and the performance modelling for players that age isn't kind. He wanted to finish his career with the Blue Jays, but how to thread the needle on a contract that rewards the player without hamstringing the franchise? "There's not one answer to that," answered Shapiro. "It requires a very delicate set of compromises and understandings from both a player and the team, and ultimately probably involves some inefficiency of the contract at the end. And so, you need a market that's big enough to withstand that. Even then, like with [star quarterback] Tom Brady, the player has to feel the same thing as the team when it does become time for the end. That's still a challenge. The odds are very slim against that, not just because of money and contracts, but also because what makes elite players great is that they're not necessarily the most objective self-evaluators. It's tough."

Tough indeed, but they never gave themselves a chance. Bautista grinded through a turf toe injury and a left knee sprain while shoulder issues lingered throughout a tough 2016 that included an early-season brawl with the Rangers, in which Odor landed his infamous punch. Despite all that, Bautista posted an .817 OPS in 116 games, the Blue Jays won a wild-card and knocked off the Rangers again in the division series before falling to Cleveland in the ALCS.

Once free agency arrived, the Blue Jays prioritized re-signing Edwin Encarnacion, but those talks were also mishandled by both sides. A bearish market combined with a down year ahead of an age 36 season limited Bautista's opportunities. After other alternatives fell through, they reunited on a one-year deal that included a pair of options, leading to that lean 2017 campaign and his eventual departure afterwards. The lasting impact of how those negotiations after 2015 played out remains unclear. "I don't really know, truly, how that affected my relationship with the current management of the team," said Bautista. "I have to say that I have a great relationship with ownership and I'm proud of that. I don't think I have a negative or a bad relationship with current management, it's just kind of like non-existent. And that's fine. There's just not really much there, to be quite honest with you. I don't hold any grudges at all towards anybody about anything at this point in my life. The path ended up taking me where it did. I wish I could have retired playing my last game as a Blue Jay. But you can't get everything that you want in life. That's one of those things for me."

The Blue Jays feted Bautista during the home finale on September 24, 2017, a 9–5 win over the Yankees. Starter Marcus Stroman warmed up in an authenticated, game-used No. 19 black jersey from Bautista's early days with the club. Drake's *Trophies*, a walk-up song he used for years, blared at the dome when it was time to take the field. His teammates stayed back in the dugout so Bautista could run out to right on his own. After the first out of the ninth inning, Gibbons sent Ezequiel Carrera out to right field to replace Bautista, who hugged his teammates on his way off the field, waving to fans.

"If you think about it, what more could Jose have done in his career?" said Gibbons. "He maxed out what he was. Isn't that the ultimate? Isn't that what you strive for as a player? There are a lot of assholes out there. There are a lot of good guys. The bottom line is to be the best player you can be. He did that. He didn't fall short one bit on that."

The last appearances Bautista made as an active player in Toronto came on July 3–4, 2018, with the Mets. That first night, a crowd of 24,010 cheered him during batting practice, again as the lineups were announced, and then gave him a standing ovation throughout a 90-second tribute video played before the game. Bautista, nearly overcome with emotion, said, "Wow," to himself as he put his hands above his head, and applauded back to the fans. The next night he said goodbye with an RBI single and a run scored in a 6–3 win.

The love-ins "were kind of bittersweet in a way. They only happen because you're leaving, or because you left," he said. "But it's sweet because you're acknowledged, you're liked and loved and had a good track record. If you think about it, to the loyal fans, I was on their TV sets for a good part of 10 years throughout the summers. That's a long time. So it's bittersweet in that way. But after time passes, it's more happy than sad because of what you meant to people and the memories you perhaps helped create for them, especially when we were winning. Sports connects people but also pulls them out of their everyday lives or troubles they might be having. I never really thought about it or looked at in that way when I was playing. After not playing for the last two years and becoming a full-time fan again, I started looking at it that way, too. So the last home game and the day that I came back, with the fans and the teammates, it's nice to have that."

Bautista more than earned the accolades and adoration. Years later, his No. 19 jersey remains ubiquitous in the city, an enduring sign of how he was both the foundation for, and the force behind, the franchise's revitalization.

28

THE 2015 TRADE DEADLINE

Driving across Florida in mid-July, piling up the roaming minutes on his iPhone as usual, Alex Anthopoulos' master plan for the 2015 trade deadline began to take shape. The Toronto Blue Jays general manager had just spent July 13 and 14 with his family in Naples during the All-Star break, and after dropping them off at the airport, he headed to Port St. Lucie for a look at the club's Single-A Dunedin affiliate. As he zipped through the swamplands of the Everglades, talks with Colorado Rockies counterpart Jeff Bridich for shortstop Troy Tulowitzki, hot-and-cold since the previous winter, started to pick up. In May the two had discussed a loose framework for a deal that would send the superstar shortstop north for Jose Reyes plus prospects, but locking down those prospects proved to be tricky. With the July 31 non-waiver trade deadline looming, they finally started to make some headway. At the same time, discussions on a parallel track with Cleveland for starter Carlos Carrasco and a reliever also gained momentum, and the goal of adding multiple long-term pieces to the franchise's core suddenly seemed within reach. "I was hoping to get the two deals done," said Anthopoulos, without confirming that Carrasco was a target. "They were both long-term guys that were going to impact the short-term. That's what we were really spending our time on. That would have solidified things."

The pursuit of Carrasco was never realized, a trade that would have sent prospects Jeff Hoffman, Daniel Norris, and Dalton Pompey to Cleveland for the right-hander coming undone near the finish line. But 12 days after that drive across the Sunshine State, the chase for Tulowitzki came to fruition, touching off the wildest five days of trading in franchise history and ultimately propelling the Blue Jays to their sixth American League East title. The Tulowitzki stunner—which included veteran reliever LaTroy Hawkins for Reyes, Hoffman, Miguel Castro, and Jesus Tinoco—was completed late on July 27 and finalized the next day. Late on the 29th and into the 30th, Anthopoulos pulled off an even bigger shocker when he landed David Price from the Detroit Tigers for Norris, Matt Boyd, and Jairo Labourt. Then, just ahead of the 4:00 PM ET deadline on the 31st, Anthopoulos completed two more deals, getting reliever Mark Lowe from the Seattle Mariners in the morning for Jake Brentz, Nick Wells, and Rob Rasmussen, and netting outfielder Ben Revere and cash to cover the $1.2 million left on his contract from the Philadelphia Phillies for Jimmy Cordero and Alberto Tirado. In between, the Blue Jays were in on nearly every player moved in July.

By the time the dealing was done, 20 percent of their roster had been upgraded and major holes had been filled. They'd taken on two players with club control and three rental players at the total expense of 11 pitching prospects, varying in quality. There could be no doubt, they were in it to win it. "The goal is always going to be the long-term piece whenever you can, right? That's what the focus was," said Anthopoulos. "But we wanted to win, we had a chance to win, and felt strongly about the club."

The Tulowitzki deal, which satisfied the team's short- and long-term needs, was the most difficult trade to make. In fact, strong opposition from within the front office nearly nixed it just after Anthopoulos and Bridich settled on the names. For weeks the two traded proposals but kept hitting a wall because the Rockies insisted on getting Hoffman, the electric-armed righty chosen ninth overall in the 2014 draft, while the Blue Jays tried to piece things together without him. As they haggled, Reyes' defensive issues kept popping up in the field, and the opportunity to upgrade with arguably the best all-around shortstop in the game became more and more tempting. The cost in prospect capital, however, was steep. Aside from Hoffman, who had legitimate front-of-the-rotation potential, there was the Castro, who broke camp with the team at 20 and closed for a couple of weeks before getting sent down after a rough patch, and Tinoco, a hard-throwing righty with good command at low-A Lansing. Anthopoulos had been reluctant to include Hoffman, but on July 27 he phoned Bridich and told him Hoffman was on the table, quickly leading to the agreement.

"Like in any negotiation, you're going to try like hell to get the deal on your terms until you're convinced you can't get it on your terms," said Anthopoulos. "It took us that long to be convinced. Trust me, we had spent months and months and months, and we're running out of time. That's what gets deals done—momentum and deadlines. That's fact. The other thing, too, is because we had so many other things on the go, and there was a domino effect with so many assets going out the door, financial commitments, things like that. You can sit there and get paralyzed. At some point, you have to pick a direction."

After settling things with Bridich, Anthopoulos convened a conference call with six top members of his baseball operations department to discuss the deal. To his shock, the majority opposed the trade, concerned about spending so much prospect capital on a shortstop when the primary need was pitching. What if they got Tulowitzki but couldn't bolster the staff? Retread Felix Doubront was in the rotation, and there was no obvious candidate to take his place. The call lasted an hour. The final vote was 5–2 against. Anthopoulos had been gung ho going into the call; suddenly he was leaning toward pulling out. "I remember getting off the phone and saying, 'I'm all messed up right now,' because we'd been working on it for months and months and months," he said. "It was the timing. If it had come down after the other deals, it would have been different."

For about two hours he sat in his Rogers Centre office mulling things over. He couldn't remember as much dissent against a move he was so in favour of making. The only thing that was close was the $65 million, five-year contract extension for Jose Bautista in the spring of 2011. In that instance, the slugger was coming off his 54-homer breakout but had no track record of such power before that. They were betting big on his success, and opinion was split 3–3 when Anthopoulos cast the deciding vote in favour.

This time, he called manager John Gibbons and went over the scenario with him. "Everybody wanted Tulo," recalled Anthopoulos. "He was just like, maybe we should wait until [the 31st], see what other things shake out, because the risk was this might cost us somebody else." Still, Anthopoulos had been through enough negotiations to know how easily today's agreement can become tomorrow's missed opportunity. If a deal feels right, he often tells himself, don't get cute, get it done. Deep down, he strongly believed the trade for Tulowitzki was the right thing for the team in both the short- and long-term. "And that was the argument I kept coming back to," said Anthopoulos. "We had decided to make a change at shortstop. Whether it's now or come the off-season, we're making a change, this is an issue that needs to be addressed. As much as we have current needs for a starter, we do have to do something in our minds at shortstop, and this is the time to do it."

Settled in his mind, Anthopoulos called Tony LaCava, his trusted assistant GM, to let him know his decision. He also sent a group email informing everyone who'd been on the call. "It's very important to me that you show respect for the people you work with," he explained. "Just because they may not share the same thought process and opinions as you, you want them to feel like their voices are heard." Anthopoulos also dropped this at the end: "I promise you, we'll get a starter."

What he didn't tell them is that in his back pocket he had an agreement in place with Oakland Athletics counterpart and close friend Billy Beane for swingman Jesse Chavez, with Boyd going the other way. Boyd had nearly gone to the A's for the versatile Ben Zobrist, but the Kansas City Royals had made a more appealing offer. Chavez was a fallback plan if all else failed, but Anthopoulos was aiming higher.

From there, he called Bridich to tell him they had a deal—it was roughly 11:00 PM at that point—and then woke up president and CEO Paul Beeston to let him know Tulowitzki was a Blue Jay. They didn't need ownership approval for the deal since they got the go-ahead back in May when the trade first seemed possible. Then, while on the elevator from the club's offices to the clubhouse, en route to meet with trainer George Poulis, Anthopoulos phoned Gibbons back. "I'm like, 'Gib, I couldn't wait. We went ahead and did it. I need you to come in to the office.' He's like, 'What? I thought we talked about this three hours ago, and we were waiting until Friday.'"

There were more surprises to come. Having already passed on Johnny Cueto and Scott Kazmir, Anthopoulos started making a hard charge at Mike Leake of the Cincinnati Reds on July 28 (he ended up going to San Francisco). The Blue Jays also kept tabs on Mike Fiers of the Milwaukee Brewers, who'd eventually end up in Houston, and Jeff Samardzija of the Chicago White Sox, who stayed put. Anthopoulos checked in on Milwaukee outfielder Gerardo Parra and Revere, but nothing was moving. He crashed at 11:00 PM—he'd slept only 90 minutes the previous night—and didn't wake up until 9:00 the next morning. Anthopoulos started the next day by pushing hard for Leake, but in the late afternoon shifted gears when Detroit Tigers president Dave Dombrowski called him to say he was moving David Price, who was No. 1 on the Blue Jays' wish list.

Nearly every team talking trade with them asked for Norris, the eclectic left-hander with the mid-90s fastball but erratic command. Anthopoulos told everyone he wasn't available—except the Tigers. For Price, he said to Dombrowski, he'd discuss anyone. "Price was a legitimate No. 1, a culture changer. Pitched in the AL East, completely healthy," explained Anthopoulos. "The tough part with rentals is, there's no margin for error. You need health, so you can't take any risk there, and you need performance. You have to feel really good because you can't afford a slump. It's a critical time, and if you get a rental, which you're giving up long-term assets for, and you get bad performance, he's actually making your team worse."

Dombrowski told Anthopoulos that he'd get back to him, called him back late that night, and the talks went fast. They quickly settled on Norris and Boyd, haggling until about 3:00 AM, before landing on Labourt as the third piece. Wired from the stress and adrenaline rush of the negotiations, he phoned Gibbons in the middle of the night. "I couldn't believe he answered his phone," said Anthopoulos. "I'm like, 'Gib, we have David Price.' He goes, 'No way.' I'm like, 'Yeah, we got David.' He's like, 'Come on man, you putting me on at three in the morning?' I'm like, 'No, man, we got David Price.'" Unable to sleep, Anthopoulos waited impatiently until 7:00 the next morning to phone Beeston for the final approval.

The deal was announced around lunchtime, triggering euphoria within the fan base. Blue Jays players who'd been quietly wondering 'Why get Tulowitzki when the team really needed a starter?' were electrified. All the while Anthopoulos agonized over the decision, as he does after every trade. "We really like Daniel Norris," he said. "He's got a chance to be a really good starter, a front-of-the-rotation starter. But it was a chance to get a true No. 1 when we felt we had a great team that was healthy. And there aren't too many opportunities to do that."

Anthopoulos awoke the next morning, anxiously waiting for Mariners counterpart Jack Zduriencik to rise on the West Coast. He wanted to close on Lowe, and also discuss reacquiring J.A. Happ, whom he traded to Seattle for left fielder Michael Saunders the previous winter. They quickly locked down Lowe but the Mariners refused to cover the remainder of Happ's contract. The lefty went to the Pittsburgh Pirates instead. Once that was done, Anthopoulos circled back to the Brewers on Parra, but they wouldn't eat the money and instead sent him to the Baltimore Orioles. He didn't mind because he felt Revere filled more of a void anyway, and completed the deal with the Phillies to cap his wild week. "No one ever has done anything close to it in team history, maybe even in the history of the game," Beeston said afterward. "He was relentless, he was focused, he got what he needed, and he deserves all the credit."

The accolades came from every direction, from awed players who were disappointed when a year earlier the team's only move was the acquisition of utility man Danny Valencia, to fans who embraced the Blue Jays like they hadn't in two decades. A 43–19 close to the season sealed the club's first trip to the postseason since 1993. They finished two wins short of reaching the World Series.

"Everything we do, prospects, drafting, going to the Dominican, GM meetings, winter meetings, the goal is to win a World Series and there aren't too many years where you can say you have a World Series–calibre team," said Anthopoulos in 2015. "You might have a team that has a chance to get to the playoffs, or with some luck things can go well. We had a great team this year—not a good team, a great team—and we had a World Series contender. Over the course of the franchise, other than the World Series–champion teams, I don't know that there was a better team than this year. Whether that sounds self-serving or arrogant, that's the truth. This was a no-doubter, World

Series–calibre team. For that to happen, you need some health, you need guys to have good seasons. It's not easy, so you better take that shot because that's why we're here. We're not here to have the top prospect ranking, or to have a sustainable .500 or above .500 record. We did that for 21 years, it didn't move the needle on the franchise. The needle got moved this year and that's what this was about for me. What we experienced, that's what this was all about."

29

EE'S
NINE-RBI GAME
AND AN UNLIKELY PATH
TO STARDOM

Amid the din of a sellout crowd in total elation, Edwin Encarnacion smiled in the Toronto Blue Jays' dugout the way a child does when struck by a moment of enchantment. Minutes earlier, he'd hit a grand slam to right-centre field off Detroit Tigers reliever Alex Wilson, sending the 46,444 at Rogers Centre into bedlam with his third home run of the afternoon. In the process, he matched the franchise single-game record with nine RBIs. Fans chanted his name as he circled the bases; pounded the hands of teammates Jose Bautista, Cliff Pennington, Justin Smoak, and Troy Tulowitzki after touching home; then skipped his way through a parade of hands in the Blue Jays' dugout. Before he could sit down, Bautista gently pointed him back to the field for a well-deserved curtain call. Encarnacion hopped out of the dugout, leaping with arms up before coming back and taking a seat. The noise didn't stop, and all he could do was sit there and beam. "It was an exciting moment, very emotional for me because of the way I've played and where I've come from," said Encarnacion. "It's one of my top moments in this game, and to see something like that is very satisfying."

Satisfying, for sure, but also, briefly, puzzling. Smoak had taken two balls from Wilson once things settled, but play was interrupted again when hats started raining down on the field. For hockey fans the gesture is, no pun intended, old hat—they doff lids and flip them onto the ice whenever a player scores three goals in the same game. It's known as a hat trick. The tradition never really made its way to baseball until August 29, 2015, when a stream of caps littered the warning track. "I asked why they did that," recalled Encarnacion. "Dioner Navarro explained to me that they do that in hockey games. After that I started looking for videos on YouTube to see it."

Encarnacion's memorable performance in that 15–1 victory also quickly found its way to YouTube, which is funny because the only other time a Blue Jays player had driven in nine runs in a single game, ESPN was still two years away from being created. Roy Howell's exploits in a 19–3 victory over the eventual World Series–champion New York Yankees on September 10, 1977, travelled to the masses via newspapers and wire-service dispatches. It was a rare highlight in what was otherwise an inaugural season of struggle for an expansion franchise.

Howell was a stalwart in the middle of the lineup during those days, but is a bit player in team history when measured against Encarnacion, an elite slugger whose walk-off homer in the 2016 wild-card game is among the franchise's greatest moments.

His path to such lofty status was anything but straightforward. Encarnacion was forced upon the Blue Jays in the 2009 trade that sent Scott Rolen to the Cincinnati Reds, the cost of doing business to get Zach Stewart, a well-regarded right-handed pitching prospect at the time who was their primary target in the trade. That Encarnacion became a three-time All-Star while Stewart flamed out is one of the happiest accidents in franchise history.

Still, there were numerous twists and turns along the way, and any of them could have led him to wash out like countless other talented players before him. Consider that between his acquisition on July 31, 2009, and his breakout 2012, Encarnacion was optioned, outrighted, placed on waivers, claimed, non-tendered, and twice re-signed.

The nadir, though, came on May 18, 2011, in a 6–5 loss to the Tampa Bay Rays, when he made two errors at first base and could easily have ended up with three additional misplays on his tab. Without any offensive production to lean on and a new set of fans turning on him, his conversion to first base looked hopeless in only his eighth game at the position. In the midst of a home run drought that would stretch to 37 games, he was very clearly a player in crisis.

"The mind is hard to control sometimes, you know?" Encarnacion said of those troubled times. "Especially when you're in the big leagues, everybody's on you. You've got to trust the process, and it's very difficult for any young player. You've got to be tough mentally, you've got to continue to be positive and believe in yourself, because if you don't believe in yourself nothing's going to change. So I just continued to believe in myself. I just relaxed my mind and started working with my offence and started to change my career."

Encarnacion's progress was slow and methodical. One important moment for him came just after the All-Star break in 2011, when then

GM Alex Anthopoulos visited him in the clubhouse and pointed out that during his best year, in 2008, he'd walked 61 times. Midway through that season, he'd walked only nine times in 258 plate appearances, and because he was so talented a hitter, he was swinging at and making contact with pitches he really shouldn't have been chasing. Anthopoulos remembers Encarnacion replying, "I know. I've got to be more selective."

In the final 64 games of the season, he walked 34 times, ripping 17 doubles and 11 homers in the process. His play in the field at first base also stabilized, and while no one was going to confuse him with Mark Teixeira around the bag, Encarnacion became more than capable.

Those two elements fed into each other. No longer carrying his defensive miscues with him to the plate, he was better able to relax and be more selective, focusing on hunting the pitch he wanted and passing the baton when he didn't get it. "I understood [moving from third base] was going to be better for me because I could get my mind right again," he said. "It had been affecting my offensive side too, and when we made that move everything started working out again."

In much the way teammates recognized a real shift in Bautista in 2009, they saw that Encarnacion was legitimately turning the corner in 2011. A $3.5 million club option for 2012 that at one point seemed laughable quickly started looking like a bargain. "A thing people need to take into consideration is not just numbers—that always gives you an idea what he can do—but different circumstances that a player is surrounded with at a particular time and place allow him to do better or worse at his job," said Bautista. "Maybe not being at the defensive position that he was best suited for, being on a team going through changes, mistakes on the field weren't going to be so blown out of proportion [made the difference].... But that's not the reason I believed in him; I believed in him because I saw with my own eyes what he can bring to the table as a ballplayer and I saw the damage he could do at the plate. Given the right circumstances, I knew he could get back to that."

After the strong finish in 2011, he worked out in the off-season back home in the Dominican Republic with local hitting coach Luis Mercedes. The move finally brought everything together. A former big-leaguer who also worked with Robinson Cano over the winter, Mercedes told Encarnacion that even after the adjustments he had made, his swing was too long; his bat path went around the ball rather than directly at it. The solution was simple: finish his swing with two hands on the bat instead of releasing his top hand at the end, creating a shorter path through the zone while keeping him more inside the ball. After trying it out, Encarnacion loved it: "That made my swing have more impact on the ball," he said.

Once the 2012 campaign opened, Encarnacion came out slugging and didn't stop, posting a 1.054 OPS in April, with eight homers and 21 RBIs. On July 26, he set a new career high with his 27th homer of the season, a three-run shot off Oakland's Tommy Milone. He picked up No. 30 two weeks later off Phil Hughes of the Yankees; hammered No. 40 on September 13 off Seattle's Felix Hernandez, a three-run shot that pushed him past 100 RBIs for the first time; and finished things up with No. 42 off Miguel Gonzalez of the Orioles on September 26. It was a season worth waiting for.

"I knew I could hit 30 home runs and drive in 100, that always was on my mind, and that year finally I did it," said Encarnacion. "With the hard work I did all off-season, and I kept positive with myself and telling myself I know I can do it, I was very happy with that."

From then on, the big numbers kept coming. His 239 home runs rank third in Blue Jays history, trailing only Carlos Delgado's 336 and Bautista's 288. He's fourth in slugging percentage, sixth in RBI, fifth in walks, eighth in runs, and among the top 10 in several other offensive categories.

The nine-RBI game is among his many Blue Jays highlights, although none will be as enduring as his 11th-inning rocket to win the 2016 wild-card game against the Baltimore Orioles. As it turned out, the home run was his last big moment with the club. Bungled negotiations when he became a free agent after the season led him to sign with Cleveland.

In his first trip back to Toronto the next year, the walk-off homer "was the first thing that came to my head" when he arrived at the field. "It was something unbelievable, you never think you're going to hit a homer to go to the next round. I had the opportunity to do it and I really enjoyed it."

Just like his time with the Blue Jays, hat tricks and all.

30

FRANCHISE ICON: DAVE STIEB

Apartments were hard to come by during the spring of 1979 in Syracuse. Dave Stieb, the outfielder-turned-pitcher with all of 12 games at Single-A Dunedin under his belt, had just been promoted to Triple-A by the Toronto Blue Jays, and the local real estate market was proving to be more of a challenge than opposing batters.

In seven starts with the Syracuse Chiefs, he went 5–2 with a 2.12 ERA. He'd allowed only 39 hits and 14 walks in 51 innings. For a guy who had only pitched a handful of times at Southern Illinois University before being selected in the fifth round of the 1978 Draft, the 21-year-old right-hander was really good on the mound. The pitching-starved Blue Jays noticed. Shortly after he finally settled his living arrangements, Chiefs manager Vern Benson called Stieb into his office and told him he was going to the Show. "You know what I said to him? 'Are you kidding me? I just found an apartment here. I just got settled,'" Stieb said, laughing at the memory. "That's what I said to him. I was just so, I don't want to say naïve, it was just such a whirlwind. I couldn't believe it, like, 'No, no. There's no way I'm going to the big leagues.' He's like, 'Do you want to call your parents?' I'm like, 'Sure.' What an experience that was. It just happened so fast."

Not only did Stieb's ascension to the Blue Jays happen fast, but it happened through such an unlikely series of events that he may very well be the luckiest break in franchise history. In the spring of 1978, scouts Al LaMacchia and Bobby Mattick were dispatched to take a look at Stieb, then an outfielder at Southern Illinois University. His team was taking on Eastern Illinois University, who featured a shortstop of some interest named Jeff Gossett, and SIU fell in a hole. Late in the game, SIU called on Stieb to move from centre field to the mound. The school had suffered some injuries to its pitching staff, and Stieb had legit stuff. LaMacchia and Mattick didn't think much of him with the bat, but they loved what they saw from him on the mound. He threw hard, with natural sink. His command was pretty good. He was raw and unpolished, but they thought there might be something there. After the game they approached SIU manager Richard "Itchy" Jones for more background on the outfielder from Santa Ana, California. Jones then introduced them to Stieb. "The conversation was that they were scouts with the Blue Jays and they liked the way I pitched," said Stieb. "I said, 'Well, I'm not a pitcher. I'm an outfielder.' And they said, 'Well, we like the way you pitch.' Then, one of them said, 'Well, the quickest way to the majors is to be a pitcher.' And I'm thinking, 'Oh, God, this is a line to lure me in.' After that, one of them said, 'If we draft you, would you become a pitcher?' It was like a no-brainer to me, I've got nothing to lose by saying yes, and I'd never been drafted before, so I wanted to give myself that chance. So I said, 'Yeah, but you've got to let me play outfield, too.' They were like, 'Okay,' and then they said it again: 'So if we draft you, you'll become a pitcher?' And I go, 'Sure.' That was pretty much the discussion. I left there thinking nothing was going to happen. Probably."

Stieb was wrong. The Blue Jays picked him 106th overall, one spot ahead of Gossett, who was selected by the New York Mets. Gossett played two minor-league seasons before bailing on baseball to focus on a career in the NFL, where he spent 15 years as a punter for four teams, including the Raiders for nine seasons. Stieb, meanwhile, only agreed to sign if the Blue Jays let him play the outfield on his non-pitching days, and they indulged him, knowing his only hope of progressing lay on the mound. He went 19-for-99 in 35 games with Dunedin in 1978 and that was it, his arm offering a path forward his bat did not.

On June 29, 1979, just a year after he was drafted, he made his big-league debut, allowing six runs, five earned, over six innings in a 6–1 loss at Baltimore. Stieb's second outing went better, as he allowed four runs in six frames at Detroit, and then three straight complete games followed, two of them wins, in which he allowed a total of only four runs. He finished the season 8–8 with a 4.31 ERA in 18 starts, the only pitcher on the entire staff to finish without a losing record.

Given all the different things a pitcher needs to manage on the mound, it wasn't supposed to be as easy as it was for someone as raw and unrefined as Stieb. "I didn't make it way more complex than it is," he said. "That was the beauty of it for me, I had never done it before, so I had nothing to fall back on. My only attitude was 'throw as hard as you can but throw strikes.' I had a very simple delivery. I would explode towards the plate at the end and I had good control. It was like a perfect storm for me. I had never pitched before but had a strong arm, and then I had this natural movement on my sinker. And I was able to throw with control right away. So, it was just throw to the glove. I was no picture of a guy carving out there or really thinking about what he's doing."

For an expansion club starved for pitching, Stieb was like a gift from the heavens. In 1980, he went 12–15 with a 3.71 ERA and 14 complete games in 32 starts, logging 242.2 innings, earning his first of seven All-Star selections. In the strike-shortened 1981 season, he went 11–10 with a 3.19 ERA in 25 starts, and a still-dreadful Blue Jays team began regarding his starts as win days.

Yet even as he sawed through opponents, he spent a lot of time burning and rebuilding bridges with his teammates because of his infamous tantrums on the mound. As teammate and friend Lloyd Moseby put it, "When he's on the mound, listen, David's not a very good person, okay? So if anyone wants to try put some sugar on that, you can't. He was fired up. He was out there for one reason, to win a damn game, and he'd do some things that kind of irk you. But if you really knew his motives, you laid off of him for a while. Then you would see him on the bus and say, 'Dave, don't ever do that again,' and we'd kind of clear it up there. But you understood, when he has a Blue Jays uniform on he's not very sane."

Not everyone understood, and some labelled him selfish. But intriguingly, it's here that his inexperience on the mound manifested itself more than in any other area. Driven by a compulsive perfectionist's streak, he simply didn't know how to handle the struggles of others. "When I played outfield, whether I had a good game or bad game, I understood it was all on me," Stieb said. "If I make an error or strike out, there's no one else to look at. But when I took that mound and I'm in a game and I realized that my outcome rests in these guys' hands and we made some bad mistakes, I didn't take it well the first few times it happened. I demanded perfection from them like

I demanded it from myself. It was hard for me to hold it back and not react.

"The worst instance was [with] Alvis Woods in left field in the corner, he couldn't pick the ball up. I don't know what he was doing over there, it was just so blatantly bad. My whole mind-set was, 'this is the major leagues, and I've got a guy out there who can't even pick up the ball in the corner?' So I threw my arms up like, 'What are you doing?' Oh, I got chewed out for that. A lot of people thought, 'You're bad. You're showing up your teammates. What's the matter with you?' I was like, 'Do you understand my mind-set? I'm not used to my success hinging on this guy not doing that out there.'"

Over time, Stieb got better at containing his frustrations, although his angry glares at teammates still get laughs today. Also, the supporting cast around him improved, as players like Moseby, Jesse Barfield, Willie Upshaw, George Bell, Damaso Garcia, and Tony Fernandez started displacing the roster placeholders. That's when Stieb really took off, and in 1985, when the Blue Jays won the American League East for the first time, he led the league with a career-best 2.48 ERA. "He was the best right-handed pitcher I ever caught," said longtime catcher Ernie Whitt. "Some pitchers you would go out and jump on their ass. He was a pitcher that you had to go out and calm down, and be a little more soothing on him, encourage him that 'You've got the best stuff in the league, just throw it, and don't let the little things affect you.'"

Over time, Stieb's slider became known as the best in the American League, a filthy put-away pitch that hitters couldn't do anything with most of the time—even if they knew it was coming. Mark Newman, the pitching coach at Southern Illinois University who first invited Stieb to throw a bullpen, initially gave him the pitch. But in 1979 at Dunedin, roving pitching instructor Bob Humphreys helped refine the grip and make it a weapon. "When he showed me that, oh my God, it was over. It was instant," said Stieb. "Now against a right-hander, I had my sinker running in on his hands, my four-seamer, and then that slider. That thing broke nasty down and away. And I had the equalizer."

His goal with the pitch was to throw it down and away to righties as if it were a fastball. His best ones started at the bottom of the strike zone and then dropped way out. At times he'd miss inside and watch it break back over the plate for a called strike. "I ran into Greg Maddux and he said, 'Man, one thing I always loved about you was that backdoor slider you threw to righties. I've got to ask you, did you do that on purpose?'" recalled Stieb. "And I wanted to say yeah, because that's what he was impressed with, but I said, 'No man, most of those were mistakes, I got all jacked up, let go too soon, it froze them and it broke in there for a strike.' He had this look like he was so disappointed. I almost felt like I should have lied to him."

By the end of the 1980s, there was an ongoing debate as to whether Stieb or his 1992 Blue Jays teammate Jack Morris was the pitcher of the decade. Over 331 starts, Stieb posted a 140–109 record with a 3.32 ERA and 92 complete games. Yet he never finished higher than fourth in voting for the Cy Young Award. The next decade opened with more promise, when he won a career-high 18 games in 1990 and finally threw a no-hitter. But things turned definitively during his ninth start of the 1991 season. In the first inning of a 2–1 loss at Oakland, Ernie Riles kneed Stieb in the head during a collision at first base. "I went back out to the mound, Pat Borders calls a curveball, and I couldn't remember how to throw my curveball," he said. Stieb missed his next start, ended up on the disabled list for the first time in his career soon after, and didn't pitch again for the rest of the season. The culprit was a ruptured disc in his spine that led to other complications. He underwent surgery that December, hopeful to regain past form. That didn't happen.

Stieb made 14 starts in 1992 before making seven appearances in the bullpen. That's when his shoulder flared up—in previous years it had been an on-and-off issue—and he didn't pitch after August 8, missing the stretch drive, the postseason, and the first World Series championship. "I'm not even on the roster," he said. "It was like my name was nowhere to be found."

The Chicago White Sox signed him as a free agent in the fall and he made four appearances before getting released May 23. The Kansas City Royals gave him a minor-league deal after that and he pitched in nine games at Triple-A Omaha before walking away, cursing an umpire he felt was squeezing him in his final game. "He was really screwing me, man," said Stieb, who at that point thought he was done with baseball.

After four seasons away, there turned out to be one last spurt left. The Blue Jays invited him to be a guest coach at spring training in 1998, and fooling around one day, he got back up on the mound and the ball sizzled out of his hand. "Roger Clemens goes, 'God, dude, you should still be pitching,'" said Stieb. A couple of days later, he threw a side session to Sal Butera, who told him, "You got to go talk to Skip."

Manager Tim Johnson embraced the idea. Stieb signed on, made 12 minor-league starts, and on June 18 returned to the big leagues with a scoreless inning at the end of a 13–6 win at Baltimore. He ended up pitching in 19 games, three starts, putting up a 4.83 ERA in 50⅓ innings, with one win and two saves. At season's end, the Blue Jays told him he'd be welcome to return as a reliever in 1999. He passed.

"I started my career with the Blue Jays, I had that crazy time with the White Sox and then the Royals that I thought was the end of my career, and I would have never expected that 4½ years later I'm pitching at 41 with the Blue Jays again," said Stieb. "I was done. I'd come full circle."

Stieb walked away as the franchise's all-time leader in wins (175), innings (2,873), strikeouts (1,658), starts (408), complete games (103), and shutouts (30). And to think that if he hadn't by chance come in to pitch during that one game back in college, it might never have happened.

31

THE BEST OUTFIELD IN BASEBALL

Born 16 days apart in the fall of 1959, they came of age together, driving the nascent Toronto Blue Jays forward. Their distinct personalities embodied the spirit of a burgeoning club. George Bell, all fire and drive. Lloyd Moseby, all fun and infectious enthusiasm. Jesse Barfield, all determination and serious professionalism. From 1984 to 1989, they became known as the "Best Outfield in Baseball," a stirring combination of power, speed, and defensive ability that dazzled fans and opponents alike. "We three had the most fun in five straight years together than anyone else in baseball," said Bell. Few will argue. "A lot of times I whipped Jesse, and another game I would be whipping George," said Moseby. "We just had good camaraderie, we had a great friendship. It was something that you can't duplicate."

The Blue Jays haven't had an outfield perform in the same way over such an extended period since. Timing the progress of players to have them peak together can sometimes be an impossible task, but managers Bobby Mattick and Bobby Cox integrated the trio over a period of three seasons before they took off. Moseby, the second overall pick in the 1978 Draft, broke in first, logging 114 games as a 20-year-old in 1980. A gifted athlete born in Portland, Arkansas, and raised in Oakland, he developed a technique of sliding in centre field to steal hits while avoiding turf burns from the gruesome rug at Exhibition Stadium. "Lloyd was the best centre fielder I'd seen in years, no doubt," said Barfield. At the plate, he consistently hit double digits in home runs, topping out at 26 in 1987, and was a menace on the bases, twice swiping 39 bags. Often he played ringmaster between the polar opposites who flanked him on the field. "Jesse was not a clowner, but some days he would be clowning you around if it was what you needed for that day," said Moseby. "Georgie was angry a lot of days, so my job was to be a therapist sometimes. It was a lot of fun doing that because you had to really read your guys, and you had to know when to say what too. You just can't keep rambling with Georgie like

that, because he would just tell you to go f— off somewhere.... It was complicated, but it was lot of fun."

Barfield and Bell both got their first tastes of the big leagues in 1981, but Barfield was the first to stick, playing regularly in 1982. A ninth-round pick in 1977 from Joliet, Illinois, the right fielder with the cannon throwing arm exceeded expectations, skipping Triple-A entirely on his way up the ladder. While he posted 22 steals in 1985, his only time in double digits, power was his game, and he became the first Blue Jays player to lead the league in home runs with 40 in 1986. An uppercut swing meant a lot of strikeouts to go with that pop, but the trade-off was worth it. Defensively, his throwing arm routinely left rivals in awe. He'd pick up balls by the outfield wall and fling a dart to the plate to nab a brave but foolish runner. From 1982 to 1988, Barfield amassed 111 assists, even with opposing teams knowing it was plain dumb to challenge him. "His arm was strong, and it was accurate, man," said Bell.

By far the most reserved of the trio, Barfield's staid nature ended up making him a target for ribbing from his fellow outfielders. "Jesse could get mad, because Jesse was so serious most of the time. You cannot joke with him sometimes. We tried to play games with him and he'd get real upset," said Bell. "When we changed pitchers, Lloyd used to walk all the way to left-centre field and I walked all the way there, so we left Jesse by himself in right field, and he used to get mad for that." Still, the good-natured fun ultimately helped Barfield, teaching him to take some of the edge off. "Lloyd made me a better player, and a better person as well," he said. "Here was a guy who could be 0-for-12 or 4-for-4 [and] you couldn't tell the difference, and that made me understand you have to take one game at a time, one at-bat at a time, one situation at a time and understand this game is going to get you at times."

Bell, on the other hand, never reined in his fiery competitiveness. A Rule 5 pick from the Philadelphia Phillies in December 1980, the native of San Pedro de Macoris, Dominican Republic, got 168 at-bats in 1981 while being kept on the big-league roster all year so the Blue Jays could retain his rights. The next year he was back in the minors for more development, but his season at Triple-A Syracuse was truncated by a beaning that broke his jaw. He spent most of 1983 repeating the level before finishing the season in the big leagues, and thrived from that point forward. While his talent with the bat was obvious, his power only began to emerge as he got stronger and smarter at the plate. "I never lifted weights in my life. Never," said Bell. "The only thing I lifted was my little wife. She's four foot eleven." Bell hit 26 homers with 87 RBIs in 1984 and kept pounding from there, peaking during a 47-homer, 134-RBI campaign in 1987 that earned him American League MVP honours. "George was definitely the best hitter I ever played with, and I played with some good ones," said Barfield. "Heart of a lion." Bell roared like one too, which is why Barfield quips that, "George thought he was in charge." In many ways, he was.

TORONTO BLUE JAYS

The Best Outfield in Baseball was broken up on April 30, 1989, when Barfield was traded to the New York Yankees for left-hander Al Leiter. Moseby left for the Detroit Tigers as a free agent after that season. And Bell departed for the Chicago Cubs as a free agent after the 1990 campaign. None recreated the success they enjoyed in Toronto. "It was just easy chemistry between us," said Moseby. "I can't really describe it, but it was just very simple, very fun."

32

THE 1987 COLLAPSE

A blown save that led to a 3–2 loss to the Detroit Tigers in 13 innings on September 27, 1987, should have been no biggie. The Toronto Blue Jays had already won the first three games of the four-game set, and even after the sweep-preventing setback, keyed by Kirk Gibson's game-tying homer off Tom Henke in the ninth, their lead atop the American League East stood at 2½ games. Considering they entered a tension-filled weekend just a half game up, they'd accomplished what they needed. Their second division title wasn't quite in the bag, but they looked to be sitting pretty with only six games left to play.

Baseball, of course, teaches you to take nothing for granted, and that missed opportunity proved very costly for the Blue Jays, who proceeded to suffer the worst collapse in franchise history. They dropped each of their remaining games to finish the season with seven straight losses. The final three came in Detroit, handing the Tigers the American League East crown. A masochist might debate which hurt more, failing to close out the Kansas City Royals in the 1985 American League Championship Series or blowing the division in '87—a case could be made either way. But the slow, methodical fashion in which the division slipped through their fingers over the final week was simply gutting, and it all started with that extra-inning setback. "That was the big game," said Pat Gillick, the general manager at the time. "We win that game, we're up 4½. It was a two-game swing, and I think Detroit would have put their heads down if we [had] won that game. But that's baseball, that's what makes it great. You have to take your lumps."

The Blue Jays took them all right. The playoff miss scarred the club for years. Although when viewed in isolation, the events of the week shouldn't have played out the way they did. Things started out innocently enough, as they so often seem to do when such collapses happen. But the combination of injuries and tough losses within the crucible of a playoff race allowed things to snowball on one of the most talented groups the organization ever assembled. "I've said all along that the best team I ever played on was the '87 team, even though we didn't win it," said catcher Ernie Whitt. "It was very frustrating, needless to say."

While the September 27 loss may have been at the root of the collapse, Tony Fernandez's season-ending injury in the third inning of the series opener against the Tigers was the seed. Bill Madlock led off the frame with a single and when Gibson followed with a grounder to second, he slammed into the shortstop with a rolling block to prevent a double play. Fernandez fell to the ground, his elbow crashing into the wood-framed seam that surrounded the dirt cutouts around the bases. A few hours later, he underwent surgery to repair a displaced fracture in his elbow, his season over.

"He went way off the base path, but I guess that was customary in those days," said Fernandez. "It could have cost me my career." Several Blue Jays felt the play was dirty, and the ill will added some extra spice to the series. A 4–3 victory that night plus consecutive walk-off victories in the next two games against Detroit became sweeter as a result. Manny Lee covered in Fernandez's absence, but there was no way to fill the entire void. "It hurts because Tony is so great both offensively and defensively," manager Jimy Williams said at the time.

Teams typically can survive the loss of one impact player, but when two or more go down, even deep clubs take a real hit. The Blue Jays found themselves in that spot on September 29, after suffering their third straight loss 5–3 to the Milwaukee Brewers. Again, a takeout slide at second base was at issue. Whitt led off the sixth inning with a single and when Jesse Barfield followed with a grounder to third, he slid into Paul Molitor at second to prevent a twin-kill. "His knee hit me in the ribs," said Whitt. "I'd never had a rib injury before so I never really knew that all your movements come out of the middle part of your body, the breathing, the coughing. If you had to sneeze, forget about it." The Blue Jays held out hope for a quick return but it didn't happen. The most complete offensive season of Whitt's career was cut short. In a span of six days, they'd lost their starting shortstop and catcher, two pillars both in the field and at the plate. "Ernie contributed a lot to the team as a left-handed hitter. And catching, he was smart enough to deal with the situation behind the plate with the hitters," said left fielder George Bell. "It cost us."

The Blue Jays lost that game 5–3, and combined with Detroit's 10–1 win over Baltimore, the division lead was cut to 1½ games. The next night the Brewers completed a three-game sweep with a 5–2 win behind a complete game from Juan Nieves. Detroit won its game in hand on October 1, 9–5 over the Orioles, and the lead was down to just one game going into the final weekend at Tiger Stadium. "I never dreamed we'd be only one out," Tigers manager Sparky Anderson said ahead of the opener. Even the Blue Jays' journey to the Motor City was ominous, as their initial flight had to return to Toronto as a precaution when a bird was sucked into one of the plane's engines. "Just as the wheels left the ground passengers heard a loud thump," Dave Perkins wrote in the *Toronto Star*. "The cabin lights began blinking on and off and there was a big orange flash in the left engine. The jet began to shake."

Pretty soon, the Blue Jays began to look shaky themselves, suffering losses that would highlight the absences of both Whitt and Fernandez. Doyle Alexander, who won the game that clinched the American League East for the Blue Jays in 1985, beat them in the opener. Jim Clancy couldn't hold a 3–1 lead Lee provided with a three-run homer in the second, although two of the four runs charged to him were unearned. Reserve catcher Greg Myers hit into a game-ending double play against Mike Henneman to end it, and Whitt's left-handed bat with the short porch in right would have created some drama. The following afternoon, Mike Flanagan allowed two runs, only one earned because of a Lee throwing error, over 11 brilliant innings but in the 12th the Tigers loaded the bases with one out against Jeff Musselman. Mark Eichhorn took over and induced a double-play ball to short from Alan Trammell, but the ball skipped through Lee's legs for a generously scored single that delivered a 3–2 win. (Fernandez would almost certainly have turned two, and who knows?) Then, in the season finale, Frank Tanana made Larry Herndon's second-inning homer off Jimmy Key stand up in a 1–0 win,

Garth Iorg hitting a weak squib three steps off the first-base side of the mound to end it.

The Blue Jays sat on the edge of the dugout, staring blankly as the Tigers celebrated a trip to the American League Championship Series (which they would lose in five games to the Minnesota Twins). The American League's third-best offence scored a total of 16 runs in the seven straight losses. Bell, the American League MVP with 47 home runs and 134 RBIs, went 3-for-27 with four walks during that week of misery. "He kind of expanded the strike zone a little bit and he tried to carry the team himself, and of course the other teams were saying, 'We're not going to let this one guy beat us,'" said Whitt. "They pitched around him, and that was frustrating to see him go through because he's such a competitor."

To this day, the pain lingers. "With everything we were going through, we made a lot of mistakes," said Bell. "We made a lot of pitching mistakes, we made a lot of mistakes in the field, a lot of base-running mistakes, but that's part of the game, and it cost us going to the playoffs. I'm going to remember that for the rest of my life."

33

THE BLUE JAYS' WILDEST PLAYOFF GAMES

In the aftermath, with the music blaring and bottles popping and cigar smoke wafting, Mark Buehrle stood off to the side of the Toronto Blue Jays clubhouse, sipping champagne, trying to make sense of what went down. "Just when you think you've seen everything in baseball, you really haven't," said the veteran of 16 big-league seasons, shaking his head. "Crazy things happen." Crazy doesn't even begin to cover it. The Blue Jays' series-clinching 6–3 victory over the Texas Rangers in Game 5 of the 2015 American League Division Series was well beyond that, featuring a seventh inning that is perhaps without peer in postseason history. It featured everything from an obscure ruling on a freak play to Jose Bautista's epic bat flip, with the benches clearing twice for good measure. Rarely, if ever, has the Rogers Centre been as raucous. It all elicited the kind of raw emotion that stays with you for a while. "This is going to go down as one of the greatest games that we've ever played," said then-GM Alex Anthopoulos, and even that's an understatement.

For the purposes of context, the only postseason game in Blue Jays history comparable in terms of its sheer audacity is the 15–14 win over the Philadelphia Phillies in Game 4 of the 1993 World Series. That night at Veterans Stadium, the Blue Jays squandered leads of 3–0 and 7–6 before rallying back from deficits of 12–7 and 14–9. Starter Todd Stottlemyre—dissed beforehand by Philadelphia mayor Ed Rendell, who said, "If Frank Thomas could hit a ball 430 feet off Stottlemyre, I could hit one 270. I'd like to bat against him"—allowed six runs on three hits and four walks in two innings before getting yanked. He also banged his chin on the ground while getting thrown out trying to go first to third in the second inning, pitching the bottom half with an open gash. Like their pitcher, the Blue Jays got up after getting bloodied. They rallied for a six-spot in the eighth inning, capped by Devon White's two-run triple off Mitch Williams, and then watched relievers Mike Timlin and Duane Ward record the final six outs in order to seal the deal for a 3–1 series lead. "Oh, it definitely turned the series for us," said Pat Hentgen. "It was almost like a high school championship game in football, where we had 25 grown men clapping. It was one of the greatest thrills of my career."

As wild as that was, Game 5 against the Rangers raised the crazy to a whole other level. The Blue Jays dropped the opening two games of the series at home before rallying back with a pair of road wins at Globe Life Park to force a decisive fifth game. Marcus Stroman, the right-handed phenom who returned in September from what was supposed to be a season-ending knee injury, got the start for the Blue Jays against ace lefty Cole Hamels. The Rangers struck first, eking out a run in the opening frame on a fielder's choice by Prince Fielder, and went up 2–0 in the third on Shin-Soo Choo's solo shot. The Blue Jays got one back in the bottom half on Jose Bautista's RBI double, and then knotted things up in the sixth when Edwin Encarnacion pummelled a first-pitch fastball into the second deck, setting the stage for the drama to follow.

Aaron Sanchez took over from Stroman in the seventh and promptly surrendered a single to Rougned Odor, a pest on the bases who nearly singlehandedly undid the Blue Jays in the series. Chris Gimenez sacrificed him over to second, a Delino DeShields groundout moved him over to third, and then things got wacky. Choo came up and, after Sanchez missed inside to even the count 2–2, Russell Martin relayed the ball back to the mound the way he had thousands of times during his career. Only this time, the ball happened to strike Choo's bat, deflecting down the third-base line, allowing an alert Odor to score. Home-plate umpire Dale Scott incorrectly ruled the ball dead, and after a discussion with Rangers manager Jeff Banister, he conferred with the rest of the umpiring crew before counting Odor's run. The decision turned a buoyant crowd of 49,742 riotous. They threw water bottles, beer cans—basically anything disposable—toward the field while manager John Gibbons came out to argue with Scott. The grounds crew could barely keep up with the torrent of garbage, and the multiple warnings made by public address announcer Tim Langton only led to new streams of trash.

When Gibbons said the Blue Jays would protest the game, Scott decided to double-check the rule interpretation with replay officials in New York. They confirmed the relevant rule, which reads:

If the batter interferes with the catcher's throw to retire a runner by stepping out of the batter's box, interference shall be called on the batter under Official Baseball Rule 6.03(a)(3) [former OBR 6.06(c)]. However, if the batter is standing in the batter's box and he or his bat is struck by the catcher's throw back to the pitcher (or throw in attempting to retire a runner) and, in the umpire's judgment, there is no intent on the part of the batter to interfere with the throw, the ball is alive and in play.

Scott said he erred initially by calling time, but then remembered the rule. Once he did, "my interpretation was there was no intent and [Choo] wasn't out of the box. That was my judgment to make sure I had the rule correct, which we did. My judgment was then there was no interference, [Odor] scores."

After speaking with replay officials, Scott called over Gibbons and explained the situation, Gibbons issued the protest, and after an 18-minute delay Sanchez went back to work down 3–2, having allowed one of the most bizarre runs in recent memory. Choo struck out to end the frame, and the dome felt like a powder keg. "We were pissed," said Josh Donaldson. "Everyone was pretty upset about it. No one wants to win or lose a game in that manner." Added Buehrle, "If that's what it came down to it would have been ridiculous."

With some help from the Rangers, it didn't. Martin led off the bottom half with a grounder up the middle that shortstop Elvis Andrus booted. Kevin Pillar followed with a chopper to first baseman Mitch Moreland, who easily had the lead runner at second but bounced a throw that Andrus couldn't handle. Ryan Goins followed and he bunted right to a hard-charging Adrian Beltre, who fielded and fired to third base well ahead of pinch-runner Dalton Pompey, but a covering Andrus inexcusably dropped the ball. Everyone was safe, leaving the bases loaded. Ben Revere followed by hitting into a fielder's choice before Sam Dyson came on to face Donaldson, who flared a ball just over Odor's head at second base, allowing the tying run to score. The Rangers still got an out at second as Revere had to hold up in case

Odor made the catch—it's a play he should have made, even with the infield in—leaving men on the corners for Jose Bautista. A 98 mph sinker was fouled off for strike one, another 98 mph fastball was low for ball one, and then Dyson tried to go in with another 98 mph sinker—only this one stayed up, Bautista turned on it, and the Rogers Centre shook as the ball smacked the facing of the second deck in left field.

The rest is the stuff of GIFs, memes, and opportunistic T-shirt makers. Bautista, snarling, stared forward, whipped his bat, and circled the bases—an iconic image destined to be a highlight-reel fixture like Carlton Fisk waving his 12th-inning, walk-off homer fair in Game 6 of the 1975 World Series and Joe Carter kangaroo-hopping his way around the bases after winning the 1993 World Series with his Game 6 homer. Bautista smacked hands with Goins at home, did a double-five with Donaldson, flexed his biceps with Encarnacion, chest-bumped Stroman, slapped hands with Martin (who later clasped his hands to the sky in gratitude), hugged Chris Colabello, and then stomped his way through the dugout.

On the mound, Dyson took exception. Even as more trash rained down and Encarnacion, the next batter, raised his arms in an attempt to urge calm, the pitcher seethed. As they waited for calm to be restored, he walked to the plate and began barking at Encarnacion, who turned around confused, took in what was being said, and then angrily waved him away. "I told him that Jose needs to calm that down, respect the game more," Dyson explained later. The dugouts cleared, angry words were traded and eventually order was restored. "This has just been a crazy half inning. Emotions are at the all-time high," Harold Reynolds said on the FOX Sports 1 broadcast, and he was spot on.

Encarnacion and Colabello followed with singles before Troy Tulowitzki popped out to end the frame, but even that couldn't pass without incident. Dyson charged to the plate to cover home as the ball was caught, and once it settled in Gimenez's glove, he tapped Tulowitzki on the backside. He meant it to be a friendly sign of respect, but Tulowitzki wasn't having it. He turned around, asked him what he was doing, and the dugouts emptied a second time. "It was just a nice gesture on my part," said Dyson. "That's what I thought."

The seventh inning lasted 53 minutes. Sanchez came back out for the eighth, left with one out and two on, and rookie closer Roberto Osuna proceeded to strike out four of the five batters he faced to close out one of the most exhilarating victories a team can experience. "It was unbelievable competition," said Bautista. "Everybody was trying to win for their team, and you see it on a slide at second base, a reaction after a strikeout, a reaction after a base hit, and that's what baseball's all about. Just play with your heart, play with emotion, and just try to win."

The clubhouse celebration afterward was an emotional release from all the stress, which spiked exponentially during the seventh inning. "I've never seen anything like that, that whole inning, in 19 years of playing," said R.A. Dickey. "I was talking to Buehrle and even he's never seen anything like that. That's almost 40 years of experience between us." The game defied reason and explanation, turning from an event into an experience, a seminal moment that people will brag about attending decades down the road. "The game of baseball, if you try to figure it out you'll drive yourself crazy," said Donaldson. "You look at what happened, there are a lot of crazy people out there."

34

DEVO'S CATCH AND THE TRIPLE PLAY THAT WASN'T

The catch portion of the greatest defensive play in Toronto Blue Jays history is sheer artistry: Devon White gliding back gracefully in pursuit of David Justice's drive to deep centre field, leaping at the warning track, snaring the ball on the backhand, splattering against the wall, and holding on after impact. The context surrounding the epic grab ensures its magnificence is timeless. It happened in Game 3 of the 1992 World Series, and led to a double play that should have been a triple play, with the score 0–0. Yet underappreciated are the flawlessly executed subtleties that allowed it to happen: White's perfect read, landing, and immediate relay to Roberto Alomar in short centre; the second baseman's laser to John Olerud at first base; the subsequent dart across the diamond to Kelly Gruber at third; and, at the end, right fielder Joe Carter and Alomar backing up Manny Lee at second, with White charging in behind them. Every little detail was textbook perfect.

"The catch was a big deal, but what transpired after the catch was even better," said White. "And that's what I preach to young guys: know where to throw the ball, hit the cutoff man. And the way the ball was thrown around, that shows you how professional we were. Not missing the cutoff man. Robbie throws a strike to Olerud, Olerud throws a strike to Gruber. You don't see that very often at this stage of the game anymore. It just seems like guys are constantly missing the cutoff man, and those were things that were embedded in us from the way we played as a unit. I would go over to whoever it is and say, 'Hey, you've got to hit that cutoff man. You've got to make that play.' We governed each other."

The benefits of their discipline showed up on that play, a pivotal one in a game that helped swing a World Series tied 1–1 against Atlanta in the Blue Jays' favour. Juan Guzman and Steve Avery held both offences in check through the first three innings when the speedy Deion Sanders opened the fourth by beating out a little squib to the pitcher's mound. Terry Pendleton followed with a line drive over Alomar's head at second, bringing up Justice, who turned on the first pitch and spanked it to deep centre.

Off the bat White, shaded ever so slightly to the left-handed hitting Justice's pull side, turned to his right, put his head down, and began running to the spot where he believed the ball would land. That allowed him to pick up more speed and make up more ground than if he'd had his head up the whole time. Twice during his run back to the wall he peeked up to adjust his path, setting himself up for a leap on the track. Once there, he was in good position to cover the remaining gap with a jump. "I was always able to take my eyes off the ball and know where the ball is going to come down, because that's something I practised most of my career, just being able to run with my head down to a spot and look up and pick it up," said White. "When you're getting to the track and going full speed, it's like a point of no return, you have to go all out, and that's kind of what I did. It's just like, if it's going to hit the wall and I miss it, so be it. But I'm not going to get caught in between playing it off the wall. Knowing my environment, I knew it's not a critical moment where I'm going to get hurt because the wall is padded. So there's hope I hit it on the soft spot instead of the metal behind it."

His glove hand, raised above his head, cushioned the impact as the rest of his body met a soft spot on the wall. On his way down to the ground, he spun to land facing the infield, took one step, and fired the ball to Alomar instantly, knowing that Sanders was on second and fearing he would try to tag up and score. "For the hell of me, I can't remember how I got it to the infield that quick," said White.

Atlanta was shocked that White had caught the ball at all. While Sanders played it a bit more cautiously on the base paths by stopping and breaking back, Pendleton did not, flying past his teammate on the way to third. The miscue led to an automatic out, even though he ran back to first. Alomar didn't realize that, collecting White's relay, and immediately fired to first to ensure the second out. As he did that, Sanders inexplicably decided to try and take third, and was out by at least 40 feet when Olerud fired to Gruber. Sanders stopped and ran back to second as Gruber chased him down. But rather than relaying to

Lee, who had an easy tag, Gruber dove for the runner and appeared to clip him on the right heel as Sanders slid headfirst into the bag. Umpire Bob Davidson called him safe, a bewildered Gruber argued briefly to no avail, and the first World Series triple play since Cleveland's Bill Wambsganss pulled one off unassisted against Brooklyn in Game 5 of the 1920 Fall Classic never was.

It didn't end up mattering. Guzman proceeded to strike out Lonnie Smith to end the frame, the Blue Jays ended up winning the game 3–2 on Candy Maldonado's bases-loaded single in the ninth, and their first championship followed soon after. But the triple play would have been gravy. "I'll take what we have," said White. "We have a banner, we have a trophy, and we have rings."

35

FRANCHISE ICON: JOE CARTER

Let the new-age revisionists debate Joe Carter's merits, point to his WAR and OPS, and argue that his numbers really weren't all that elite, especially given the lineup that surrounded him. The first World Series championship for the Toronto Blue Jays ended with the ball in his glove. The second finished with a ball off his bat. During big moments, he was there. He delivered. Without him the only two titles in franchise history probably wouldn't have happened. That's why his name is on the wall at the Rogers Centre. That's why it belongs there. "Every time I come back here they still talk about it," Carter said of the magic from 1992 and '93. "It's been a love affair from day one and it'll always be that way. Toronto... is like a second home to me."

As well it should be, given the mark Carter left during his seven seasons with the Blue Jays, and his enduring popularity within segments of the fan base who bore witness to his exploits. It's worth remembering that when he was acquired with Roberto Alomar from the San Diego Padres on December 5, 1990, in a deal that literally caused gasps when it was announced at baseball's winter meetings, a lot of fans weren't sure what to think. Gone were slugger Fred McGriff and beloved shortstop Tony Fernandez, two players who grew up in the organization and became big-league stars. Alomar was a talented youngster at second who was relatively unknown on a national level, and Carter was an outfielder with a track record of driving in runs, more than anything else.

Some of the initial reviews of the deal weren't particularly encouraging, either. "I think it's a very good trade in favour of San Diego," Boston Red Sox general manager Lou Gorman told reporters at the time. "McGriff is a bona fide 30-home-run hitter and Fernandez is an outstanding shortstop." Pat Tabler, who signed with the Blue Jays as a free agent the previous day, remembers thinking, "What? They traded McGriff and Tony Fernandez?" Add in that Carter would replace

George Bell, who left for the Chicago Cubs via free agency and both he and Alomar were stepping into a difficult situation.

"I was disappointed I was traded, but, once I got over the initial shock, I told my wife, 'Look, we're going to Toronto. This place is awesome. You got all those fans, you'll absolutely love it, and it's going to give me a chance to win a world championship,'" said Carter. "That was the epitome of what a baseball player wanted to play for. So I knew coming in we would have a chance to go to a lot of playoffs, and it happened my very first year, in '91. We won the AL East, but we got beat in the ALCS. And then it kept getting better and better and better. Coming in my expectations were to win a world championship, and winning those two world championships was great."

The second overall pick in the 1981 draft by the Chicago Cubs, Carter was already well acquainted with big deals by the time the blockbuster with the Blue Jays went down. In June 1984, the Cubs included him as part of a seven-player deal with Cleveland that netted Rick Sutcliffe. Then on December 6, 1989, Cleveland sent him to the Padres for catcher Sandy Alomar Jr., infielder Carlos Baerga, and left fielder Chris James.

It was in Cleveland that Carter became an everyday big-leaguer, playing in 143 games in 1985 before really breaking out in 1986 when he slashed .302/.335/.514 with 29 homers and 121 RBIs, a career best he matched in 1993, and 200 hits, his only time reaching the plateau. Tabler and Carter were both in the Cubs' system together before reconnecting in Cleveland, and the first time they met, Tabler remembered, "Joe was playing Space Invaders at the team hotel."

"He was very talented," he continued. "In Chicago, his swing was very long and he had to go to the minor leagues, obviously, and find his game. Then in Cleveland, when we traded Rick Sutcliffe for him, he came and [manager] Pat Corrales said, 'You're going to be our guy.' He put him in the lineup and he was a run producer."

What Carter learned during that time is something Cito Gaston preached over and over to all his hitters: have a plan in the batter's box and keep your cool. That mind-set helped Carter enjoy a slight uptick from his overall slash line (.259/.306/.464) to his slash line with runners in scoring position (.271/.338/.467) over his career.

"I would say I was a little bit the same, but I knew that pitchers were different," Carter said of hitting with runners in scoring position. "I knew they were going to pitch me different with guys on base. I knew that as soon as I came up, the first thing that comes their mind is, 'Good RBI guy. Don't let him beat you.' So now the pressure's on them because they're thinking that 'I can't let this guy beat me.' That's a negative thought. My thinking was, 'You have an opportunity. This is what I thrive on, he's worried about me.' So I just reversed the pressure, and I knew he's trying to hit his spots and make the perfect pitch. You may make the perfect pitch once, but you can't do it two or three times. If you did it with one strike or no strikes, then you're kind of at my advantage. So I just turned the tables."

Riding that approach at the plate, "he was a bona fide All-Star" in Tabler's eyes by the time Pat Gillick traded for him. Fittingly, Carter earned All-Star honours in each of his first four seasons with the Blue Jays, four of his best in a 16-year career, while mostly batting third. His performance in 1991 may have been the most complete of the bunch, as he played in all 162 games, and slashed .273/.330/.503 with 33 homers and 108 RBIs, while adding a career-best 42 doubles plus 20 stolen bases (it's often forgotten Carter posted a 30-30 season with Cleveland in 1987). A solid showing against the Minnesota Twins in the five-game loss in the American League Championship Series—he hit a homer, two doubles, and drove in four—followed.

The next year, Carter slashed .264/.309/.498 with 34 homers and 119 RBIs in 158 games, adding three homers and six RBIs in the 12 postseason games en route to the franchise's first World Series title. He was at first base in Game 6 at Atlanta to catch Mike Timlin's relay when Atlanta speedster Otis Nixon bunted into the game's final out, leaping into teammates' embraces once the title was clinched.

Just like that, however, free agency hit and Carter nearly leapt to the Kansas City Royals, who had pursued him aggressively that fall to try and bring him home. Carter's wife, Diana, is from the area and they lived there. He was on the verge of accepting when he dreamed of Devon White at the dome and awoke to the chirping of birds. "When the Lord shows me the way, then I'd decide," Carter told the *Kansas*

City Star in 2013. "Then I had the dream, and I woke up and saw blue jays in my backyard, and I knew. That's how it happened."

That White was involved was in a sense fitting since Cleveland considered sending Carter to the Angels for White and infielder Johnny Ray before they instead traded him to the Padres. Oddly enough, a year later he went from being traded for one Alomar to being swapped with another.

Regardless, only the second home run to ever end a World Series came that close to never happening—but unfortunately for Mitch Williams and the Philadelphia Phillies, Carter stayed and came up in Game 6 of the World Series in Toronto, lining a 2–2 breaking ball over the wall in the left-field corner for an 8–6 win. If Carter needed any affirmation that he made the right choice, *boom*.

"I mean, to be at first base and catch the last out, I thought that was great," said Carter. "A year later, signing as a free agent to come back, and to do it one step better, do it with the bat this time, and with a home run that's only been done twice in the history of the game, it's awesome."

So too was his tenure with the Blue Jays, even if the team's fortunes slipped during the back end of his stay. Carter's numbers remained steady—he drove in at least 102 runs in six of his seven years in Toronto—but without a sufficient supporting cast around him, it didn't really matter. He signed with the Baltimore Orioles for the 1998 season, lured by Gillick, but faded. He was dealt to the San Francisco Giants that July 23, and finished out his career with two months by the bay. The next summer, Carter and Gaston became the club's third and fourth members of the Level of Excellence, a fitting place, no matter what the modern analytics say.

36

THE TRADES FOR DAVID CONE AND RICKEY HENDERSON

On July 31, 1993, Paul Molitor experienced one of the perks of being in baseball's upper crust. That night the Toronto Blue Jays, trying to lock down yet another division title, acquired the greatest leadoff hitter of all time—Rickey Henderson, from the Oakland Athletics—just ahead of the trade deadline. Molitor was ecstatic. A year earlier, he could only watch with envy when on August 27 the Blue Jays picked up ace David Cone from the New York Mets in an effort to seal the deal in a tight American League East race. After 15 seasons of toiling away for the Milwaukee Brewers, where such luxurious midseason splurges were far out of reach, a taste of the high life with Toronto was something to savour.

"We didn't have a lot of chances in Milwaukee, but when we did we rarely did anything. It was just kind of the way it was with the market," said Molitor. "The only time [a deadline move was made] in Milwaukee, we traded for Don Sutton in 1982, which was a big addition. But I've seen other teams go out for a long time and make valuable acquisitions late, and I almost learned to use it as motivation that, 'I don't care what they do, or who they are, we're going to try to win with what we have.' So you're almost prideful on that a little bit. But coming over here after the '92 experience, we were in it for a while there, and Toronto did what they did and they went on to win. And then I was here. I saw how making a change, adding a Rickey Henderson, what it can do to bolster a team. And it was nice to be a part of a team that was willing to go out there and make that kind of bold move to go ahead and try to put you over the top."

Those kinds of deals were par for the course for the Blue Jays back in the day. In 1985, general manager Pat Gillick added Al Oliver and Cliff Johnson prior to the trade deadline. In 1987 he picked up Juan Beniquez and Mike Flanagan. In 1989, Mookie Wilson and Jim Acker helped push the Blue Jays over the top. In 1991, Tom

Candiotti, Cory Snyder, and Candy Maldonaldo were the big gets. The acquisitions of Cone and Henderson, however, were by far Gillick's finest and boldest season-finishing touches.

The Blue Jays led the Baltimore Orioles by just 2½ games with the Brewers 5½ games off the pace when they acquired Cone for infielder Jeff Kent and outfield prospect Ryan Thompson. While the former ended up having a Hall-of-Fame calibre career, it was the latter Gillick was hesitant to trade. Still, the chance to pick up someone of Cone's talent in August, when players must first pass through revocable waivers in order to be traded, was rare. He wasn't willing to let it pass. "That was a funny deal," said Gillick. "Once in a blue moon a guy will slip through waivers, and he slipped through. We made a call and they came back to us and said, 'Well, we would be prepared to move Cone, but this is what the deal has to be.' You know, 'We're not going to negotiate if you aren't prepared to do this deal.' To me [Cone] kind of put us over the hump and got us where we had to go."

News of the trade was stunning. "I was walking to breakfast with my wife and somebody out on the street said they just heard the Blue Jays traded for David Cone," recalled Pat Tabler. "I'm like, 'Oh my gosh, they're serious about winning this.' It was like a bolt of lightning went through the clubhouse and everybody was like, 'We're not trying to just win the division, we want to win the whole thing.'"

They ended up needing Cone to do both. However, his time with the Blue Jays started inauspiciously. He joined the team in time for a 22–2 drubbing by the Brewers. And the next day he gave up seven runs in 6⅔ innings in a 7–2 loss. "He was like, 'What did I get myself into coming over here?'" quipped Tabler. Then Cone went 4–2 in his next six starts, the Blue Jays managed to fend off the Brewers (who closed out the season with a 17–5 run that pulled them within two games with three to play), and then the team won three of Cone's four playoff starts en route to a World Series title.

Molitor was on the wrong end of things that time, but after joining the Blue Jays as a free agent that off-season, he relished what Henderson did for the team. (Steve Karsay and Jose Herrera were sent to Oakland for Henderson.) The top of the American League East was crowded when he arrived, as the Blue Jays and New York Yankees were tied for the lead and the Boston Red Sox were only 1½ games off the pace.

Despite the banner acquisition, integrating Henderson was a delicate piece of business, since he would disrupt WAMCO atop the batting order. Manager Cito Gaston was sensitive to his players and sought their insights about a new batting order. White, who'd been the team's leadoff hitter since his acquisition from the California Angels on December 2, 1990, appreciated the overture. "It was definitely a respect to his players," said White. "I don't think any of us had any issues with Henderson coming over here and leading off. Cito said to me that it's going to affect me the most because I have to move out of the leadoff spot. And my comment was, 'It doesn't matter as long as we continue to be successful and do what we were doing.'"

For the most part, what the Blue Jays did was bat Henderson leadoff and bump WAMCO down one spot, with Alomar and Molitor swinging between batting third and sixth, depending on whether a lefty or righty was on the mound. Gaston's preference was for as little disruption as possible. "You like to keep guys where they're comfortable," he explained. "As a player, when I played there was a restriction in the way you'd wear your uniform and just a little thing like that, where if to me you're not comfortable in the way you look, it can affect you in other ways. So my thought was I wanted to make sure these guys felt comfortable about where I was going to put them in the lineup. They pretty much came back [to me] with the lineup I was thinking."

Despite staying the course, the Blue Jays couldn't shake the Yankees until a nine-game win streak from September 10 to 21 put the division out of reach. Henderson then proceeded to help Toronto claim a second straight World Series title.

"We were going to win a division both times, and it was almost like, 'How did we pull those guys out of the hat?' because they were some of the best," said Jack Morris. "David Cone was a huge part, and he pitched some big games down the stretch for us.... Then when we got Rickey late, it was like, 'Oh my God, [our opponents] have no chance now.' They were unbelievably talented teams, not only on paper, but they went out and showed it and they proved it every day."

37

JACK MORRIS AND PAT HENTGEN WIN 20

The win stat for pitchers is considered meaningless in many baseball circles these days, particularly among those on the evaluative side of things, where the emphasis has shifted to measures directly within a hurler's control. Logically, that makes sense. A starter can surrender 10 runs over five innings and still get a win, or can give up a single run over nine innings and lose. The decision tells you nothing beyond the game's result. Still, there's an intangible meaning to earning a win that carries weight for pitchers. Sure, having a low WHIP and a strong ERA mean a pitcher is contributing to his team, but at the end of the day it's the victories that count, and a win in the decision column means a win for the club.

That's why becoming a 20-game winner remains such an enduring mark of status. Wins are becoming increasingly harder to get for starters in this age of monitored workloads and specialized bullpens, and anyone who reaches the plateau has done lot of things right. You don't get there by accident, and you don't get there if you aren't worthy. And even if you are worthy, it still may not happen.

The Toronto Blue Jays can certainly attest to that. It wasn't until their 16th season that they boasted their first 20-game winner, despite a decade of dominance from Dave Stieb. That Jack Morris, a free-agent mercenary signed to help get the team over the hump in 1992 after tormenting the organization for years, became the first pitcher to reach 20 always seemed somewhat out of place. The honour should have belonged to Stieb, who topped out at 18 wins in 1990 and three times won 17. It didn't happen for him, underlining the random element attached to the stat. In 1996, Pat Hentgen would become the first homegrown Blue Jays pitcher to reach 20 wins, an achievement that felt more rewarding. But it was Morris who delivered the milestone first, during his penultimate regular-season start of the '92 campaign, when he threw six shutout innings in a 12–2 thumping of the New

York Yankees in the Bronx. (Stieb was on the disabled list at the time, his last pitch of the season coming August 8, when the Detroit Tigers clubbed him.)

"It was unfair," said Morris. "Dave Stieb was a great pitcher here, he's on that Level of Excellence and he deserves to be, but he was hurt that year, and he took a lot of ribbing, which I didn't really like. As much as I battled him as an opposing pitcher, I was looking forward to his contribution and wanted him to be healthy, and he took a lot of heat because he wasn't. I know a couple of my teammates, and I'm not going to mention names, basically cheered me on to win 20, and it was more of an 'In your face' to Dave Stieb, which was kind of sad. I didn't like the way it came down."

Morris and Stieb traded a few barbs during the 1980s, when the former was the brash front man for the Tigers and the latter was the ace of the emerging Blue Jays. Given the rivalry that existed between the teams, and competitive nature of the two men, the bad blood is no surprise. "We wanted to beat the heck out of one another," admitted Morris. But once he signed with the Blue Jays—a US $10.85 million, two-year deal that at the time was the richest in team history—the animosity disappeared. Instead, his focus was on delivering the goods, which he more than did, going 21–6 with a 4.04 ERA while logging 240⅔ innings over 34 starts.

"I was proud of what I did," he said. "You know, you get a big deal and you want to make sure that you're not looked upon as somebody who shut it down, and I wanted to make sure I did everything within my means to do my best. And I think that I can look back and say I did just that. I took the ball deep into games and I had a great team. My ERA was a little bit high that year, but we had a lot of run support, a lot of great defence, and I ended up winning the 21 games."

A byproduct of the Morris signing was that Hentgen, an up-and-coming 23-year-old at the time, was pushed down the depth chart and ended up being relegated to the bullpen, where he went 5–2 with a 5.36 ERA in 28 games, two of them starts in 1992. He broke into the rotation during the 1993 season thanks to a Dave Stewart injury, pitching so effectively he forced the Blue Jays to keep him there. "It was hard to break in as a starter at that time," said Hentgen. "Pat Gillick could build pitching staffs."

Hentgen won 19 games that year, his emergence playing a pivotal role in the club's second straight World Series championship. He credits a spring training conversation with reliever Mark Eichhorn for helping to set him on the right path. "Our lockers were beside each other, he'd just pitched in a game, and I said, 'Hey, how'd it go?'" Hentgen recalled. "He said, 'It went well. I was wild in the zone.' And I said, 'Wild in the zone?' I remember driving home and thinking, I'm just happy to be *in* the zone. Man, I'm looking at this the wrong way. I need to start challenging myself in the box, as opposed to being happy about just being in the box. I was lucky my stuff was okay, I could be wildly effective in the box, but that was really the turning point for me mentally."

Things really came together for Hentgen in 1996, when he enjoyed his finest season in the big leagues, one that was rewarded with the franchise's first Cy Young Award. He made 35 starts that season, logged 265⅔ innings, threw 10 complete games, struck out 177, and won 20 games with a 3.22 ERA, all career bests. He closed with a flourish too, winning his final three starts and allowing just three runs in 23⅔ innings of work. Milestone win No. 20 came on September 29, the final day of the season, when he threw 7⅓ innings to beat the Baltimore Orioles 4–1. "You know what I remember from that September? I had a lot of innings and we weren't in the race," said Hentgen. "The last game of the year, Brady Anderson led off with a home run, his 50th of the year, but we won the game. I'm proud that I was able to stick it out there for 20 wins, and it's something I'll never forget. It's not easy. It's definitely a team achievement for sure."

38

SEVEN BLUE JAYS AT THE 1993 ALL-STAR GAME

Venomous boos rained down from the stands in Baltimore. Chants of "Cito Sucks" reverberated through Camden Yards. Cito Gaston sat in the dugout, shaking his head. The 1993 All-Star Game, a 9–3 American League victory over the National League, ended in controversy for the Toronto Blue Jays, as simmering anger at their manager's stacking of the roster with seven of his own players, and his refusal to pitch local favourite Mike Mussina, boiled over. The repercussions from that July 13 night are still felt in the way Midsummer Classics are handled today, with managers making sure to highlight hometown players, whether the game calls for them or not, lest they suffer a similar fate. And even years later, bitterness lingers. In 2008, when a reporter came earnestly to query Gaston about Mussina for a story about the right-hander, the rebuke was immediate. "Mike Mussina can kiss my ass—and you can print that."

To a certain degree, the malice is the lasting memory from that All-Star Game from a Blue Jays perspective, which is a shame. Coming off their first World Series championship, they came out hot in 1993 with one of the finest offences in team history. The top five hitters in their lineup, dubbed WAMCO—based on the surnames of Devon White, Roberto Alomar, Paul Molitor, Joe Carter, and John Olerud—blistered opposing pitchers. Pat Hentgen and Duane Ward were forces on the mound. Gaston, in charge of the American League club by virtue of his trip to the World Series the previous fall, made sure to take care of his guys. Others felt snubbed, but there are always All-Star snubs. To the victor go the spoils.

Alomar, Carter, and Olerud were elected starters in the fan vote. Ward, Hentgen, Molitor, and, most controversially, White were the additions, giving the Blue Jays a full quarter of the 28-man American League roster. No other team had more than two players. The predictable uproar ensued.

"Got a lot of heat for that, a lot of heat—but they all belonged there. They're all All-Stars." Gaston said defiantly. "Some people said I did it for their bonuses. I did it because they belonged there, and what they had done for the Blue Jays that year."

Regardless, the furor made for an awkward entry into the All-Star Game. So too did the 10 losses in 11 games the Blue Jays suffered on the way in. Add that they were hated in Baltimore at the time, in addition to the feeling that some of their Orioles should have been on the All-Star team, and the scene was toxic. Ward, a first-time All-Star, discovered that while walking to Camden Yards in the morning. A fan mad that Gregg Olson didn't get picked "was screaming at me," he told the *Toronto Star* at the time. "I told him, 'Hey, buddy, I got no control over that. I'd like to help you, but sorry.'" Ward would later find himself in the middle of a much bigger storm.

Two Orioles made the American League roster—shortstop Cal Ripken, elected a starter by fans and who would go 0-for-3 before Travis Fryman took over; and Mussina, a manager's pick who 11 days earlier came off the disabled list following a bout of shoulder soreness. Gaston also made a point of selecting Frank Thomas, left off a year earlier by Minnesota Twins manager Tom Kelly, and as a result, he had only nine pitchers. "I had a meeting with Mussina and Pat," Gaston recalled, "and I said, 'Mussina, you and Pat will only get to this game if it goes to extra innings.'"

By the eighth it was clear extra innings weren't going to be needed. Alomar hit a solo shot in the third that tied the game 2–2, and in the sixth White's RBI double opened up a 6–3 lead for the American League, and he later scored on a John Smoltz wild pitch to make it 8–3. In the seventh, Terry Steinbach's RBI double made it 9–3.

Gaston turned to Twins closer Rick Aguilera in the eighth and during that inning, Mussina began warming up in the bullpen, to the delight of Orioles fans. The problem was he was warming on his own—Gaston planned to use Ward in the ninth. After Juan Gonzalez struck out to end the bottom of the eighth, fans began chanting "We want Mike," and then booed Ward when he entered.

After a Gregg Jefferies strikeout and Tony Gwynn groundout, the boos got even louder when fans realized Gaston wasn't even going to give Mussina the final out. Ward proceeded to catch Mike Piazza looking to end the game, and the brouhaha began, Mussina telling reporters that he was simply getting his work in. "I was like any other baseball fan at that moment. I wanted to yell and scream, 'C'mon, let Mussina get the last out,'" Ripken told reporters. "This is a strong baseball town, a real Orioles town. The fans wanted to let [Gaston] know, 'We're going to come after you.' I don't think they're going to hold it against Cito until the day he dies, but I don't think they're going to forget about it anytime soon."

They didn't, and the ensuing vilification of Gaston in Baltimore even spawned a T-shirt emblazoned with Cito Sucks in Orioles orange and black. "My name's been booed in Baltimore ever since," said Gaston. "[Mussina] upset me because there's a lot of things said about me that weren't true. And it's not like I didn't tell him. This guy here knew what he was doing. I don't know why he would want to get up and throw. When they came in and asked him, he should have told the truth. 'Cito said I wasn't pitching.' I don't pitch Wardo? I got a lot of bad calls [at the hotel] whenever I went to that city."

The seven Blue Jays at the 1993 All-Star Game remains a team record. Five went in 2006, when Roy Halladay, B.J. Ryan, Troy Glaus, Vernon Wells, and Alex Rios all went to Pittsburgh. Managers Carlos Tosca, John Gibbons (twice), and John Farrell have served as coaches. None have inspired a spiteful T-shirt.

39

TOP
THREE HITTERS
IN 1993

From across the diamond, Paul Molitor had long admired John Olerud's swing. Short and quick with a perfect path through the strike zone, the stroke was art, a brilliant product of honed athletic ability, strong hand-eye coordination, and precise physics. After signing with the Toronto Blue Jays as a free agent on December 7, 1992, Molitor got his first look at Olerud's swing as a teammate at spring training in 1993, and became even more impressed. "I asked him if he ever thought about winning a batting title," recalled Molitor. "He was still a young player (24), and he was like, 'I don't run well. There's no way I'm going to win a batting title.' And I said, 'I really think you can.'"

Olerud proved Molitor right that season in a big way, winning the only batting title in franchise history with an average of .363. Ironically, the runner-up that year was Molitor, who finished 31 points behind, thanks in large part to a late-season swoon by Olerud. It didn't matter, the race had been over since June anyway. "Not only does he go on to win the batting title, he runs away with it," said Molitor. "I always joked that if I knew I was going to finish second, I would have waited another year to tell him."

Jokes aside, the achievement was made all the more special when Roberto Alomar collected three hits in the season finale at Baltimore to finish at .326, just edging out Cleveland's Carlos Baerga by .0009 for third spot. That left Olerud, Molitor, and Alomar as the first teammates to finish first, second, and third in the batting race since Billy Hamilton (.380), Sam Thompson (.370), and Ed Delahanty (.368) of the Philadelphia Phillies did it in 1893. The feat is so rare that the commissioner's office made up a special trophy for what it dubbed the once in 100 years accomplishment, a memento that sits inside a reception-area display case at the Blue Jays' offices, directly across from another prize bagged in '93: the World Series trophy.

Olerud, Molitor, and Alomar played pivotal roles in making that happen as three-fifths of the Blue Jays' famed WAMCO lineup, the American League's second-most-productive offence, with 847 runs. Big seasons were expected from all three, but Olerud's breakout was remarkable. It was by far the best offensive year of his career. "I'd not seen anybody hotter and it was a pleasure," said reliever Duane Ward. "We all sat there and marvelled at his swing, also, just saying, 'What's a pitcher thinking after getting through the first two or three guys and then having to face No. 9?' I mean, the guy was hotter than a firecracker and was that way all year.... To be able to sit back and watch it was nothing but awe-inspiring."

A third-round pick in the 1989 draft out of Washington State University, Olerud is among the small handful of players to skip the minor leagues entirely and go straight to the big leagues. He and Fred McGriff split time at first base and designated hitter in 1990 and Olerud took over at first the following year, when McGriff was sent to the San Diego Padres with Tony Fernandez for Alomar and Joe Carter. He batted .265, .256, and .284 in his first three full big-league seasons and, despite his sweet swing, he was best known league-wide for wearing a helmet on the field, a precaution he started taking after an aneurysm led to brain surgery in college. His reputation changed when he burst out of the gate in 1993, his average sitting at .458 on May 1, .400 on June 1, .407 on July 1, and .402 on August 1. Bolstering his national profile was a 26-game hit streak from May 26 to June 22, during which he went 40-for-92 with 22 walks, nine of them intentional, fuelling talk that he could deliver baseball's first .400 season since Ted Williams' .406 in 1941.

The focus on him—even two decades before the public's demand for content became insatiable—was relentless. "Olerud is one of the best young hitters I've seen in a long time. It's amazing how well he has handled the tension so far," sage Detroit Tigers manager Sparky Anderson told the *Toronto Star* that August. "But this club is in a pennant race. That's enough pressure for anybody without having the whole sports world watching to see if he's going to bat .400."

Olerud's batting average dipped under .400 for good after an 0-for-3 night at Yankee Stadium on August 3, his 106th game of the season. He batted only .295 over his final 52 games, with a still-healthy OPS of .857. His final stats looked like something out of a video game: a slash line of .363/.473/.599 with 200 hits, 54 doubles, 24 home runs, and 107 RBIs. He walked 114 times, a league-leading 33 of them intentional, against just 65 strikeouts. Afterward, he summed it up to reporters in his typically understated manner: "It was a busy year. There was a lot of stuff going on. There's not really one thing about it that sticks out."

Molitor, of course, felt differently. In 1982, Robin Yount (210), Cecil Cooper (205), and Molitor (201) gave the Milwaukee Brewers the top three hit totals in the American League, a feat no teammates had managed since Ty Cobb, Sam Crawford, and Bobby Veach of the 1915 Detroit Tigers. Twenty-one years later, he knew he was "part of something that was special."

"Those are two things that happen rarely," he said, "and I was fortunate to be a part of both of them."

40

FRANCHISE ICON: CARLOS DELGADO

The Toronto Blue Jays groomed Carlos Delgado to be next in the franchise's long line of homegrown superstars, a fearsome slugger to replenish the team's golden-era core. His first taste of the big leagues came in 1993, with the club at its peak. Soon, the team would crater. And when Delgado blossomed, the organization wilted, making him the first superstar of the Blue Jays' lost generation. From 1996 to 2004, nine seasons of elite production were squandered when a suitable supporting cast couldn't be assembled around him. "It was a big challenge in front of you," said Delgado. "You're competing with the Yankees and Boston and Baltimore, with a team that has a much smaller payroll. Obviously, when you're looking on paper, you try to be optimistic, but you know they seemed like better ballclubs. You still have to go out and work, and that was my approach. I wanted to go out and try to beat everybody. Sometimes you've got to play the hand that is dealt to you."

The imposing Puerto Rican with the welcoming smile and a gentleman's grace did precisely that, delivering at least 25 homers and 91 RBIs in each of those nine years. The Blue Jays never once finished better than third in the American League East. He bears no responsibility for that. In 2000, when Delgado hit 41 homers with 137 RBIs and an OPS of 1.134, the Blue Jays finished 83–79, a mere 4½ games out of the playoffs. In 2003, when he hit 42 homers with 145 RBIs and an OPS of 1.019, the Blue Jays finished 86–76, 15 games off the pace. And those were Delgado's best chances at the playoffs in Toronto. "Carlos and I would talk about what it would be like to make the playoffs here," said Roy Halladay, whose best years also weren't leveraged into a playoff berth by the Blue Jays. Both had to move on to experience the postseason, Delgado as a free agent after the 2004 season, Halladay via trade after the 2009 campaign. "I didn't feel like the team showed enough commitment to try to keep me, and I understand," said Delgado, who signed a $52 million, four-year deal with the Florida Marlins. "It's part of the business, so I moved on, and I can tell you today, like I said in that moment, I was very grateful for the opportunity. But sometimes the situation moves otherwise, and that was the case when I left."

The real shame is in the unrealized promise—from a team, not a personal perspective. Signed at 16 as an international free agent, Delgado is among the last of Latin American scout Epy Guerrero's great finds, and it was the team's history in the region that tipped the scales in the Blue Jays favour. A catcher at the time, Delgado points to the relationship the team then had with Latin ballplayers, with names like George Bell, Tony Fernandez, Manny Lee, Juan Guzman, and Junior Felix either on the club or in the system, as being a key selling point. While the money was there, "you're going to a different country, you're going to go speak a different language. You have a tough challenge ahead of you, which is going through a minor league system to make it to the big leagues. You want somebody that is going to give you a fair chance," he explains. "I'm not saying that other teams don't give you a fair chance, but it's nice when it's noticeable, because what does a kid from Aguadilla at 16 know about how 30 organizations work? But on paper it looked like the Blue Jays were patient and they had enough confidence to deal with Latino ball players."

Delgado's pro career started at low A St. Catharines, Ontario, in 1989. "We rented bikes to get to the stadium. Outside the clubhouse there must have been 20 bikes, $25 a bike," he recalled. And in the coming years he'd play alongside Guzman, Pat Hentgen, Ed Sprague, Shawn Green, and Alex Gonzalez, becoming particularly close with the last two. All of them were expected to eventually help turn over the big-league roster and keep the Blue Jays' winning ways going. "I remember my first year with Shawn in 1992 [at Single-A Dunedin], and our first year with Alex in 1993 [at Double-A Knoxville]," said Delgado. "That's all we talked about in the minor leagues, that we want to make it to the big leagues, and hopefully we can make it together, hopefully we can make an impact. And we pretty much made it all at the same time, and we all had three decent careers. It would have been nice to go into the playoffs and win a championship or win a pennant and obviously leave more of a legacy like George Bell and Lloyd Moseby and Tony Fernandez, but they had a better team."

Delgado appeared in two games as a September call-up in 1993 and then surprisingly broke camp with the Blue Jays in 1994 as a left fielder, a position he was playing for the first time. No matter. He clubbed eight home runs in his first 18 games and the move looked brilliant. Then a 15-for-82 slide with just one home run followed over his next 30 games, leading to his demotion to Triple-A Syracuse, where he resumed catching. "It was sort of crazy, but it was exciting, because I was in the big leagues," Delgado said. "Cito Gaston came up to me in spring training and asked, 'Would you rather play left field in the big leagues or catch in Triple-A?' We all know the answer to that. When they sent me down I knew I had some work to do. I went to Triple-A, and I remember the first game I had a terrible game. And I told myself, 'I will not play here any longer than what I absolutely have to. I want to go back to Toronto,' and I went to work."

During that time, Delgado focused on the tools he'd need to hit at the big-league level. The early homer barrage was a product of his raw talent, but he quickly realized ability and power would only take him so far. He worked to learn how opposing teams were pitching to him, how to maximize his swing to counter that, and ways to tailor his approach to his skills. Blessed with a good eye, he learned to walk too. Gaston's tutelage was vital. "He was very influential on what to look for, pick up tendencies, how these guys are trying to get you out," said Delgado. "When you're 22 and you have bat speed, it doesn't matter, you go out there look for a ball and try to hit it and you hit it. But when you're 32, 33, you don't have the same bat speed and then you just think, 'Well, I've seen this guy 20 times and last time he just pounded me outside. Why not look outside?' It sounds easy, but when you're in the heat of the moment, you have very little time to make adjustments."

The next spring, a bout of knee soreness during spring training led to a position switch, this time to first base. He understood that meant more time in the minor leagues, a fate he accepted since he wasn't going to learn the position in the majors. In September he was called up, and aside from injury rehabs, he never saw the minors again, playing 27 games at first in 1996 and 119 there in 1997 before taking over the position full time. "When I moved to first base, I committed to it and wanted to be the best I could. I worked my ass off," he said. "I wasn't a Gold Glover at first base, but I got better over the years. It was probably the best career move that I ever had."

While he was developing, so were the Blue Jays. Green and Gonzalez grew into building-block regulars; Shannon Stewart, Jose Cruz Jr., Chris Carpenter, and Kelvim Escobar broke through; and free agents like Roger Clemens and Darrin Fletcher were added to bolster the process. In 1998 the Blue Jays won 88 games but still finished 26 games behind the 114–48 New York Yankees in the American League East. They only finished four games behind the Boston Red Sox for the wild-card, but Clemens demanded a trade after the season, manager Tim Johnson's lies to players about his war-veteran past were exposed, and the Blue Jays spun their wheels while the Yankees and Red Sox engaged in years of one-upmanship on the free-agent market.

Uncertainty over the team's direction led Delgado to include the option to demand a trade in a $36 million, three-year contract extension in December 1999. That clause led to a then-record $68 million, four-year extension that was the first major move under the incoming ownership of Rogers Communications Inc. Still, a sideways 2001 led to the firing of general manager Gord Ash and a rebuild was embarked upon under his replacement, J.P. Ricciardi. As the payroll was cut into the $50 million range, Delgado's payroll hits of $17.2 million in 2002, $17.5 million in 2003, and $18.5 million in 2004 became a financial albatross, even as the team surged unexpectedly in 2003. But without the financial wherewithal to augment the roster, the Blue Jays instead rolled the dice on various free-agent flotsam hoping to bet right, biding time until Delgado's free-agent departure created the needed financial flexibility. He signed with the Marlins on January 26, 2005, a couple of months after Rogers purchased the SkyDome in a deal that created additional revenue streams for Ricciardi to work with. By the time he loaded up for a run at the 2006 season, Delgado had been peddled by the Marlins to the New York Mets, where he reached the playoffs.

"It would have been nice [to reach the postseason] in Toronto, but I can't say that it hurt, because I look back now, and being completely open-minded and neutral about it, we just didn't have enough to compete," he said. "I'm not saying we had bad teams. I'm saying that in those years, the AL East was what the NL Central is today. It was the best division in baseball. You don't want to admit it too much, because you're fighting those guys, but you look back and those were the times where those teams were loaded, and they were good."

Delgado played through the 2009 season, when a hip injury got the best of him, leaving him 27 homers short of the 500 mark in his spectacular career. On July 21, 2013, the Blue Jays added him to their Level of Excellence. He is undeniably the best offensive player developed by the farm system. There's a case to be made that he isn't appreciated the way he should be, likely because he never led the Blue Jays to the playoffs, but that's unfair. He's one of the best Blue Jays ever, end of discussion.

"Toronto gave me a chance to do what I love to do, that's play baseball, and the city treated me like family," said Delgado. "There are so many good memories and moments that I will always remember, from the most important game or the biggest accomplishment on the field, to having a security guard say 'hello' and giving you a hug. That's the most important thing."

41

TWO YEARS WITH ROGER

In December 1996, the Toronto Blue Jays picked Roger Clemens from George Steinbrenner's pocket. Two years later the Rocket forced them to finally put him in the New York Yankees' stable. In between, he delivered two of the most brilliant seasons ever pitched in Blue Jays history, each resulting in an American League Cy Young Award. Later, those performances were tainted by allegations of steroid use.

Such is the complicated legacy left behind from Clemens' short but eventful stay with the Blue Jays. Had the team fared better during the 1997 and '98 seasons, perhaps he might not have invoked a "handshake" clause allowing him to demand a trade, and finished out the $31.1 million, four-year contract he surprisingly signed to come north. Instead he forced general manager Gord Ash's hand, eventually leading to the February 18, 1999, trade to the Yankees, whom the Blue Jays had beaten out for his services in free agency. In exchange they got David Wells, Homer Bush, and Graeme Lloyd. The return of Wells led to another debacle after two solid seasons from the outspoken left-hander, who criticized the organization and ripped the team's fans. Shortly after, Ash traded him to the Chicago White Sox. Mike Sirotka, the primary piece coming back, arrived injured and never threw another pitch in the majors again. It's an ugly branch of team history rooted in the Clemens signing, which at the time triggered so much optimism.

The Blue Jays, back then, were trying to emerge from a rebuilding period that followed the back-to-back World Series championships in 1992 and 1993. Pat Hentgen, Ed Sprague, Carlos Delgado, Shawn Green, and Alex Gonzalez were developing into the team's new core. A quick return to prominence felt within reach. But interest in the team sagged, particularly after the 1994 players' strike led to the cancellation of the World Series. Then the club's ownership changed when Labatt was swallowed up by Belgian brewer Interbrew S.A. And the bold 1995 reacquisition of David Cone failed miserably. Clemens was looked at as someone who could reinvigorate the entire franchise.

Even better, signing Clemens meant getting the better of the Yankees and Steinbrenner, their larger-than-life owner. New York had just won the World Series and was looking for another title. The Boss personally visited Clemens at the ace's Houston home in an attempt to woo him. Things went swimmingly, and afterward he phoned Blue Jays president Paul Beeston to brag. "He'd eaten dinner with the family, he'd signed a lot of Roger's memorabilia because Roger has a great collection of that," Beeston recalled. "And I just took it all in because I knew that we were still in on the deal."

What Steinbrenner didn't know is that a similar visit November 20 from Beeston had gone just as well, if not better. When push came to shove, Clemens opted for Toronto. His agent, Randy Hendricks, told reporters at the time that Clemens had spurned more lucrative offers from two teams, one of them believed to be the Yankees. It was a stunning upset. "When we got Roger, I phoned George before we announced it," said Beeston, "and I said, 'Listen George, when we were down there we did some signatures too, except we got Roger's on a contract.' I can't repeat what he said, but I think he kind of admired the competition. He was in, we were in, we won, he'd lost, he wasn't happy, but at the same time it was okay."

Once the deal was announced, Clemens told reporters that Beeston's visit made the difference. "He sat on a chair in front of me and looked me right in the eye and said, 'They talk about Atlanta being the team of the '90s but did you know we sport one more world championship ring than they do?'" Clemens relayed. "I told Paul it was a point well taken. It sunk in with me that it could happen here again. He also made the statement that if July rolls around and we're where we're supposed to be, we'll do whatever we need to do to fill spots if it's needed to top things off. He said to me, 'We're going to get back to where we were.'"

That July, despite Clemens' best efforts, the Blue Jays unfortunately weren't where they were supposed to be. On the 27th, a five-game win streak came to an end with a 3–2 loss to the Kansas City Royals, leaving them 50–50 and 12½ games back of the American

League East–leading Baltimore Orioles. They proceeded to lose another five straight and eight of their next nine, never to be heard from again. Manager Cito Gaston was fired with five games remaining. While Clemens went 21–7 with a 2.05 ERA and 292 strikeouts in 264 innings over 34 starts, a nine-player blockbuster in November that had bagged Dan Plesac, Orlando Merced, and Carlos Garcia flopped. The Blue Jays finished 76–86, last in the division, 22 games back of the Orioles and 20 behind the wild-card-winning Yankees.

The next season, after a potential sale of the team failed, the Blue Jays tried to load up around Clemens, adding Darrin Fletcher, Jose Canseco, Mike Stanley, and Randy Myers. They hired Tim Johnson as manager, starting with a clean slate. Optimism abounded, but for three months they spun their wheels, taking off only after Stanley, Myers, Tony Phillips, and Juan Guzman were purged at the deadline. By then it was too late. Johnson walked into controversy after controversy, feuding with coaches and players. His credibility was undermined by lies about serving in the Vietnam War. Clemens, who went 20–6 with a 2.65 ERA in 234⅔ innings over 33 starts, grew wary of the dysfunction. Though the Blue Jays went 88–74, they finished 26 games back of the Yankees and four behind the Boston Red Sox for the wild-card.

In December, after more of Johnson's lies came to light, Clemens requested a trade. It didn't happen until the following spring. Speaking with reporters after his acquisition by the Yankees, he said of the Blue Jays, "For their sakes, I hope they get everything straightened out. We had a conversation with Gord Ash over the winter and he basically outlined to us that the team was having some problems. It was to my amazement when I was there how so many non-baseball things trickled down to the clubhouse and had an effect on guys."

Clemens helped the Yankees win the next two World Series while the Blue Jays treaded water.

About a decade later, former Blue Jays strength and conditioning coach Brian McNamee made allegations of steroid use by Clemens in the 2007 Mitchell Report, prepared by former U.S. Senator George Mitchell, probing the use of performance-enhancing drugs in baseball. McNamee said he began injecting Clemens in 1998, during their time together in Toronto. Clemens denied the allegations, later insisted before U.S. Congress that he never used PEDs during his long and storied career, and in 2012 was acquitted of perjury charges that were based on McNamee's testimony.

The outlook on Clemens' tenure with the Blue Jays had soured long before then, but it only added to the morass. On the one hand, his signing had been a bold attempt to try and revive a fading franchise and push it over the top. On the other hand, the "handshake" clause given him allowed him to bail out at the first sign of trouble—which is what he did, leading to a detrimental chain of events. The steroid allegations only made everything even more distasteful. Ultimately, the dysfunction of the time was merely a hint at what was to come, as the World Series years quickly gave way to two lost decades in baseball's wilderness.

42

VERNON WELLS' 215 HITS

Vernon Wells' place in the pantheon of great Toronto Blue Jays is complicated. A quick glance at the franchise's all-time offensive leaderboard makes it clear he is one the most dominant players the team ever fielded. The fifth overall pick in the 1997 Draft out of Bowie High School in Arlington, Texas, ranks second in hits (1,529), fourth in home runs (223), second in doubles (339), second in RBIs (813), third in games played (1,393), and first in at-bats (5,470). A three-time Gold Glove winner, he played centre field with a grace not seen at the dome since Devon White. And in 2003, he set a club record with 215 hits. He was an elite player for a long time—nobody flukes his way to those kinds of numbers.

Yet the love for Wells isn't there, at least in the way it should be. That's partly because the teams he played on never reached the postseason, but in large measure due to the $126-million, seven-year contract he signed following the 2006 season. That deal remains, by far, the biggest in franchise history. It eventually became the only prism through which his performance was judged, and neither injury nor good work in the community could change that.

When Alex Anthopoulos pulled off the stunning January 21, 2011, trade that sent Wells and the vast majority of the $82 million that remained on his contract to the Los Angeles Angels for Mike Napoli (subsequently flipped to the Texas Rangers for Frank Francisco, who in turn became a compensatory draft pick used on Matt Smoral) and Juan Rivera, the general manager was celebrated as a genius. With the team in transition at the time and building toward a new competitive window, the parting of ways made sense, and the financial flexibility allowed the Blue Jays to sign Jose Bautista to a contract extension that was pivotal in the build-up to 2015. Still, Wells deserves more appreciation than he receives and it's unfair to scapegoat him as the reason the Blue Jays failed to reach the playoffs during his tenure. Wells looked forward to helping Anthopoulos complete his rebuild;

it wasn't meant to be and he understood that, waiving his no-trade clause for the Angels deal to happen.

"As an athlete, of course you want to be able to win in a place where you spent so many years, but I'm one to look at everything the way it's laid out in front of you and understand through the good and the bad that sometimes it's not about what you want, it's the way things played out," said Wells. "I knew that in 2010. I was looking forward to coming in, playing for John Farrell when the organization made changes for 2011 and being a big part of that. I had talked to Alex over the course of the off-season and I had the feeling he was feeling me out on some things and I was answering accordingly. And when he brought the trade to me and told me, 'Hey, this is what we have,' I knew for the organization, if they were able to shed some of the contract, it would be valuable for them to move forward and make some of the changes that they wanted to make. For me, it was going to an organization in Anaheim that had a chance to win at that point. It was the right move, and whether you want to look back and say it worked out or didn't work out it doesn't really matter. We try to enjoy our time wherever we were, and you're in a place for a reason. I had the chance to be around some good young players and help them as they made their transition to the big leagues, and you try to find the positives in all situations."

Wells didn't always have that outlook, and before he broke Tony Fernandez's single-season hit record of 213 during an unexpectedly successful 2003 season that also included Roy Halladay's Cy Young campaign and what should have been an MVP award for Carlos Delgado, it took him some time to find the right mind-set. In 1999, he played in 24 games after debuting as a 20-year-old, but appeared in only 33 more big-league games over the next two years. He finally established himself in the majors in 2002, when he played in 159 games and hit the 100-RBI plateau for the first time. Those formative years were difficult and pivotal.

"The first time I got sent down I didn't handle it well. I didn't use it as an opportunity to understand what I needed to do to get better," Wells said. "I got to the big leagues at 20. I thought I had it all figured out and I sulked my first time in Triple-A [in 2000]. I went back to

Vernon Wells rounds the bases in the eighth inning of a two-homer game against the Orioles. (Frank Gunn)

spring training in '01, played really well again, and got sent down, and that's when I started to realize there just wasn't a spot for me. We had three guys that were fully capable of leading that outfield, and I handled the situation completely different. I went down to Triple-A, played well, and used that opportunity to get better. When I got called up in 2001, I played every day and tried to just show them that I was ready to be there on an everyday basis, and it happened after that."

The 2002 season was another period of transition for the Blue Jays, as Gord Ash was fired as GM following the 2001 campaign, J.P. Ricciardi took over with a mandate to cut spending, and the roster was aggressively turned over. Wells was a pivotal part of that new future alongside Delgado, Halladay, Eric Hinske, Orlando Hudson, Reed Johnson, and Josh Phelps. Veterans like Frank Catalanotto, Greg Myers, and Mike Bordick were sprinkled in around the group for the 2003 season, and while the pitching staff behind Halladay and Kelvim Escobar was a mess, the offence mashed its way to a club-record 894 runs, good for second in the American League. Behind the bats, a team with few expectations finished a surprisingly strong 86–76, even if they were outgunned by both the New York Yankees and Boston Red Sox in the AL East.

Batting third in front of Delgado, Wells was in the middle of it all. "Our lineup top to bottom was fun to be a part of," said Wells. "You knew guys were going to get on base, and if they weren't, you were going to get on base for the guys behind you. It was that way from the start of the season to the end. We had so much fun as a group because we knew each other so well. We knew who was hitting in front of who, because our lineup stayed the same pretty much the entire season. Having that continuity in the lineup was really a blast to be around, and we put up the numbers that not too many American League ballclubs could put up."

While critics would point to Wells' remarkable ability to make contact with a wide variety of pitches as a reason for his inconsistencies later in his career, in 2003 everything Wells touched seemed to touch green. In the opening month of the season he collected 29 hits, at the All-Star break he had 121, and by the end of August he was sitting at 180. From there he slowly started leapfrogging franchise giants on the Blue Jays' list of most hits in a single season. Roberto Alomar collected 192 in 1993, Delgado dropped 196 in 2000, George Bell had 198 in 1986, John Olerud put up 200 in 1993, and Paul Molitor delivered 211 in 1993. Finally there was Fernandez's 213 in 1986, a mark Wells matched against Cleveland in the series opener on the season's final weekend when he hit a ground-ball single to right field off Jason Stanford. He broke the mark the next day with an infield single to third base off Terry Mulholland in the first inning, and added a double to centre off the left-hander in the third, coming around to score on Mike Bordick's single to tie the game at 2–2. The Blue Jays eventually won 5–4, Roy Halladay throwing a complete game to earn win No. 22 on a milestone day for the entire team.

"It's definitely a neat accomplishment, especially with the names at the top of the list, when it comes to that organization," said Wells. "But at the time, having Carlos behind me, and knowing my role was to really get on base for him and allow him to drive in 145 runs, that was the fun part about it. I mean I really wasn't too happy with him sometimes when he'd hit a double and I'd have to score from first, I was far happier when he hit home runs and we could both jog around the bases. But that was more so the exciting thing for me, that I knew when I got on base, there were going to be runs being scored with the group of guys that were behind me." Wells scored 118 runs in 2003, the only time in his career when he reached triple digits.

Despite winning 86 games that year, the Blue Jays finished 15 games behind the AL East–champion Yankees, and nine games behind the Boston Red Sox, who won the wild-card. In 2006, the Blue Jays won 87 games but finished 10 back of the Yankees and eight back of the wild-card Detroit Tigers, while in 2008, when they led the league with a 3.49 earned-run average, they actually finished fourth in the AL East, 11 games back of the Tampa Bay Rays, and nine behind wild-card Boston. During the first decade of the 21st century, the Blue Jays never sniffed the postseason.

"If you go back and look, there were some of those seasons where our pitching was really good and we didn't support them offensively and vice versa. There never really was a season where we put it together," said Wells. "Whether it was due to injuries, or us not doing our jobs, we just never had that season, and you have to have that season where everything came together at the right time in order the compete in that division. We didn't have the depth to withstand some of the injuries like other ballclubs did, because at that time you had the Yankees and Red Sox, whose [rosters were] deep enough to have guys on the bench who could be starters on other teams. We weren't afforded that luxury."

Like Delgado and Halladay, Wells was a great player trapped in the wrong decade for the Blue Jays, with several great seasons, including a record-setting 215-hit 2003, lost in the dead zone of his team's mediocrity.

43

FOUR SEASONS WITH JD

Josh Donaldson hit the Toronto Blue Jays like a bolt of lightning. Upon arrival, his scintillating swing and truculent competitiveness transformed a team that needed his grit as much as the production that earned him the 2015 American League MVP. The mad 10th-inning dash and head-first slide home—popping up with his left arm skyward before leaping into the arms of Troy Tulowitzki—to beat the Texas Rangers in the 2016 American League Division Series became a signature moment. But his power began to fade when a calf injury the following spring truncated his 2017 season, leaving behind a haunting sense of what-might-have been. More calf problems in 2018 sapped what remained of the initial surge, and complicated a split that turned bitter all around.

The entire experience was mesmerizing and dizzying, a vertiginous ride from the euphoric highs of the 2015 AL East championship to the gutting anguish of a full-on rebuild. Roberto Alomar's five-year run in the 1990s is the only stretch in Blue Jays history comparable in terms of immediate, game-changing impact, tenure, and an emotionally fraught departure. In each case, the exit coincided with the dawn of dark days and hard times.

"Josh was the key guy in changing our mentality," said John Gibbons, the Blue Jays manager throughout Donaldson's four years. "He was a loud guy from the get-go there; he wasn't afraid to ruffle some feathers, that's just his personality. But he said all the right things, you know? He had the pedigree, the background, the mentality, and the toughness to back it up. He'd done it. He was vocal, and the team needed that."

Alex Anthopoulos, then the general manager, discovered all of that during their first conversation on November 28, 2014. Donaldson had just been jarred from a chill Friday playing video games by news that the Oakland Athletics had traded him to Toronto. Typically, Anthopoulos avoids inundating players he's just acquired with too much information. He prefers to let the trade sink in and allow players to acclimate at their own pace. On that call, he simply told his new third baseman how excited he was to have him and explained why he acquired him. "If there's anything you need, let me know," Anthopoulos said at the end. Before hanging up, Donaldson replied: "The one thing I know how to do is win. Ever since I was a kid I've always won. I've never been necessarily a great loser, but I don't want to be. You can handle it the right way as far as class is concerned, but you don't ever want to get used to that. My thing is I want to affect the clubhouse in a positive way. I want those guys in the clubhouse to not just believe in me, but to enjoy being around me."

For someone trying to transform a team that was continually less than sum of its parts, the message immediately resonated. Anthopoulos and assistants Tony LaCava and Andrew Tinnish had talked about changing the club's culture in their private box at Camden Yards as the Baltimore Orioles celebrated clinching the American League East against the Blue Jays in 2014. They felt their team might be more talented. But the tenacity and togetherness of the Orioles brought better results. "You want talent," explained Anthopoulos, "but you want those other components, too."

By focusing on talented players who were also good teammates and made winning a priority, the Blue Jays changed the heartbeat in their clubhouse. A bond between teammates developed that was so strong even veteran players earnestly said they had never before experienced anything like it. Russell Martin, another centre-piece of Anthopoulos' off-season makeover, and the midseason additions of Troy Tulowitzki (who immediately connected with Donaldson) and David Price only augmented a leadership core that included mainstays Jose Bautista, Edwin Encarnacion, R.A. Dickey, and Mark Buehrle. "The road to success has a recipe," said Martin, signed to an $82-million, five-year deal 10 days before Donaldson's acquisition. "One, you have to stay healthy. Two, you have to believe in what you have. Three, you have to compete and get the job done. Obviously, you need the weapons.... I've seen that be a winning combination throughout my career."

It was again with the Blue Jays in 2015 and 2016, with Donaldson as the team's pulse. "Once I had the key guys on the team who I felt comfortable with, I wanted to come out and be that guy, to be the lightning rod for them to talk to," he said. "I want those guys in the clubhouse to know I'm here today, it's good. It's almost like a persona. You want to take that façade of you're the guy to answer the bell each and every day. For the most part, I feel like I accomplished that. There were times where not everybody on this team felt great body-wise, physically, and for myself that was the case at some points. But you go out there and grind it out for your teammates. I think that's something that's changed, that it's become, 'Hey, I might be 70 percent today, but I'm going to go out there and give it my all for my teammates, and I'm going to do my best to help us win the game.'"

Josh Donaldson pops up after his slide home beat the Rangers in the 2016 ALDS. (Chris Young/The Canadian Press via AP Images)

Donaldson won the Blue Jays plenty of games, especially in that first season, putting up a good chunk of his gaudy numbers—a .297/.371/.568 slash line with 41 home runs and 123 RBIs—when it mattered most. He hit three walk-off homers, a club record; 28 of his homers either tied the game or put the Blue Jays ahead; 15 came in the first inning, regularly giving his team a jump. Defensively, he was relentless. His most memorable play was a dive into the stands at Tropicana Field on June 24—safety be damned—to catch a David DeJesus popper and extend a Marco Estrada perfect-game bid. In the dugout, his brooding, sometimes fearsome intensity repeatedly set the tone, and he demanded as much from his teammates as he did from himself. "The environment when I first got to Toronto was very individual-based," said Donaldson. "Like, 'Hey, I'm going to do this,' or, 'If I'm an All-Star, it's okay, and if we don't win, maybe we're not that good.' At the end of the day, on any team I've been on that had a chance to win, there are sacrifices to win that have to be made. One of those sacrifices is having communication between everybody so that the mindset is always on winning and has nothing to do with individual accomplishments."

Nothing illustrated that better than when, in May 2015, he made one of the more important declarations in recent Blue Jays memory. In the midst of a four-game sweep by the Astros, after yet another bullpen implosion led to a loss, he calmly told reporters, "This isn't the try league, this is the get-it-done league. Eventually they're going to find people who are going to get it done." Privately beforehand, he made the same point to some teammates—that what was happening wasn't good enough, and it wasn't to be tolerated. It was a mentality that became mantra. "At that time, we had a bunch of younger guys out there who were still trying to find their way and find their roles and how they were going to be a part of this team," said Donaldson. "What I wanted these guys to understand was that, 'Hey, we're not going out there trying to win, we're going out there expecting to win, and if we don't, that's not a good thing.' I needed the expectations of our team to be raised, and the bar to be raised, as far as what was going on."

Eventually, the Blue Jays collectively gained ground, carving out a new identity that carried through to the wild-card run of 2016.

Donaldson again was in the middle of the club's success, especially in big moments. In the wild-card game against the Orioles, his base hit preceded Encarnacion's walk-off homer. In the division series, he scored from second on a Martin grounder to short that the Rangers couldn't turn into an inning-ending double play. In the American League Championship Series, he gathered his teammates in a circle and spoke about playing their hearts out ahead of a 5–1 Game 4 win that, for a day, pushed back elimination. "You could see the intensity just by the look in his eyes," Martin said afterwards. "You could tell that nobody wanted it more than him today."

The same held true most days, but the trajectory of both the Blue Jays and Donaldson's time with them was altered in the spring of 2017. One morning early in camp he was doing a sprint drill and his right calf popped. Though he started the season on time, he reaggravated the injury 10 days later, returning only in late May. It took him a couple of months to get his legs under him, but over his final 50 games, he posted an eye-popping 1.108 OPS with 22 homers and 47 RBIs. That fuelled a surge that pulled the Blue Jays within three games of a wild-card spot on August 17, but too many injuries and too thin a supporting cast meant that was as close as they got. "I've never torn a muscle in my body before and to have a tear in my calf from doing an exercise that I probably shouldn't have been doing at the time, that's part of the learning process," Donaldson said after the season. "Learning what I need to do this off-season, and then build up to the point that I'm not just sprinting right away after I haven't really run in three or four months. It just wasn't the smartest of things."

Adding to the tension was that Donaldson would be eligible for free agency after the next season. About two weeks before the season ended, he told GM Ross Atkins that he wanted to talk. "I let him know where I stand and where I stand is: I want to be a Blue Jay," he said. "I love Toronto, I love playing there. By the same token, I understand their side of it and both sides have got to match." As things moved along, it became clear they did not. Donaldson took control of his training, working outside the team's high-performance framework. Meanwhile, the Blue Jays explored trades for the slugger before engaging on some extension talks. Early in the new year there appeared to be some momentum, but the discussions blew up after the gap between them turned out to be far wider than either had realized. Just before spring training started, Donaldson shut down the talks to focus on the season. "There really haven't been numbers per se, any definite type of numbers that have been thrown around," he said. "But we've had conversations about it and I just think that we are not quite there."

Given that the Blue Jays were headed toward a full-scale rebuild, that wasn't surprising. While they retained Donaldson in the hopes a low-percentile outcome in 2018 would propel them to one last postseason run with him, there was little belief it would actually happen. The opportunity to return a bounty for him at the trade deadline seemingly offered insurance to the Hail-Mary approach.

Though a 13–6 start suggested promise, Donaldson's season quickly went awry after a shoulder injury sidelined him 12 games into the season. The Blue Jays treaded water in his absence and seemed positioned to leap forward when returned in May. But he didn't finish the month, tweaking his left calf running the bases May 28 in Boston. "I don't think I injured it seriously at all," he said afterward. Unbeknownst to everyone, it was his final game with the Blue Jays.

Over the next three months, as the club's fortunes collapsed and a deadline sell-off neared, his rehabilitation was the subject of secrecy and constant conjecture. Slow progress and generic updates made it more suspicious. As July 31 approached, and J.A. Happ and Roberto Osuna headlined a six-player subtraction, teams also inquired about Donaldson. He hadn't yet played in a rehab game, so nothing got done. The August waiver period presented another chance to deal him, if he could get back on the field. Given that he had ruptured the calf during rehab, that was no certainty. Still, by month's end, he was ramping up. He appeared in rehab games on August 28 and 30 with single-A Dunedin in the nick of time to make him eligible for trade. He was shipped to Cleveland just before the August 31 cut-off. The man who helped transform the franchise and delivered two of the most productive seasons in franchise history returned only a player to be named later, right-hander Julian Merryweather, who debuted in 2020. "It sucks," Aaron Sanchez, who would be traded at the 2019 deadline, said after the news broke. "He put us on his back in 2015 and took us to the promised land. We understood what it took to win ballgames and what it took to get to that next level in terms of playing for a real season in October."

The predictable uproar followed. Some of the private acrimony between the player and club spilled out publicly. Donaldson hinted at disaffection with the club's high-performance department. Atkins pointed out that the club gave him the latitude to manage his own conditioning regimen. They also disagreed on how serious their extension discussions became. Atkins said the sides talked "at length." Donaldson countered that "there weren't really contract negotiations being had" and insisted dollar figures were never exchanged. Ugly didn't begin to describe it.

"I've told you where I was at from the beginning, I felt like being a cornerstone part of that organization for the last four years, that's where I called home and I wanted to be there," Donaldson said in Cleveland two days later. "The fact of the matter is, as a player, we can only control what we can control. I'm not authorizing decisions. What I can control is, after a decision is made, turning it into a positive and trying to do the best that I can to turn the situation into a positive one."

Donaldson's time with the Blue Jays was more than positive. For two seasons he was electric, jolting a franchise in need of a shock. Then, as he was limited by injuries, the charge fizzled out. That wasn't enough to obscure the flash of brilliance. But it was enough to make you wonder, under different circumstances, how much brighter it might have been.

44

JOHN MCDONALD'S FATHER'S DAY HOMER

They gathered inside one of the patient rooms at Lawrence+Memorial Hospital in New London, Connecticut, some leaning against windows, others seated in chairs, telling stories, just like normal. In his final days, Jack McDonald was surrounded by friends and family reminiscing about this day, arguing about that game, praising one team, griping about another. Shouts, yells, laughs, as always, although everyone understood time was running out. John McDonald, son of the longtime coach, umpire, and sports official, counted himself lucky to be there. He was told by the Toronto Blue Jays to stay as long as he needed, to be with his father until the imminent end.

The remember-whens flew fast and furious, and McDonald brought up the time he was in high school, working on a season without a single strikeout, when his team arrived at the ballpark for a game and there was no umpire. The coaches knew Jack's background and asked him to suit up. He did. During the game, the count went full on McDonald and on a breaking ball father rung up his son. It was his only K that year, and it still bothered him. So he brought it up for the first time, in a room full of Jack's fellow umpires. "Daddy, with everyone here right now, well, tell me you missed the call. You got overanxious," he recalled saying. "You didn't want to give your son anything when you rung me up when I was a freshman. You can tell everybody now, what was the deal there?" The elder McDonald sat up, gave a stern look, and replied, "Son, it was a strike then and it's a strike now," without an inch of give.

That was Jack McDonald—honest, demanding, and fair, no matter who was in the box. Those traits helped instill a determination in John that allowed him to become a beloved defensive whiz in the infield who played in 16 big-league seasons. He was so gifted defensively, watching him take grounders during batting practice was worth the price of admission alone. His limitations at the plate kept him from being an everyday player, but the assortment of acrobatics he employed to steal hits made him popular beyond his role at every stop. "Johnny's one of my favourite players of all time," said Brian Butterfield, the longtime Blue Jays third base and infield coach, now with the Boston Red Sox. "He exemplifies everything that you would want in a man and in a big-league baseball player." Countless others feel exactly the same way, which is why John McDonald's pinch-hit Father's Day home run on June 20, 2010—a mere five days after his dad died, fulfilling his final request—still resonates. Under any other circumstances, a garbage-time homer in a 9–6 loss midway through a mediocre season wouldn't be even a footnote in the franchise annals. But given the person and the situation, McDonald's rare long ball became one of the most touching and emotional moments in team history.

At the beginning of spring training that year, McDonald was at a restaurant eating dinner with his wife and daughter when his dad phoned with some news. In November, doctors discovered some issues with his liver and he had undergone some treatments, but a new series of tests determined that he had liver cancer, and it was bad—he had six months, maybe a year if things went well, to live. A tsunami of emotions struck. "Get home to Connecticut," McDonald thought. The next morning, he walked into the manager's office and told Cito Gaston along with coaches Nick Leyva and Butterfield what was going on. "Go home as soon as you can," Gaston told him. While the arrangements were being made, McDonald joined his teammates for a workout that morning. By then word had filtered out to Vernon Wells, Aaron Hill, and Lyle Overbay, three of McDonald's closest friends on the team, through trainer George Poulis. On the field during stretch, they could see McDonald was in distress. "I remember Vernon handed me his sunglasses and said to wear them during stretch," recalled McDonald. "I knew right then that I had a lot of people I could talk to, and that made it very comforting for me to go away from the club and to talk to people while I was away and then to come back."

During the off-season, McDonald and his dad decided to host another Father's Day event, a tradition they had started when John played for Cleveland, bringing a group of fathers to the ballpark for batting practice, brunch, plus a question-and-answer session with Jack. Planning another one after the cancer diagnosis was almost like setting a goal for Jack. "He knew he was going to have a battle, but he felt like he was going to come through on the other side and be fine," said McDonald. The Blue Jays set up an essay contest for admission to the event, the theme focussed on why people wanted to bring their dads to the Father's Day game. Holly Purdon Gentemann, the team's beloved manager of community relations, collated the 25 winning essays into a booklet she eventually gave to John. He still has it to this day.

As Father's Day approached, however, it was clear that not only would Jack not be well enough to attend the event, he might not make it that long at all. On June 4, McDonald again left the team to be with his father, spending day and night with him talking, reminiscing, enjoying one another as much as possible. The kibitzing over the high school strikeout took place during that time. And when the subject of the Father's Day event came up, Jack insisted that his son attend on his behalf. "I told him, 'I'm not leaving you. I'm not leaving you while you're still with us,'" recalled McDonald.

The visits from his many friends in local baseball, football, and basketball circles started to pick up, as did the stories, and the back and forth. "Basically we were just trying to bust each other's balls in the room," said McDonald. "I was like, 'What else you got for me, Dad?' And he said, 'I want you to hit your next home run for me. And I want you to cross home plate and I want you to point to me.'" This time, he wasn't joking. Things got quiet. "It was inevitable [what was] going to happen, and for him to say that, he could have said it to me, but he said it in front of 10 other guys. And we're thinking, at least I was, that it's pretty neat that he said that, but I'm like, 'I don't know, Dad. They're not that easy to hit,' and he's like, 'You know, that's fine, that's what I'd like you to do,'" McDonald remembered. "For my dad to ask that, he was always saying when you step on the field, you run hard, you try not to show anybody up, you try not to show emotion and if you do show emotion it's short-lived, do your job. So that was a bit out of character, but it sat in the minds of everyone in the room. I said, 'All right, I'll do my best. I don't know how long it's going to take.'"

Not long after that conversation Jack McDonald died, on June 15, after fighting cancer for nearly eight months. Three days later John delivered the eulogy at his funeral, a day after that he flew back to Toronto, and on the Sunday morning, Father's Day, he stood in for his dad at the event they both were supposed to attend. The Blue Jays offered him an out given the circumstances, but McDonald insisted on following through, meeting fathers and sons, listening to their stories of adversity and survival and of the bond they all shared through baseball. After all he'd gone through, it was draining. "But it was very therapeutic too," said McDonald. "It was good for me to see other people and just to do that event, because that's what my dad wanted us to do. To me, that was kind of like his wish."

On his way down from the suites level at Rogers Centre to the Blue Jays' clubhouse, McDonald felt good about things. The event went well, a game against the San Francisco Giants loomed, and though he wasn't in the lineup and hadn't swung a bat in a couple of weeks, he started to get dialled up to play. Before the Blue Jays hit the field, Gaston called a team meeting and invited McDonald to join him in the centre of the room. Everyone had signed a jersey with his dad's name on it as a show of support, and the manager presented it to his player. "After he handed me the jersey we talked a little bit, I spewed out of my mouth for a couple of minutes just about what it meant to me to be home during that time, and then to be back, and what it meant to be around them, being with the guys again and doing something that I love to do, that my dad loved for me to do."

McDonald was on the bench as Shaun Marcum took the mound against the Giants, trying to anticipate whether he might come in as a pinch-runner or defensive replacement. Through the first five innings, that seemed possible as the Blue Jays held a slim 3–2 lead, but then a five-run sixth opened things up for the visitors, they added two more in the eighth, and they were on cruise control from there. Gaston subbed McDonald in for Aaron Hill at second base in the top of the ninth. He fielded an Aaron Rowand groundout for the first out of the inning, and once David Purcey got out of the frame, he was due to bat second in the bottom half. Immediately, en route to the dugout during the changeover, his father's words popped into his mind.

"I was pacing up and down the dugout with a bat in my hand because I wanted an at-bat pretty badly," recalled McDonald. "Lyle Overbay looked at me and was like, 'What are you doing, man? You need to calm down.' And I said, 'I'm calm.' He's like, 'Relax,' and I said, 'I'm relaxed. I'm just going to go up there and go deep!' I remember us both kind of laughing and then getting ready to go hit." There was good reason to laugh, as McDonald had all of 13 career home runs to his name at that point (he retired with 28), which isn't exactly the type of track record that suggests a hitter should go to the plate looking to drive the ball out of the yard.

Fred Lewis opened the ninth with an infield single off Jeremy Affeldt, bringing up McDonald, and now his father's words were really in his ears, although he also managed to focus on the task at hand too. He recalled that Affledt's fastball had life on it, so he needed to shift his load back early. He remembers thinking, "If it's a heater, don't take it. You're not taking a heater. You haven't swung the bat in four weeks. Get the head out and try to hit one as hard as you can hit it." The first pitch was a fastball down the middle and McDonald fouled it straight back, just missing it. Still, the swing felt so good it encouraged him to keep hacking aggressively. For some reason, he felt comfortable in the box and ready to hit, which wasn't always the case. And then there was his dad. "I wasn't going to go down flipping it up with a lazy bat," he said, "I was going to swing it hard."

Affeldt's next pitch was a curveball and McDonald swung as hard as he could again, this time ripping the ball to left field. "I knew I hit it good but I didn't crush it," he said, "I'm running to first base and kind of watching it, and you think he's going to catch it, and then it keeps on carrying." He'd just rounded the bag when the ball cleared, pumping his right fist before settling into his trot, the crowd erupting. "Wow, I've got goose bumps," analyst Pat Tabler said on the Sportsnet broadcast. Still, McDonald's initial elation didn't last long, as the haunting finality of death hit him hard. "It was more emotional hitting second base and thinking 'That's it, that's what I wanted to do, and he's gone,'" he said. "It was also like, 'Wow, I can't call him here, and that really sucks.'"

By the time he rounded third, tears had welled up in his eyes, and one photo captured McDonald shaking hands with Butterfield, his head down so no one could see. He collected himself in the final 90 feet, pointed upwards to the sky with both fingers as he touched home, and then returned to the dugout, where he was embraced by his teammates. After he sat down on the bench, another wave of emotion struck and he ran off into the tunnel leading to the clubhouse, where he broke down. Wells and Hill were among a group of players waiting for him. "It was one of the more memorable moments of my career," said Wells. "To see him come back to the dugout with tears in his eyes, a lot of us had to leave because we were going to start crying with him. We just gave him a hug. It was one of those moments that you don't see too often in this game, and truly allowing your emotions to come out, that's something I'll never forget."

Said McDonald, "I just needed someone to let it out with and to be comfortable enough to do that with your teammates, who text you when you're away, 'Hey, how's everything going?' and they saw how everything was going right there, the emotion flooded right back over all of us."

Lyle Overbay struck out swinging for the final out. Without doubt it's the happiest loss in franchise history.

"The adage is, 'Whenever you try to hit a home run, it doesn't happen,'" said Butterfield. "Here's a guy who doesn't hit home runs, who wanted to hit a home run on that particular day for his dad, and he did it. It was divine intervention. Other than the World Series, it's the greatest moment that I've had or seen in the big leagues."

The home run was McDonald's first of 2010. He finished the season with six. "I think Johnny Mac is leaving out that later in his career he was trying to go deep all the time," Wells said, laughing. "The game was out of hand, and it didn't matter what the scoreboard read. When he walked up to the plate and went deep, no one cared about wins and losses. It was a moment you wanted to soak in. It was a special time for him, and we were all glad we could sit back and watch it unfold."

The emotions of the day still hit McDonald in the same way. He doesn't often discuss the home run, at least not in great detail, and when it crosses his mind he's filled with joy. "But I'd rather have my dad back," he said.

During spring training before that season, New York Yankees manager Joe Girardi had reached out to McDonald after learning of his father's illness, and the two had spoken on a couple of occasions. Girardi talked about how the best way to honour his father was in the way he lived his life, in the way he treated others and in acting the way his father raised him to act. The words comforted McDonald, as did the time they managed to spend together before the end, leaving him with no regrets.

"So many people pass away and you think I probably wished I would have asked one more question. What else would I have asked?" he said. "And I didn't have anything else I would have asked my dad. The home run was the ending of it as far as a lot of the things that we talked about. It was, 'Wow, I just did something else for my dad, and he's gone.' Not that many people get to do that."

45

FRANCHISE ICON: TONY FERNANDEZ

Alfredo Griffin could see Tony Fernandez coming long before he ever left the Dominican Republic. The young shortstop, then employed as a groundskeeper by the country's professional league, regularly dazzled when he worked out in the infield in San Pedro de Macoris. Griffin, a gifted defender in his own right, noticed immediately. "I saw him taking ground balls off the bat, with no shoes, no shirt, and like a cotton glove, and he just picked it clean," remembered Griffin. "I thought, 'Man, this guy's going to be a good player one day.'"

Indeed, Fernandez impressed all who saw him. Ray Knight was one North American player who regularly lent him some leather, and gave him some time. "I was known around the stadium because I used to use everybody's glove, whatever was available," said Fernandez. "Being around all those guys really helped my career." Eventually Fernandez, who died in 2020 after suffering from kidney disease, proved Griffin right and took his job with the Toronto Blue Jays.

The skinny beanpole of a kid signed by scout Epy Guerrero in 1979—the year Griffin was co-winner of the American League Rookie of the Year—could hit a little bit too. Fernandez sped through the Blue Jays' farm system, skipping Double-A entirely. His first taste of the big leagues came in 1983. He spent most of 1984 in the majors, though largely in a part-time role. In 1985 he took over as the everyday shortstop, with Griffin dispatched to Oakland for bullpen help. By the time his 17-year career came to an end, Fernandez amassed 2,276 hits, five All-Star selections and four Gold Gloves—the vast majority of it over four different stints with the Blue Jays. Not bad for a kid from humble beginnings. "He's in the minor leagues with us, and next thing I know he's knocking on the door chasing me out of there," said Griffin. "I went, 'Wait a minute.' That's fine. It felt good because I had a chance to move on, went to another organization. He stepped in and we were both in the big leagues at the same time."

Fernandez moved with a grace and fluidity that belied his gawky 6′2″, 165-pound frame. Defensively, particularly early in his career, he seemed almost to float from side to side, swallowing up grounders and flipping the ball to first in a single motion. Great plays looked routine, almost effortless. At the plate, the switch-hitter dangled his bat limply over his back shoulder until loading up and whipping the bat head at the ball with a short, compact stroke. His 213 hits in 1986 stood as the club record for nearly two decades. Once on base he was a threat to run, too, topping out at 32 stolen bases in 1987. And while he played with a flair that bordered on art, he played with an artist's whim, at times, as well. The most famous example of that came September 23, 1989, when he infamously missed an at-bat, Kelly Gruber leading off the sixth inning instead in his spot. "Tony, you know, he's either going to be late one day, he's going to try to go first to third when you shouldn't go first to third, he's going to try an inside-the-park home run on a double—there was always something happening," said centre fielder Lloyd Moseby. "We loved him. We laughed. We'd fine him in kangaroo court every day and he hated that. I mean, he hated getting fined. We weren't really fining him, we just liked to see him mad. He was a different kid, that definitely goes without saying, but we realized that different kid was just an incredible damn player."

Getting to that point wasn't easy. When he first came over to North America in 1980, reporting to Single-A Kinston in North Carolina at age 17, Fernandez fought loneliness and homesickness. He couldn't speak the language and struggled to communicate. His style of play also drew criticism, as happens too often when young Latin players enter pro ball and encounter old-school coaches. "I had managers screaming at me, saying I was flashy, but that was the way that I played," said Fernandez. "John McLaren was one of my minor league managers and coaches here. John told me this once: 'When you are yourself, you're one of the best players. You'll be a great player, just be yourself, smile, have fun. That's the way you should play the game.' I was fortunate to have coaches like that in my career who understood my style of play. Latin players have to play like that. As long as you do what it takes to help the team win ballgames, go and do it."

Critical in helping him overcome his initial growing pains was Guerrero, who'd regularly check in on his progress up the ladder. The two had a bond that formed when they first met. Fernandez was 14 and had a bone chip in his right knee that turned off other scouts. Guerrero suggested he see a doctor. Fernandez's mother took him to an orthopedic centre in Santo Domingo, where he underwent surgery. His movements improved, and two years later Guerrero signed Fernandez before other teams knew what had happened. "The other scouts were scared because I had a cast and then a surgery," said Fernandez. Guerrero told the *Washington Post* in 1986, "the other scouts... told me I had just signed a *tullido*, a cripple. But I knew better." That's why when Fernandez first came over, it meant so much to him that "Epy was always with us."

"I remember we were some of the first [Latin] players to come through this organization," Fernandez added. "The trainers went out of their way to please us because they saw we couldn't speak the language, there was a cultural barrier. Now when I look back, those guys were like a godsend because we couldn't communicate."

Fernandez eventually learned to communicate in English, and to better navigate the new cultural waters. Still, there were challenges. He developed a reputation for being moody. His flights of fancy led some to conclude he was selfish. *Toronto Star* columnist Dave Perkins once described him in a column as a "chicken-hearted, self-centred clown." But he was also dedicated and driven, repeatedly coming up with different contraptions to use for stretching or on his bats to get the most out of his performance. "Latin players are different than North Americans. We are more emotional, we do not get things as quick sometimes as others," said Fernandez. "Baseball is a business, but for us it's a game and we take things too personal. By the time we realize they don't mean any harm, it could be too late, your feelings are hurt, and you carry that with you and that hinders your performance."

The only thing to hinder his performance early in his career was the Bill Madlock slide that led to a broken elbow at the end of the 1987 season, an injury that contributed to a Blue Jays collapse in the campaign's final week. He bounced back the following year to win another Gold Glove, slumped a bit in 1989, then delivered a solid 1990

Tony Fernandez looks on during a game against the Anaheim Angels in 1999. (Larry Goren/Four Seam Images)

season before the franchise-altering trade that sent him and Fred McGriff to the San Diego Padres for Joe Carter and Roberto Alomar. "I kind of knew something was going to happen," said Fernandez, who was at home in Boca Raton, Florida, when he got the news. "Nobody wants to be traded, it's always shocking to you, but it doesn't hit you until you're with another team. That's when you realize you're somewhere else. It took me a few days to digest the whole thing, but it was expected."

After two decent seasons in San Diego, the Padres traded him to the Mets—two days after the Blue Jays won the 1992 World Series. And on June 11, 1993, following a miserable 48 games in New York, he was sent back to Toronto for outfielder Darrin Jackson in an underachiever-for-underachiever deal. The trade worked out brilliantly for the Blue Jays, giving them a shortstop they needed at the time with Dick Schofield out for the season. While his defence wasn't the same, his .803 OPS over 94 games fit right in. "It surprised me," said Fernandez. "I didn't think I was coming back anytime soon, but I'm glad it happened."

There would be two other stints for Fernandez with the Blue Jays, one in 1998–99, and another to close out 2001, the last season of his playing career. Neither reunion was as successful or as fitting as the one in 1993, when alongside Griffin, the man he displaced nine years earlier, he celebrated a World Series title. "It meant a lot to me to be a part of the World Series because I felt like I represented the organization," said Fernandez. "Many of the guys from '85 weren't able to make it who deserved to be there. I'm sure they felt that by me playing that a part of them was in there. Like Pat Gillick put it, it was meant to be."

46

THE CANADIANS

The first Canadian ever to play for the Toronto Blue Jays was in the lineup on Opening Day April 7, 1977, batting eighth and playing third base. Dave McKay, a plucky infielder from Vancouver, went 2-for-4 in that 9–5 win over the Chicago White Sox, an auspicious start for a native son playing in his home and native land. Despite the promising opening, it took two decades for a local product to make a sustained impact on the field. Paul Quantrill of Port Hope, Ontario, developed into one of the game's most dependable relievers from 1997 to 2001, logging 383⅓ innings over 348 games with an All-Star appearance during that span. Third baseman Corey Koskie of Anola, Manitoba, became the most accomplished Canuck to have played for the Blue Jays when he signed a $17 million, three-year contract December 14, 2004. But without doubt the best Canadian ever to wear the uniform is Russell Martin, who agreed to an $82 million, five-year deal November 18, 2014. His .240/.329/.458 slash line, with 23 homers and 77 RBIs in 129 games, combined with the defensive value he provided in 2015, also gives him the most productive season any local boy has delivered for the Blue Jays, as he played an instrumental role in the club's sixth American League East championship. "It feels good," he said the day the division was clinched, celebratory cigar in hand. "I feel like I can really share with the fans how it feels. I remember '92, '93, and if we can just bring that back, that would be a dream come true for me."

Up until Martin's arrival, the best all-around run for a Canadian position player with the Blue Jays arguably belonged to Matt Stairs, whose short but sweet stay of 230 games from 2007 to his August 30, 2008, trade to the Philadelphia Phillies produced 32 homers, 108 RBIs, 100 runs, and 85 walks. The native of Saint John, New Brunswick, embraced every bit of playing at home, demonstrating the kind of modest blue-collar sensibilities that made him easy for fans across the country to connect with. "I'm a person that's very outgoing and is not afraid to go out to a bar and have a drink with fans," he said, "so I was right at home." And he played the game with the so-called hockey mentality some baseball executives and scouts tend to attribute to Canadians, competing with the type of hard-but-fair edge inherent in the most relentless of National Hockey League checkers. "We're laid back, we don't show a lot of emotion, we don't do the big bat flip, we don't sit there and admire home runs, and I think it's because we knew how hard it was for Canadians to get to the big leagues and we respected the road it took to get there," said Stairs. "I don't know if it's because a majority of us were hockey players. I think a lot of it has to do with how much we respect the game and other peers, but the bottom line is, don't piss off a Canadian."

Alex Rodriguez learned that the hard way during some of Stairs' most memorable moments in Toronto, in the midst of a feud that played out over several months of the 2007 season. The New York Yankees superstar triggered the bad blood during the ninth inning of a 10–5 loss May 30 at the dome, when he screamed "Ha" as he ran past third baseman Howie Clark, who was camped under Jorge Posada's two-out pop fly. Confused and concerned that shortstop John McDonald was calling him off, Clark backed away at the last minute and the ball dropped in. Instead of the final out, that "hit" triggered a rally that put the game out of reach for the Jays. McDonald exchanged words with Rodriguez afterward, and while no blows were exchanged, the Blue Jays were livid. Stairs, who was in left field that night, became all the more enraged once he returned to the dugout and learned the details of what went down.

"I remember my ears getting very, very red from being pissed off," recalled Stairs. "It wasn't what A-Rod did to Howie Clark—whatever, it happens, it won't be the first time, it won't be the last time—but what really pissed me off was that when John McDonald said something, A-Rod, quote, replied, 'Who the [expletive] are you?' That pissed me off for disrespecting another major league player. That's why I wanted to say something. Disrespecting another major league player, that's what I have a hard time with."

The Yankees scored twice more in the top of the ninth before the inning's end, and Stairs batted second in the bottom half, grounding out to second base against Mariano Rivera. But rather than simply returning to the dugout, Stairs rounded the bag at first base, looped wide toward the middle infield, and, as he crossed the diamond toward the Blue Jays dugout, directed a few indelicate adjectives toward Rodriguez at third base.

At that point it was clear that the discourse would be continued, and after a four-game July series in New York was uneventful, things heated up again when the teams met in Toronto in early August. Jesse Litsch threw behind Rodriguez in his first at-bat in the series opener, and, because he missed, Josh Towers made sure to do the job in the second game, clipping A-Rod on the left calf on the first pitch of his second at-bat. Rodriguez took a few steps toward the mound before home-plate umpire Angel Hernandez blocked his path, and both benches emptied. Yankees first baseman Andy Phillips blocked Stairs from getting at Rodriguez during the fracas.

Once the field cleared and the umpires conferred, things picked up again when Towers and Rodriguez exchanged words. Yankees first base coach Tony Pena intervened. Towers took exception. "I heard somebody chirping when I was talking to Lyle [Overbay, the Blue Jays first baseman] and I didn't think it was Alex and I asked who it was," Towers told reporters afterward. "Tony Pena is running his mouth off and I was like, 'What's this guy running his mouth off for?' This dude is a quitter. He managed a team and quit in the middle of the season because he couldn't hack it. He's going to run his mouth off? So I ended up getting into it with Alex a second time."

Stairs sat atop a cooler in the dugout, angrily staring out at the field afterward. "When it all happened the first time, [Rodriguez] was like, 'Stairsy, what's going on?' And I'm like, 'He hit you because you're a dick. What you said is disrespectful,'" said Stairs. "The second time it happened was because of Tony Pena at first base. You get in that thing—and I've been in many hockey fights—you get in the heat of the moment and a lot of things are said and you forget what was said. But I remember him asking, 'What's the deal? Why did they hit me,' and that's why I said, 'Because you're a dick.'"

The Blue Jays lost that game 9–2 and finished the season at 83–79, 13 games behind the Boston Red Sox in the AL East and 11 games back of the Yankees for the wild-card. They ended up 86–76 in 2008 but dropped to fourth, 11 games behind the division champion Tampa Bay Rays, who lost in the World Series to Stairs and the Phillies. Ironically, Stairs' pinch-hit homer in Game 4 of the National League Championship Series against the Los Angeles Dodgers played a pivotal role in helping Philadelphia advance.

Still, his tenure in Toronto, limited as it was, remains a special time for Stairs. "Every time you'd take the field, you'd look around and see the signs like STAIRS FOR PRIME MINISTER. There was a lot of support that people give you," he said. "I remember doing an autograph signing at the Bay, and they said it was the largest in the history of signings at the Bay. You came to the ballpark every day and you knew there was a kid waiting to see you and look for an autograph because you were Canadian. For me that was the biggest joy, seeing young kids wearing your jersey or wanting your autograph, or them telling you where they're from and having a conversation with them to tell them I've been there before.

"Every time you put on that jersey you were very proud, especially playing at home, when your name was on the scoreboard it had a Canadian flag beside it. You felt proud. Not a lot of people have done it. You're very honoured, very humbled putting the jersey on knowing you're helping represent Canada."

Stairs, and the 28 other Canadians to play for the Blue Jays through the 2020 season, did it well.

47

THE WIN STREAKS

In the midst of a winning streak that would run to a team-record-tying 11 games from June 2 to 14, 2015, with excitement increasing and perspective declining, Mark Buehrle offered some sage words of caution. When asked what could be drawn from the string of victories, he said, "It's going to be telling when we lose a game or two, how we rebound from that. Are we going to get our heads down, or are we going to keep our heads up, keep grinding?"

Those following along may remember that the plain-spoken and insightful left-hander made a similar pronouncement the previous time the Blue Jays won 11 in a row (June 11 to 23 during the club's ill-fated 2013 season). That stint was a mirage built on a series of outliers—Chien-Ming Wang delivered three solid starts; Esmil Rogers dominated in two victories; Josh Johnson pitched well twice, earning one of his two wins all year; Munenori Kawasaki homered late to tie one game, the only time he's gone deep in North America. The Blue Jays resumed losing immediately afterward, dropping 8 of their next 11, with a seven-game losing streak soon to follow. Aside from providing a period of joy amid a stretch of misery, the 11 straight wins were ultimately meaningless. So when the Blue Jays hit that mark again, 2013 was in the back of their minds. "You don't want to take that bait," said R.A. Dickey. "We have enough guys who were on that team, who experienced that, to not take it for granted, and to know that you've got to bring your game every day."

The 2015 Blue Jays, helped along by success at the trade deadline, validated their first run with a second 11-game winning streak, from August 2 to 13, a stretch that carried them all the way atop the American League East, a place they hadn't been that deep into a season since 1993. In doing so, they became the first team with multiple 11-game streaks in the same year since Cleveland in 1954, and became the first American League club with multiple win streaks of 10 or more games since the 1977 Kansas City Royals.

During their first run, the Blue Jays bludgeoned their opposition, outscoring them 88–40; the second time, the bats did some bashing, but the pitching did the heavy lifting, as the collective score was 59–22. "The only word to describe it is fun," said Ryan Goins. And the fun kept coming for the Blue Jays after that streak, as they closed out the season at a 29–17 clip to clinch their first division title since 1993. The 2015 streaks were as meaningful as the 2013 stretch was meaningless.

What's remarkable is that the Blue Jays pulled off three 11-game win streaks in the span of three years after accomplishing it just twice previously in franchise history—from June 2 to 13, 1987, and August 27 to September 7, 1998. Like the 2013 club, neither of those teams reached the postseason, although both were in the thick of the hunt right up to the end. Factor in that the Blue Jays also pulled off a nine-gamer from May 20 to 28, 2014, and that's an unusually high number of extended win streaks in a concentrated period. Coincidence? Probably, and it's worth remembering that "even a bad team goes on a nice little streak once in a while," as manager John Gibbons often pointed out.

The first 2015 streak started after the Blue Jays dropped to a season-low seven games under .500 in the opener of a doubleheader against the Washington Nationals, falling 2–0 as Jordan Zimmermann held them to six hits over eight shutout innings. Tensions were high between games before the clubhouse was darkened for players to nap, and things didn't look good when they awoke to face Max Scherzer. Then Kevin Pillar, in a 12-for-81 slide coming in, became an unlikely hero by hitting a pair of homers off the ace, the second a three-run shot that erased a 3–1 deficit and carried the Blue Jays to a 7–3 win. Buehrle threw a six-hit shutout the next day, and suddenly they were rolling.

"I remember feeling like absolute garbage after that first game. We were in a bad spot, and then Pillar hit the two home runs off Max Scherzer," said first-base coach Tim Leiper. "There was a definitive low point after that first game, and then having to sit around and wait for that second one. To me, that was a huge turning point for us." Added Gibbons, "We were on the ropes, seven games under .500 at the time, against a guy who has thrown two no-hitters this year and Pillar took him deep twice.... We really could have disappeared, but we regrouped against maybe the top pitcher in the game."

The Blue Jays rallied from two runs down in the ninth for a 7–6 win June 7 that completed a three-game sweep of the Houston Astros. Jonathan Villar's collision with a ducking Jose Reyes at second base on a Jose Bautista pop-up set the stage for Chris Colabello's game-winning two-run single. Edwin Encarnacion's walk-off two-run homer against Miami's A.J. Ramos—the first long ball he'd allowed since May 28, 2014—pushed the streak to seven on June 9. But the most memorable win of the streak was No. 9 on June 12 at Fenway Park, when they erased an 8–1 deficit in a 13–10 triumph. The Blue Jays scored three in the fifth and then exploded for nine in the seventh, capped by Russell Martin's three-run triple and Justin Smoak's two-run homer. "That's where this offensive unit realized how good we really are, that there's no deficit we can't overcome," said Pillar. "On the flip side, I think our pitchers realized it's okay to give up some runs, as long as it's within reach to give our offence a chance to come back. I think that was a big turning point for us."

The second 11-gamer of 2015 started the day after Mark Lowe surrendered a three-spot in the eighth inning of a 7–6 loss, with Dickey delivering seven innings of two-run ball in a 5–2 win that gave the Blue Jays three of four from the Kansas City Royals in a wild series. David Price, just acquired before the trade deadline, made his debut the next day in a 5–1 win over Minnesota, the first of four in a row against the Twins. "We got crushed," Minnesota veteran right fielder Torii Hunter said afterward.

The Blue Jays then went into Yankee Stadium and allowed just a single earned run over 28 innings in a three-game sweep of New York that gave them a 1½-game lead atop the division. A three-game sweep of the outclassed Oakland Athletics followed before the streak came to an end August 14, when Aaron Sanchez gave up a three-run homer to Carlos Beltran in the eighth inning of a 4–3 loss to the Yankees. The game ended with Troy Tulowitzki striking out against Andrew Miller in a riveting 12-pitch at-bat. "I was running out of gas there," said Miller. "I changed locations and angles. I didn't execute everything I wanted to, but I practically threw him a curveball on one pitch.... He's just a good hitter. Fortunately, I figured out one that worked."

The at-bat was reflective of how the Blue Jays played both during and after the streak. As Tulowitzki noted at the time, "I like to say that if you respect the game, the game will respect you back. I think at the end of the year, the team that respects the game the most is usually the team that's on top. We're doing things the right way and hopefully that will pay dividends later on in the season."

It most certainly did.

48

THE OWNERS

At the turn of the century, Interbrew S.A. no longer wanted to own the Toronto Blue Jays, but couldn't find anyone to buy them. The Belgian beer maker inherited the ballclub when it purchased the Labatt Brewing Company in 1995, assuming control soon after the resumption of play following an ugly players' strike. By then the team's on-field fortunes had turned dramatically for the worse. Attempts to sell the club in 1997 failed, it was pulled off the market, and the outlook for what was once a model franchise turned dire. "The strike literally killed us," said Howard Starkman, the longtime Blue Jays executive hired as the club's third employee. "Interbrew took over and they didn't know what to do with the team."

Eventually Ted Rogers, partly driven by a sense of civic pride, sensed opportunity in the club no one seemed to want. He had some big plans for the Blue Jays when he purchased an 80 percent stake in the team from Interbrew for U.S. $112 million on September 1, 2000. The founder of telecom giant Rogers Communications Inc. had his eye on full control of CTV Sportsnet (Rogers Inc. already owned 29.9 percent of the network, and acquired a controlling stake in July 2001), and he wanted the Blue Jays to provide it with content. It's a business model still in place today, although the club is now leveraged on multiple platforms. The deal has played out to plan, giving Sportsnet at least 162 games annually—the kind of live events coveted by advertisers as the last bastion of appointment TV after the Internet and PVR devices revolutionized consumption—while *Forbes* pegged the Blue Jays' value at U.S. $870 million in March 2015. Not bad for an asset purchased in distress. "There was really only buyer at the time," said Paul Godfrey, who helped negotiate the sale and took over as team president immediately afterward. And if Rogers had listened to his board, which was against the purchase? "There was that fear, there was that concern that the team would be moved," said Gord Kirke, a prominent Toronto sports lawyer who has provided the team with ongoing counsel. "But you didn't allow yourself to believe that. You believed that something will come along and you'll be okay."

Indeed, the Blue Jays have been okay ever since, and while Rogers' ownership often draws slings and arrows from the fan base, complaining about a team's owner is a rite of sports fandom. Labatt was widely regarded as a benevolent owner, having overseen the club from expansion cellar-dweller to perennial powerhouse and authorizing the game's highest player payrolls during the World Series championships in 1992 and '93. When times are good, what's not to love? But the business of sports was much simpler and smaller then, and Interbrew never really understood what it had. To be fair, a season-ticket-holder base of 27,000 was cut by more than half by the time it took over, and trying to rebuild the connection with fans sated by consecutive championships and turned off by the strike would never have been easy. "Interbrew was losing money, and the hole kept getting deeper and deeper and deeper," said Starkman. "The strike hurt us maybe more than any other team because we had the most to lose financially, and we lost it. Player payroll became an issue, players playing here became an issue, all these things became issues."

Anyone buying the Blue Jays then would inherit all those problems, and that curtailed the market. So the team sat and sat and sat. Interbrew turned away bids from Toronto real-estate developer Murray Frum and a consortium led by lawyer Lawrence Dale in 1997, leading to real questions about the franchise's future. Then the media landscape evolved to the point when Rogers became interested.

Godfrey, who left his post as publisher of the *Toronto Sun* in June 2000, had barely set up a temporary office at the law firm Goodmans LLP when Ted Rogers phoned. "'Come and have breakfast with me,'" Godfrey recalled him demanding. "I said, 'What about?' He said, 'Why, you won't have breakfast with me if there's no agenda?' I said, 'Of course not, Ted, I'm glad to come over.'" They met a few days later, and Rogers told him he planned to make a run at both Sportsnet and the Blue Jays. He asked Godfrey to help negotiate the deal. "Ted said, 'If you help me buy the Blue Jays, I want you to be the president,'" said Godfrey. "I replied, 'You know I've never run a baseball team before.' He said, 'Did you ever run a newspaper before you ran the *Sun*?' I said,

'No.' He said, 'Did you ever run a city before you ran Metro?' I said, 'No.' So he said, 'What's your problem?' I said, 'That's a pretty good point.'"

Godfrey worked with Albert Gnat of Lang Michener LLP and a director at Rogers ("One of the few guys I met who could yell and scream at Ted and get away with it," said Godfrey); Richard Wong, a Rogers mergers-and-acquisitions specialist; and teams of lawyers to get the deal done. It took nearly three months to complete, and Rogers acquired 70 percent of the team from Interbrew plus the 10 percent CIBC had owned since the team's inception. For the purposes of the deal the Blue Jays were valued at U.S. $140 million by all three sides to structure the disbursements.

Intriguingly, as the sale of the Blue Jays was coming together, another purchase by Rogers was coming apart. In February 2000, a C $5.6 billion deal to acquire Videotron was in place, but the Caisse de dépôt et placement du Québec, a 17 percent stakeholder in the Quebec-based telecom, objected and launched a counteroffer with Quebecor Inc. After months of wrangling, Videotron accepted a revised offer of C $5.4 billion from Quebecor that paid Rogers a C $241 million breakup fee. The U.S. $112 million price tag on the Blue Jays amounted to roughly C $165 million. "So Ted got the Blue Jays, basically, for nothing," said Godfrey.

Rogers bought the remaining 20 percent of the team from Interbrew in January 2004, and later that year added SkyDome to its portfolio, purchasing the stadium for $25 million, an amount many complained was basically nothing given its $572 million building cost. The decade since has consisted largely of public hand-wringing over the state of the club's payroll, which, while not perfect, is better than worrying that Interbrew would sell the team to Americans interested in moving the club.

Kirke and Pat Gillick were so fearful of that possibility that "we put together a group of people and talked to Interbrew about trying to do something," said the longtime Blue Jays general manager. "It never worked out, but I'm glad that Ted Rogers got a hold of it and kept it in Toronto where it should be." Added Kirke, "We had a feeling that if someone like Ted Rogers hadn't stepped up we would have done it. We would have raised finances principally in the United States, but we would have kept the team here. But the Rogers thing came up and it took the edge off, and we weren't going to compete with Rogers, couldn't compete with Rogers, and it wasn't necessary."

That's why a statue honouring Ted Rogers, who died in 2008 at age 75, was placed near the southeast corner of the stadium during the 2013 season. The decision remains a lightning rod to fans, but not to Alan Horn, chairman of the board for Rogers Communications. "It was Ted who stepped up to the plate, so to speak, when no one, and I can say this from actual experience of working on the deal, no one else in Toronto showed any interest in buying the team or keeping it in Toronto," Horn said on the day the statue was unveiled. "As Ted said at the time, 'How can you be a major league city without a major league team?'"

Toronto has no plans to find out.

49

SUPER SCOUTS

There is little glory beyond what gets accomplished on the field for scouts, and very little credit from the cheering masses for the work they put in. Baseball's bird dogs work long hours, travel to remote outposts, and file countless reports, usually for meagre pay and with little job security. Those who do it have to really love it. Yet scouts are in many ways the lifeblood of successful organizations, identifying present and future talent, gathering information to be exploited in trade talks or contract negotiations, and identifying opponents' tendencies in order to prepare players for games.

The Toronto Blue Jays have long been an organization that has prided itself on its scouting, starting from the crew assembled by Pat Gillick during the franchise's inception to the battalion of men Alex Anthopoulos hired when he took over as general manager. To single out only a few is a disservice to the many who deserve recognition, but there are three men who repeatedly draw praise for their work helping build up the franchise into the powerhouse it became: Bobby Mattick, Al LaMacchia, and Epy Guerrero.

Mattick joined the Blue Jays in 1976 as a scouting supervisor, was promoted to director of player development in 1978, and in 1980 took over as manager of the Blue Jays, becoming at age 64 the oldest rookie skipper ever to start a big-league season. After a 104–164 run in two seasons, he became the club's executive coordinator of baseball operations, and in 1984 was named its vice president of baseball, a position he held until his death in 2004 at age 89.

"Bob was probably one of the most visionary guys, both intelligent and intellectual," said Gillick. "He had a great mind, and he wasn't only a tremendous scout, he was an outstanding manager too. I don't know if I've ever [run] into someone that could instruct all aspects of baseball like he could."

Wearing all those hats made Mattick a father figure in the organization, although with his old-school edge he didn't suffer fools.

Former Blue Jays general manager Gord Ash recalled how he would "ask you things like, 'What comes first, success or confidence?' He'd throw that out into a group of 10 people and by the end of it there were people ready to choke each other," Ash continued. "But he did that with a purpose because that is the great debate. He did not mind the tension of an argument. He had a lot of passion for that kind of stuff."

Cito Gaston remembers Mattick initially disliking his approach to coaching hitters, but eventually the two became close friends. The key, he said, was in not taking his guff. "They used to send the major league coaches to instructional league every year, and we'd go down for a week and the other coaches would go home," said Gaston. "Al Widmar [a longtime pitching coach] stayed the whole time, but John Sullivan [a longtime bullpen coach] would go and I'd come in. The first day I came there, Bobby said to me, 'Cito, do you like frog legs?' I said, 'Yeah.' He said, 'Let's go out to dinner after the game.' So I said, 'Okay.' At dinner, he asks, 'Did you see anything we were doing that we could improve on?' I looked at him right in the eye and said, 'Yeah, the outfielders, they're standing there with their hands on their knees, they never get set to go get the ball.' And he lost it. He went off and he said, 'Damn it, we're doing the best we can.' I looked him right in the eye and said, 'Bobby, you know what? I could get on that fucking plane tomorrow and go home. I don't need to fucking be here.' And from that day on him and I were friends."

LaMacchia joined the Blue Jays in 1977 as a scouting coordinator, working his way up to an assistant to general manager Gillick in 1984. Later that year he was promoted, like Mattick, to vice president of baseball, a role he held until he left the club following the 1996 season. He died in 2010, at age 89.

Gillick is full of praise for LaMacchia's ability to project players of marginal ability into big-leaguers, and describes him as a "tremendous grassroots-type scout." A perfect example of that came in 1964, while he was with Milwaukee (the franchise would move to Atlanta following the 1965 season). He stumbled upon a summer league game on his way home in San Antonio. "He stopped at the ballpark and he sees me hit one on the street, over the ballpark, across the road," said Gaston. "I got signed that night."

Gillick and LaMacchia first met out on the hustle, in a world so competitive Gillick would sometimes hide in trees and watch players with binoculars to avoid tipping off other teams about his interest. But LaMacchia also had a cooperative spirit to him too, demonstrated during 1975, while he was with Atlanta and Gillick was with the Yankees and both were interested in drafting first-base prospect Willie Upshaw. The Yankees picked him in the fifth round, but the cousin of NFL Hall of Famer Gene Upshaw had a football scholarship he wanted to pursue and began ducking calls from the baseball team.

"So I called Al. We were competitors but good friends," recalled Gillick. "I said, 'Al, I can't get him signed. I'm going to ask you something. Will you go up there with me and try to get him to sign and try to get his parents to get his kid into baseball? If he goes to football, he's not big enough and he's going to get busted up.' So we went up there, and his parents were there and his dad said, 'So let me get this straight: You work for the Yankees, and you work for [Atlanta].' I say, 'That's right.' He replies, 'Well, I don't get it.' And Al said, 'I'm just up here trying to help Mr. Gillick sign your son, because we think he belongs in baseball. Hopefully it's going to be in the big leagues with the Yankees. Unfortunately, we didn't get him in the draft, but we think he belongs in baseball.' With that, [the Yankees] ended up signing him."

LaMacchia had a fiery side too. Gaston remembers a game at Fenway Park in which George Bell struggled with the Green Monster in left field. "Al runs down the stands screaming at me, telling me to take him out of the game," Gaston laughed. "I was yelling, 'Sit down, sit down. Leave us alone.'"

Guerrero joined the Blue Jays as the scouting supervisor for Latin America in 1978, but his relationship with Gillick ran back to the '60s, when the latter worked with the Houston Astros. The trust they had developed led to the Blue Jays following the lead of the Los Angeles Dodgers in building their own complex in the Dominican Republic; Guerrero ran it. They signed as many players as possible, especially early on, looking to infuse the organization with talent.

Guerrero was relentless too, donating equipment to poorer, remote areas and later circling back to see if any talent was emerging. No signing demonstrates that quite like his acquisition of Nicaraguan Brant Alyea, a process that seems straight out of a spy movie. A Blue Jays scout took notice of the outfielder during the 1984 World Junior Baseball Championship in Saskatchewan and suggested the organization follow up. So Guerrero made plans to go to Nicaragua. The country was closed under Sandinista rule at the time, but he arranged a visa through some officials he had met at a previous baseball tournament and said he was planning to run some clinics during his visit. Instead, Guerrero "purchased combat boots, a camouflage outfit—shirt, pants, even a Sandinista hat" so he could move about the country unfettered, remembered Gillick. He eventually signed Alyea and snuck him out of the country. It's rumoured that he paid the customs official a $3,000 bribe to ensure a smooth departure. "He was very inventive like that," said Gillick.

Cleverness aside, Guerrero also developed a reputation for being an unabashed supporter of his players. "In meetings, everybody that he talked about was a 'prospect,' nobody wasn't a prospect," Gaston said. "We'd start messing with him because we knew he'd say, 'This guy's a prospect.'"

Guerrero left the Blue Jays in 1995, shortly after Gillick's departure. He died in 2013, at age 71.

50

FRANCHISE ICON: TOM CHEEK

Amid the pandemonium that erupted after Joe Carter's World Series–winning home run cleared the wall in left field, the jubilant man of the moment hopped around the infield like a marsupial. At least that's what it looked like to Athelene Carter, a very proud mom, who turned to Mary Howarth, the wife of radio broadcaster Jerry Howarth, from her seat in the stands and beamed, "My son the kangaroo!"

Up two levels, in the broadcast booth, Tom Cheek saw it the exact same way as he relayed the historic events over the radio, leading to perhaps the most memorable call in Toronto Blue Jays history. "Touch 'em all, Joe! You'll never hit a bigger home run in your life," Cheek urged in his distinctive baritone, a moment captured so perfectly the phrase is timeless. "That really is my favourite call of all time," said Cheek's widow, Shirley. "It was so off the cuff. Tom was just an off-the-cuff guy. Whatever came out of his mouth came out of his mouth, nothing was preplanned. It was how it happened. When Joe Carter was running around those bases, it looked to Tom like a kangaroo jumping up and down, and he was mentally telling him, 'Joe, don't miss a base.' So, it was just how it came out."

The genuineness of Cheek's delightfully understated words—no catchphrases, no shtick—is the enduring legacy of a brilliant career. That's why he is among the most beloved figures in Blue Jays history, and earned a place in the National Baseball Hall of Fame as a recipient of the Ford C. Frick Award for broadcasting excellence. An unrivalled dedication to the job led him to call the first 4,306 regular season games and 41 postseason contests in franchise history. Yet when asked about his ironman run, he'd brush it off as part of his job description, saying simply, "This is where I want to be." His streak was only interrupted by the sudden death of his father, a hero in the Second World War, on June 2, 2004. Eleven days later, on his 65th birthday, Cheek underwent surgery to remove a brain tumour that had been discovered when he took ill shortly after his father's funeral. He recovered for a time and returned to the broadcast booth in '04, but the cancer returned. He died October 9, 2005, having provided the soundtrack that connected the first generations of fans to the Blue Jays.

"The thing I always remember about Tom is that he was very fundamental. He made the calls," said Jerry Howarth, his longtime broadcasting partner. "He was the sophisticated Blue Jays fan that every fan wanted to be, because Tom's calls were very high and

Tom Cheek keeps an eye on the action at Blue Jays spring training in 2005. (Frank Gunn)

emotional when the team was winning, and they were kind of down in the dumps a little when they weren't doing well. That's what the fan was too, and Tom had that sophistication. He didn't have signature calls, and he didn't want those. He'd say, 'I want to be the Blue Jays announcer for the fans, and the affiliates across Canada.' So other people had signature calls, but Tom didn't have them, nor did he want them because he was happy just being the fans' radio announcer. I always respected that."

A native of Pensacola, Florida, Cheek worked in construction after a tour of duty in the U.S. Air Force but dreamed of working in radio. He eventually enrolled at the Cambridge School of Broadcasting in Boston before starting his radio career in Plattsburg, New York. His next stop was Burlington, Vermont, where he did play-by-play in basketball, football, and hockey for the University of Vermont. That led him to a swingman role on Montreal Expos radio broadcasts from 1974 to 1976, working on nights when Dave Van Horne called the games on television. Len Bramson, president of Telemedia Broadcast Sales, took notice. When he obtained the radio rights to the expansion Blue Jays' broadcasts, he tapped Cheek to be the team's radio voice. Cheek once said the club's first-ever victory 9–5 over the Chicago White Sox on its inaugural Opening Day, April 7, 1977, ranked as his top memory. He nailed it that day, and in every game that followed.

"Tom's voice not only delivered baseball, it delivered summer," said Mike Wilner, who joined Cheek and Howarth as the third man in the booth in 2002. "He also had a huge role in teaching Toronto about the game, and his love for baseball and the Blue Jays shone through in everything he did. He was the icon who didn't know he was an icon. He just thought he was going to work every day. As great a broadcaster as he was, and he was a Hall of Fame broadcaster, he was an even better human being, and that came through loud and clear on the radio waves."

Once Cheek took ill, Wilner began actively campaigning for fans to help ensure Cheek's inclusion on the Hall of Fame's Frick ballot, which is in turn voted on by a committee composed of all living award recipients as well as four broadcast historians or columnists. Cheek was among the 10 finalists for the 2005 ballot, but Jerry Coleman won that year. "There are some names and some things that guys on that list have done that blows me away," Cheek said afterward. "And I understand that. Just having my name on that list is pretty nice, pretty nice." Wilner was more disappointed, as he hoped Cheek would be honoured before the cancer won out. Instead, it took eight years of trying.

"It was a real tragedy that Tom didn't win the Frick while he was still alive to enjoy it, and I'll never understand how that happened," said Wilner. "The reason I campaigned so hard for Tom in 2005 was because we all knew he wasn't likely to be around in 2006. He very clearly had a Hall of Fame résumé and was more than worthy of the honour, but I don't think it ever occurred to him that it was a possibility. Every Frick voter thought highly of him and knew that eventually he'd get it, but for some reason they decided that he had to wait his turn instead of bestowing a great honour upon a great man before he passed. Eight years later, they finally got it right, which was great for Mrs. Cheek, Tom's children and grandchildren, and everyone who ever listened to Tom, but we would all have much rather seen Tom himself up on that stage in Cooperstown on induction weekend so that he could see, once again, just how much he meant to us."

The Blue Jays paid Cheek a proper tribute August 29, 2004, when they added his name to the Level of Excellence, appropriately adorned with the number 4,306 beside it. During a pregame ceremony, team president Paul Godfrey read from a congratulatory letter sent by Cal Ripken Jr., baseball's "Iron Man" who played in 2,632 consecutive games. Cheek, who never saw himself in the same light, eventually addressed his health, telling a crowd of 44,702 that "I've been fighting a situation now for over a month, almost two months now. We're doing the best we can to stay ahead of it. A brain tumour. We're dealing with it." At the end, the outpouring of emotion from the stands led him to tears, yet he maintained his poise and grace. "I never could really get the point until somebody said, 'Since I was a little kid, you have been the sound of summer.' I say from the bottom of my heart, thank you and God bless you. To everybody, to everybody."

Such emotion from Cheek was rarely seen. One instance Howarth remembers particularly well came after the Blue Jays clinched their first World Series title in 1992. Cheek always called the ninth inning, but when games went into extras he and Howarth would alternate after the 10th. So Howarth was on the mic in the 11th inning of Game 6 at Atlanta when Dave Winfield hit the decisive two-run double and between innings thought to himself, "Tom has been here since day one. This is his call. This should be his call."

"So when we came back," said Howarth, "he was kind of back in his chair a little bit, and I said, 'Fans, I've had the pleasure of calling Dave Winfield's two-run double. Now here's my partner Tom Cheek to take you the rest of the way.' Spontaneous. I'd rather be spontaneous than rehearsed. He sat up, right into that microphone and said, 'We're in the bottom of the 11th inning, the Blue Jays lead it 4–2,' and I was so happy for him because he was like a kid in the candy store, and that's the way it was supposed to be. The Blue Jays win, and I see him back at the hotel. We all stayed up until about five in the morning, with the team and members of their families and parties, and Tom, if he came

THERE SHE GOES

Jerry Howarth's familiar cry of "there she goes" whenever the Toronto Blue Jays hit a home run happened for the first time at random some three decades ago. "I didn't have a home run call at all my first couple of years in Toronto, nor was I interested in one," he said. "But then one day at Exhibition Stadium, in about the third inning, it was a day game, a Blue Jay hit a home run and I said, 'There it goes.' I thought to myself, 'Hey, that's pretty close. Maybe that's something I can use.' Well, I got a break. The next inning another Blue Jay hit a home run and I said, 'There she goes.' And in those back-to-back innings I thought, 'That's for me.'" In general, Howarth believes announcers should be spontaneous rather than rehearsed. "But I always tell young broadcasters, 'If [a phrase is] natural to you, use it.'" Howarth has one other on-air trademark. Whenever the Blue Jays score their first run, he'll say, "The Blue Jays are in flight." Credit for that goes to his dad, also named Jerry, who made the suggestion during Howarth's second season in Toronto. "That was his thought, and I said, 'Dad, I love that. I'm going to do that for you,'" he recalled. "That's how that came about." Howarth retired before the 2018 season after 36 years.

up to me once he came up to me three times, emotional, eyes watery, giving me a hug saying, 'Jerry, thank you very much. I really appreciate what you did for me.' Tom was not an emotional person. But when he showed those emotions, I was so happy for him."

The next year, Howarth was next to the Blue Jays' dugout, anticipating a Philadelphia Phillies victory in Game 6 of the World Series and preparing for the postgame show he hosted from field level. He didn't hear Cheek's brilliant call until hours later, but the two chatted about it during the celebrations afterward. "I asked Tom, 'How did it go?'" Howarth recalled. "And he said, 'Jerry, it was so good, but I was afraid that Joe was going to miss first base. He was so excited, jumping and down, and that's when I said, 'Touch 'em all, Joe! You'll never hit a bigger home run in your life.' That was Tom's way. It wasn't like he was thinking, 'How am I going to sound?' That's what he saw, and that's what the fans appreciated."

Eventually, Carter asked Cheek, "How did you come up with that? What were you thinking about? Because the first thing that went through my mind was 'touch every base,'" Carter recalled. "Once I finally realized it was going out, you can see on the film that I stopped the jumping. And he said, 'I saw you jumping up and down and it was the first thing that came to mind, Joe, you better touch all the bases. And it came out like that.' So we were on the same page." Just like Cheek and Blue Jays fans.

[Acknowledgments]

Trying to pare down the Toronto Blue Jays' illustrious history into 50 men, moments, and achievements the first time was an intimidating task. There are so many more stories that deserve to be told and in putting together this update, my hope was to get the book more current. This is my latest take on the Big 50. I hope the new additions to the book spark the kind of friendly debate that makes being a sports fan so much fun. I want to thank Josh Williams at Triumph Books for presenting me with the initial opportunity to delve into Blue Jays history and then giving me a chance to bring it up to date. Editor Jesse Jordan's guidance throughout the process was again helpful. To all the Blue Jays players, coaches, executives, officials, and staff members past and present who were generous with their time and insights, thank you for sharing your memories. Everyone should be as lucky as I am to have colleagues and friends like John Lott and Mike Wilner. Their generosity with advice, ideas, and editing helped make this book better. I am beyond grateful. Jerry Howarth, Bob Elliott, Scott MacArthur, Mike Cormack, Buck Martinez, Pat Tabler, Howard Starkman, Jay Stenhouse, and Mal Romanin each helped in ways big and small. Many thanks. The cooperation and support of Sportsnet, my employer, was instrumental in the completion of this project. My lovely wife, Stacey, on top of being the best life partner one could hope for, supported me and helped out with this project in every way possible. And, as always, thanks to all the fans who let me tell stories like these.